Good luck

W Churchill

A REASONABLE

By the Same Author

A
Reasonable Doubt

BY J. W. EHRLICH

THE WORLD PUBLISHING COMPANY

CLEVELAND AND NEW YORK

Published by The World Publishing Company
2231 West 110th Street, Cleveland 2, Ohio

Published simultaneously in Canada by
Nelson, Foster & Scott Ltd.

Library of Congress Catalog Card Number: 64-12057

FIRST EDITION

WP164

CONTENTS

CONTENTS

CONTENTS

CONTENTS

FOREWORD

In this, his latest contribution in the field of legal history and bibliography, J. W. Ehrlich, the distinguished author of such masterpieces as *The Holy Bible and the Law* and *Ehrlich's Blackstone,* has successfully presented the reader with perhaps the most fascinating form of literature: the legal essay that becomes as much a statement of personal philosophy as it is a statement of law.

The contents of this book are not, as might be imagined, exclusively limited to learned discussions of the law. There are no dry and musty dissertations within these pages, nor will the pedant find points to quibble about. Instead, what the reader—whether he be an attorney or a layman—will find here is a collection of lively and humorous anecdotes in addition to many simplified discussions of some of the finer points of the law. For example, the reader will discover a gentleman in Los Angeles who unsuccessfully petitioned the court to change his name to that of a famous film star. The humanist and the criminologist will read much of interest in Mr. Ehrlich's controversial positions on such timely subjects as capital punishment and why, as he believes, the lie detector ought to be relegated to the scrap heap. The American historian, further on, will no doubt be surprised to learn of Aaron Burr's finance trick played upon Alexander Hamilton and the fact that the consequences of this piece of legal legerdemain far outlived its author, still having consequences long, long after Burr's death. One of the essays in this book deals with a killing and the judge's instructions to the jury just before they retire to decide on the defendant's guilt.

These are just a few of the many absorbing and thoroughly readable subjects that the author covers. And there are more . . .

In addition to his reportage of incidents and anecdotes of interest to all readers, Mr. Ehrlich has successfully written a philosophy of human relations that is peculiarly American. To qualify this statement, let me add that I believe Mr. Ehrlich has captured the state of mind that was the political morality—as they lived it and as they wrote it—of our founding fathers. And most important, the author appreciates that our founding fathers —Jefferson, Madison, Franklin, Paine, and the many others— were but reflections of the body politic that surrounded them, the electorate, the American people. For our laws were not written, were not conceived, by the founding fathers, alone. Our laws were, in essence, the fingerprints of the American people impressed upon the pages of history.

Mr. Ehrlich understands, as did the American people during the time of our Revolution, that there had been democracies in existence over two thousand years before ours and that these democracies were tragically short-lived, soon falling into the hands of despots and demagogues. Our founding fathers had read their histories well and during their lives they, too, feared the awful and often-inferred presence of the unenlightened majority, always in a position to trample upon the rights of the minority. The author is disturbed by this and often, within the pages of this work, as he raises his voice in an angry and outraged cry for the rights of the minority, one may correctly infer that his voice contains as much anger directed toward the *principle* of such an act on the part of the majority as it contains anger toward the *act* itself.

There are many, many things that Mr. Ehrlich says within A *Reasonable Doubt*. I shall simply touch upon a subject that is very close to me, his recognition that our constitutional framework and our Bill of Rights are—and always have been—the pattern of individual liberty under law: government, it should be said, that must be the direct expression of an enlightened electorate. Mr. Ehrlich bases many of his premises upon our Declaration of Independence, which avers that certain of our rights are inalienable because they come to us from a higher power than the state or, as our founding fathers put it, "endowed [upon us] by our Creator," that therefore these rights of the minority, these rights of the individual citizen, cannot be taken away from *any of us,* either by a mob on the street, a policeman, or by *any* act of *any legislature!*

As one peruses this remarkable book it will be found that Mr. Ehrlich has woven a consistent thread throughout his tapestry of personal declaration, a consistent demand that more than just lip service to the inalienable rights of the individual be given, lest lip service in lieu of protection and recognition lead to regimentation of the people and the ultimate magnification of the state, which would bring all of us into the coldest and darkest nights of tyranny, where we would be eternally governed by a cold and impersonal monolith that would forever compel each individual to sacrifice a portion—an ever-increasing portion— of his liberty "in the interest of the common good."

In those sections of the book where Mr. Ehrlich squarely attacks what he believes to be wrong with many of the present misguided interpretations of what our heritage of individual liberty actually comprises, it is almost as if he is re-echoing the warning of the late Justice Sutherland of the United States Supreme Court when he said: "The saddest epitaph ever carved to the memory of a vanished liberty is that its possessors failed to lift their hands to keep it while they yet had the power."

If the reader of this controversial book does not always agree with the author, the reader will nevertheless have exercised his intellect and in this very act he will have perhaps strengthened it, as an athlete strengthens his muscles by another form of exercise. The younger reader who concerns himself with the chapters that the author partially or totally devotes to a re-examination of the fundamental principles that govern our way of life will quickly detect that a cleavage exists between what he, the reader, may have been taught in school and what, perhaps, the people of an earlier and younger America actually had in mind concerning the meaning of that much-used but poorly understood word "democracy."

In conclusion, it may be said that this book is most properly the author's own, personal interpretation of that most elusive mystique "the American Dream." As long as Mr. Ehrlich and his contemporaries continue to search for it, redefine it, and cherish it each time they find it, the dynamics of the American Revolution and their continuing impact upon our society will not be lost and the liberty and the dignity of each individual will be assured.

THOMAS P. WHITE
Retired Associate Justice
of the Supreme Court of
the State of California

November 15, 1963

Magna est veritas—truth is great. Debunking the accepted liturgy of popular belief is not an easy approach to truth but *A Reasonable Doubt* will in some degree lighten the burden of disbelief.

It is against tremendous odds that man battles to destroy false gods once an idol has been built. Perhaps in the following pages you will agree that some accepted truths are sorely damaged by factual data to the exclusion of fable.

Magna est veritas.

J. W. EHRLICH

San Francisco, 1963

In Search of the Truth

IN SEARCH OF THE TRUTH

MEN ARE LIKE FINGERPRINTS; no two are alike. While many men have no choice as to the occupations they will follow for the balance of their lives, some of us are able to choose our calling, as the mariner of old chose a star in the dark of the ocean's night, following it until the dawn broke, and with it, light. I belong to this latter classification; fortune has been good to me. I was given a star to follow.

Some men are like bankers; they love money. Others like to be engineers or builders; they want to see a tangible monument to their lives. And then there are others who feel they owe mankind something. All of us represent a fraction of each of the above; the best of us try to remember that our debts to mankind are never fully discharged.

In spite of the fifty-five million laws ruling our every move, I truly love my calling—my star—the Law. It is a ruthless taskmaster, the Law, for within this arena where conduct is governed by these fifty-five million laws, human rights can be quickly forgotten and man fast relegated to the Kafka-esque role of the tiny cog within a wheel, within another wheel. The Law tries, sometimes impersonally, to make us do what it tells us to do. In the cold, bleak, barren sentences that run together and blend into legal jargon—words found in our lawbooks—there is little or no understanding, compassion, or love for the abstract man. As a nation, and considering the heritage of freedom and civil obedience that good men fought to hand us, untouched, we are the greatest police state in the world.

And I say that if we are a police state as a result of the Law, the Law is still my calling; it is a first love, for the Law, per se, is no better and no worse than a loaded pistol. Guns do not kill people; people kill people. In concept the Law should be as plastic, as putty in the hands of a sculptor who first makes a mold before he begins to slash at granite. I love the Law because it could, with an enlightened public, become the grandest instrument of their will; it could become the living embodiment of all the fine emotions that, like cruel emotions, are the heritage of man. Carpenters have their tools; writers have their tools; both work with their tools as they see fit. It is thus with the lawyer; his tools are books and words, and he does the best he can to stand between man and the laws man thinks he ought to have. A lawyer is a kind of legal gunsmith; without him you cannot fire true on target. Without him, you may be handling a weapon with a cracked breech, a weapon that could, when fired, blow up in your face.

As a lawyer I feel a deep obligation to my client and his cause. Whatever his alleged sins, whatever my client's background, regardless of his creed, he is my client. He has retained me because he is alone and frightened in a land of badges or torts, bars or bankruptcy. Regardless of what my client has done, the Law and a sense of moral obligation charge me to do my very best for my client. And while I do not justify harming in any way another human being, I have seen enough murder to understand why it is that one man kills another. And so would you, I think, had you listened to, talked with, and hand-held as many murderers as have I. Each murderer—like each man—is a kind of spiritual fingerprint, apart from and unlike any other being; you will not know him until you understand his feelings, his hurts, his loves, his every waking thought.

When I walk into court, when I take meals with my friends, when I speak at gatherings, and say, "Never plead guilty," I am doing nothing more than acknowledging that it is a human being I am defending, not a robotnik. I am telling the State: "Take your best shot, if you will; we will give you nothing. You must prove all." I am operating, in criminal actions, always with the conviction that our police state—and it surely *is* a police state we are headed for, if not living in—prove its charges. I take no policeman's word, no prosecutor's protestations, to mean a thing, if my client has come to me and has told me: "My hands are clean."

A trial is a fascinating thing. Each time I walk into court I see, in the spectator's sections, old, familiar faces; people who spend each day going from one courtroom to the other, listening to arguments, direct examinations, and the like. It is an instructive way to spend a day, even if you are a layman, for there is much to be learned in a court of law.

The defendant, in a criminal action is, all too often, in a position that some call: "Up for grabs." The State and its functionaries have claimed the defendant is guilty of some offense, hence the trial in the first place! And while the prosecution must prove the charge of a criminal act to a moral certainty, and beyond a reasonable doubt, the Duncan Do-Right who reads the newspaper smacks his lips and gloats each time the State shoves another wretch into a criminal court. "Got to be guilty," says Duncan. "Wouldn't be there in the first place if they didn't have the right man!"

Thank God that Duncan Do-Right has never done a wrong thing, never made a mistake, never told a lie. By the way, if you would like to meet a Duncan Do-Right, spend some time in your local municipal court; Duncan will be the complainant, alleging that another party sold him a gold brick or, possibly, the Brooklyn Bridge.

Many factors enter into a trial. Trying a case, standing on your feet and searching your brain for quick answers, is a heady wine for the best man; he who is a slow lawyer may have a dead client. Also, there are many more factors to be encountered in a court of law than one would imagine, has he not spent much time in trial; this includes many lawyers who have never actually tried a case, limiting their life's work to scholarly research, legal writing, or other extra-courtroom occupations.

The business of witnesses against the defendant is something too many people place too much faith in. Here, I am not necessarily saying that witnesses lie; most of them do not. But they are suggestible and, like little children, sometimes have the tendency to say anything that the prosecutor puts in their minds. For that matter, not even lawyers make good witnesses in court; experience with people in matters under litigation has made them much more aware than other persons that man's perceptive powers are, at best, somewhat unreliable. Having found, by cross-examination of witnesses, how no two persons perceive the same event with the same set of eyes, the lawyer is often the first to admit his own perceptions could be in error.

Many factors we have only recently discovered tend to unduly influence a witness. The studies made by psychologists have taught us that feelings, suggestions, emotions, empathy, association—all tend to influence the witness's capacity for accurate, objective perception. And because we really have few tests, at the early stage of a trial, to determine a witness's reliability, an innocent man may be sent to the penitentiary by an honest but thoroughly biased witness.

The history of the courts' placing the witness's credibility under scrutiny goes as far back as the fourteenth century, and surely further, should we care to look. But during the 1300s, judges maintained that the indispensable requisite to form an opinion on the trustworthiness of a witness was that he, the witness, appear personally before the judge. The court could then gain certain impressions as to the witness's manner of answering questions, his reactions, behavior, and physical appearance. Following the examination, the judge would then put into the record his reactions to the witness; that the witness stammered or hesitated in replying to specific questions, or showed fear during the examination, as well as any other circumstances about the witness that the judge felt impelled to record.

The natural and acquired shrewdness and experience by which an observant judge forms an opinion as to whether a witness is lying or telling the truth are by far the most important of all the trial judge's qualifications; no doubt, infinitely more important than any acquaintance with the Law. Insofar as the judge's abilities to perceive truth, falsehood, or simply addled confusion in a witness are concerned, I assure you that no school of law, no set of books, will so qualify him. Such knowledge can only be learned by experience, and here the judge may be handicapped, as he has probably had little of it in this most subtle art of all: detection and preservation of the truth when dealing with a witness. People come before him with their cases prepared and give evidence which they have determined they shall give. Like untidy housekeepers, many persons come before the judge with clean floors; all the dirt is hidden away, under the rug. It is for the judge to do a little rug lifting, if he is to find the truth.

As I have said earlier, the observations of witnesses are either generalities too vague to be of much practical use, or they are so narrow and special that they can be learned only by personal observations and practical experience. The most acute observer would never be able to catalogue the myriad tones of voice, the passing shades of expression, or the unconscious gestures which he has, by tradition, learned to associate with falsehood. And this is the plight of the trial lawyer in court, standing before a judge with limited experience in matters of ascertaining the truthfulness of a witness. By and large, the English and American traditional procedures of examination are doubtless entitled to high praise, but on the whole it is the rarest and highest personal accomplishment of a judge to make allowance for the ignorance and timidity of witnesses and to be able to see clearly through the confident and plausible liar.

Without a doubt, the result of our courtroom procedure is to vest the trial judge with immense power not always subject to correction later on, when the case may be appealed. The judge's estimate of a witness's oral testimony as regards credibility may frequently stem from an absurd rule of thumb: the assumption that when a witness wipes his hands profusely during his testimony he is lying. But unless the judge somehow reveals, in his record of the trial, that he has used such an irrational and high-handed method of determining witness credibility, the higher courts can do nothing to correct his error; they will have to assume that the trial judge used some infallible system not governed by human vagaries.

To understand better why trial lawyers—who love the Law but are still driven to despair by some of its facets—sometimes have a sour disposition, let us see what actually happens when oral testimony is being heard by a judge and jury.

When an honest witness testifies to something he saw, what does he do? He represents, under oath, that he accurately saw or heard something of importance to the case—some past event or thing—that now, in the courtroom, he accurately remembers to the most finite detail. Our witness would like us to believe he is a combination movie camera and tape recorder. Well, insofar as his initial observation of the event, his memory of the observation of that event (for now, some time has passed between the event and the trial), and his verbal communication in the courtroom . . . error can enter, and often does.

When a witness says: "I saw," or "I heard," what he really means is: "I believe I saw," or "It is my opinion I heard." His testimony consists of nothing but a report of his beliefs, and this report is not a documented series of facts, just a series of now-moldy recollections that have been colored by the passage of time as well as the talks he may have had with the district attorney or the police.

I think William James best expressed the state of mind of the average witness when he said: "Whilst part of what we perceive comes from the object before us, another part (and it may be the larger part) always comes out of our mind. . . ."

Now, judges and jurors also fulfill the function of a witness—a witness as to what goes on during the trial. They must decide the facts of the case from what they see and hear; that is, from the words as well as the demeanor of the testifying witnesses. Reduced to absolutes, the judge and the jury are witnesses of the witnesses and, if those who testify are not to be likened to scientific observers, neither are the judges nor the jurors: they make the same mistakes the testifying witnesses make.

If a judge or a juror has a hearing defect, he is bound to miss some important point, or misunderstand defense testimony about defense's alibi. The communication process between a key witness and a partially deaf (or dozing) judge or juror may be likened to a conversation that takes place between a Swahili and a Swede; little, if anything, will get through. Similarly, defective eyesight may interfere with the juror's observation of an important witness's demeanor; say, the spectacle of the State's witness testifying against the defendant, with a smirk on his face.

Deficient memory of the testimony that has taken place in the courtroom will surely lead to error later on, in the jury room. And don't think that because twelve jurors have heard the same testimony the majority will necessarily have understood it. Usually, it will be the mistaken juror whose bray will eventually bring the others around. Every practicing lawyer is familiar with the daily recurring spectacle of lawyers and judges disagreeing as to what testimony has been given by a witness just a short time before! Thus, even men with trained minds in such matters, whose attention is constantly riveted upon the witness, who realize the importance of every word, may receive erroneous or inconsistent impressions of a witness's narrative. And if these trained and skilled practitioners of the Law make such mistakes, what say you of the mistakes a juror could make?

That the truth will out, alas, is not invariably true. It is often untrue because our jurors have no adequate guides for determining which witness speaks the truth and which speaks with a forked tongue. Cross-examination, as a pure wind that blows away the smog of lies, prejudices, and mistakes, has been greatly overrated. To evaluate the reliability of a witness's testimony would in most instances require a knowledge of his personality that the jury could not possibly acquire from seeing and hearing him just a brief time in court.

The best cure for our legal inequities, of course, would simply be if more people were aware of the frailties and unreliabilities of our so-called powers of perception. Knowing how unreliable the best of us can be when it comes to memory, we should all be far less positive about things and, by the same token, more tolerant of the other's honest mistakes. For no man who is honest with himself can ever stand pat on the accuracy of his own testimony. He not only may be mistaken, but most often is.

The problem of truth, the search for the accurate, truthful witness, is, has been, and will be going on for a long, long, time. It is not just my search; it is yours too. It is a fascinating search, for it may lead you into the strangest lands, onto the most distant shores of human experience. And because the truth, like the search for the truth, is purely a human experience, it must have within it all of man's faults and virtues. For the truth is man, and both are the Law; among the three we have civilization, and without them we should have nothing but the darkest of nights, the coldest of worlds.

YOUR WITNESS!

IF GIOVANNI JACOPO CASANOVA DE SEINGALT had been as adept in the art of cross-examination as he was skillful in the science of seduction, he would today be regarded as history's greatest lawyer as well as its greatest lover.

Surprisingly, the ways to winning over a witness and wooing a woman are similar. In each case the conquest must be carefully planned and executed. In the waging of such wars the lawyer and the lover fight a common enemy: hostile suspicion.

Similar, too, are the dangers to be avoided. The greatest of these is proceeding too far too fast.

Many a lawyer is of the theory that cross-examination should never be undertaken. I am not of that school, although I know full well that it can prove to be fatal as well as fruitful. In the hands of the expert trial lawyer, cross-examination is a broadsword to victory. In the hands of the inexperienced, it can be a boomerang.

Unfortunately for the lawyer, when he takes a case to court he must also take a client with it. In many an instance it is the client who demands that his attorney take on a witness and question him as to statements made on the stand.

And there's where the danger lies. In questions? No. Not in questions, but in the one question too many.

In a California courtroom not so many years ago a personal injury suit was in trial. The plaintiff contended he had been physically and financially injured as a result of an accident. He said so on the stand in a tone of voice calculated to arouse the sympathy of the jury.

The defendant, an insurance company, was represented by an eager young practitioner who could hardly contain himself until the moment when he was able to begin questioning the plaintiff. The cross-examination went thusly:

Q. Did you, at the time of the accident, when you were asked if you were hurt, reply that you weren't hurt?
A. Yes, sir, I did.
[The questioning should have gone no further. The plaintiff had been led to admitting that at the time of the accident he had said he had not been hurt. But our hero was not satisfied and continued.]
Q. Well, sir, why have you been testifying all morning that

you were hurt, giving the jury the impression that you were still suffering from the effects of the accident?

[The why question was, is, and always will be sudden death for some lawyers. Read on.]

A. Well, Mr. Smart Lawyer, it was like this. I was driving my horse-and-buggy along the road, and along comes this client of yours in his automobile and knocks us in the ditch. You never saw such a mess in all your life. I was flat on my back with my legs in the air. My poor old horse was on his back with his legs in the air. The buggy was completely wrecked. Now this client of yours gets out of his car and looks at us. He sees my horse has a broken leg. He goes back to his automobile, gets a gun, and shoots him. Then he comes up to me and says, Now what about you? Are you hurt?

I do not need to relate the verdict of the case, nor tell you that the lawyer never made the same mistake again during a long and profitable private practice that began immediately after the insurance company learned of the incident in the court-room.

An even more dangerous undertaking is the cross-examination of what the law terms an expert witness, a person so qualified that his testimony is considered to be beyond question.

An example of the folly of tackling the testimony of an expert witness occurred in a drunk driving case. The arrest had been made by a police officer whose employment record showed the defense attorney that he had only been on the force a short time. The cross-examination began:

Q. Patrolman Murphy, do you think that a year's experience as a police officer qualifies you to state that my client was intoxicated?

A. No, sir.

[Again, the questioning should have stopped, but it didn't.]

Q. Upon what, then, do you base your assumption that my client was drunk?

A. Fourteen years of bartending.

While cross-examination can be the curse of a lawyer's life, so can the interrogation of your own client bring disaster, the pitfall being the same—asking that one question too many.

In a dispute between a landlord and a tenant a lawyer made just such a mistake. The landlord wanted his tenant, an attractive young widow with a child, evicted on the grounds that her conduct was questionable. He complained that she made too much noise and had too many visitors at all hours of the day and night.

In this instance, cross-examination proved to be beneficial. Our lawyer got the landlord to admit grudgingly that he had made similar accusations against previous tenants that had been proven unfounded.

The mood of the jurors indicated to courtroom observers that the case would be decided in favor of the attractive widow. There was no need to put her on the stand, but, of course, our hero did just that:

> Q. What is your name?
> A. Mary Jones.
> Q. What did you say to Mr. Flowers in connection with renting the apartment?
> A. I told him I was a widow who needed a home for me and my little boy.
> Q. What is your son's name?
> A. James Smith.
> Q. Oh, is he your son by another husband?
> A. No, by a friend.

It is easy to see that Pandora's box can be opened with a question as well as a key.

UNDUE INFLUENCE

THERE ARE A NUMBER OF WAYS in which he who is searching for a black eye or a bloody nose may be accommodated. A political discussion on the relative merits of a Republican candidate, held at high noon deep in San Francisco's Mission District, is almost guaranteed to lead to a severe degree of physical disfigurement. A case of roving hands on a crowded bus, the taking of another's parking place, and cutting in at the head of the box office line on the night a highly touted musical opens are also guaranteed to do the trick.

And if all else has failed to produce the desired result, you can always precipitate an argument, at least, about the female and her influence over the male.

It is an undisputed fact that the female sex does have the power, in many instances, to exercise a dominating influence over the male of the species. The peacock fans out the iridescent glory of his plumage all the more brilliantly when the peahen stands beneath the near-by mulberry bush. That, my friends, is female influence.

A tired workman, home from the shop after a hard day's work, tries to get in an hour or two of sleep. He weighs two hundred and twenty pounds. His wife, on the other hand, weighs one hundred soaking wet. She wants him to put the curtains up. The curtains go up after a certain amount of hinting relative to dinner, the budget, and the chances of getting a new car. That, too, is female influence.

Every schoolboy knows of Edward VIII giving up his throne for "the woman I love." If that is not female influence, I defy you to show me what is! And, finally, we read of King David deliberately sending a man to his death in the front lines of battle as a shapely woman, who bathed across the way, darkens the doorway of the palace. This is surely female influence.

In the Law, there are two degrees of influence—due and undue influence—and, further, there is a distinction between reasonable and unreasonable influence. Finally, there are further distinctions between opportunity and exercise of influence.

Since all this has been purely an academic discussion and intended solely for entertainment, don't put it to the test; you may be influenced.

EYEWITNESS

SOMETIME THIS YEAR the following scene, with modifications, will be played out in one of our universities.

Some twenty students sit in a classroom, their heads bent over examination papers. Suddenly the door pops open and a young woman, about five feet tall and dressed in levis, a plaid hunting shirt, and a green Tyrolean hat, bursts into the room. She quickly levels a carrot at a student seated in the first row and shouts: "Federal Herring! You stole my marks!" Outside, in the corridor, a popping sound is heard.

A student in the front row clutches his breast, screams, and falls to the floor. As the assailant runs out, two men dressed as ambulance attendants enter the room, drag the victim to his feet, and quickly carry him away.

The whole scene has taken almost one minute from the time the assailant entered until the victim has been removed.

When the class has quieted down the instructor rises to his feet and says: "Ladies and gentlemen, I want all of you to take a fresh sheet of paper and describe *everything* that just took place in this room. I want you to tell me exactly what happened. I also want complete physical descriptions of the victim and the assailant, as well as of the weapons used. You will also tell me just how long it took this little drama to unfold before your eyes from the beginning to end. Commence writing."

On the face of it, this should be an easy task, especially when we know that this is no ordinary class. All of these students are graduate students majoring in psychology.

The results? One young man, who hopes to become a criminologist, writes: ". . . the killer was a big Germanic type . . . looked something like a Hollywood storm trooper . . . called the deceased an FBI man . . . said he was tired of being a communist . . . the murder weapon was a 7.5 Mauser . . . the victim was a typical-looking student in his twenties . . . white . . . seasonable dress . . ."

Another student, a young woman who hopes to become a clinical psychologist, says: ". . . the murderer was of average height . . . wearing a European-type railroad conductor's uniform . . . used a switch-blade knife on the victim . . . murderer said . . . you are a Marxist and are working to destroy our republic . . . stabbed the victim three times . . . victim was a white male dressed in khaki trousers and a blue sweater . . ."

And so on. Oh, yes! It was not mentioned by anyone that the "victim" of this assault was a male Negro, wearing an R.O.T.C. uniform!

The little episode just recounted will give you something of an idea as to the value of the eyewitness in court. As we have just seen, these students were persons highly trained in the art of observation. They had already spent at least four years studying human behavior, studying the many small nuances of the human mind. We should think that as "experts" they, if no one else, would be detached, would be able to record events with a great degree of precision. For, after all, if the experts can be wrong, what of the man in the street who glimpses, for perhaps

five seconds, another man running out of a liquor store, a bag
of money in one hand and a smoking pistol in the other. Or was
it a pistol? Perhaps it was just a cigar.

Most of us see what we wish to see, and even that none too
clearly. We live in an age of noise, of gaudy motion, of such
incalculable distraction that it is impossible for the eye to record
very much, and even less possible for the memory to retain anything thus recorded for very long.

And yet each day, in courtrooms all across the land, people
take the stand and solemnly testify to events they would like us
to believe they witnessed sometimes as much as two years
earlier.

Legal history abounds with cases of mistaken identity. Almost
weekly we read of some poor man who, after spending ten or
fifteen years in prison, is released because some eyewitness was
mistaken. Innocent men have been executed because someone
swore, under oath, that the accused was the same person who
pulled a trigger or wielded a knife or was behind the wheel of
a car.

Human memory is a frail and precious thing. Stop, for just a
moment, and see if you can remember what you had for dinner
last night. The night before? What is your driver's license number? If you are a man and you have received military training,
what was the serial number of your rifle?—the serial number
you were required to commit to memory! What is the color of
your husband's—your wife's—eyes? In which hand does the Statue
of Liberty carry a torch? Quickly, tell me which direction north
lies in! Finally, are you absolutely certain that you locked your
front door last night, before going to bed? Assuming that your
life were at stake as a result of a false answer to *any* of the above
questions, what would you say?

With all humility, you and I and all the rest of us would have
to say: "I cannot be sure, for a fact."

But what of the eyewitness in a criminal case? What of the
people's witness who takes the stand and solemnly testifies that

the accused, sitting a few feet away, was the person who held up his liquor store or who was seen running down a hotel corridor at three o'clock in the morning. How can a person be so sure?

To begin with, our eyewitness has undoubtedly seen the accused, though perhaps not at the scene of the crime. No, the eyewitness's acquaintance with the accused probably commenced sometime after the crime had been committed. More likely than not, the victim and the accused were introduced through that age-old introduction bureau, the Police Department. Let me give you an example.

You are a small businessman. You own a combination liquor store and market. As a small businessman you probably have no other employees; you open the store in the morning and close it at night. In between, you arrange stock, wait on customers, beat off persistent salesmen, and try to get your bills paid on time. You are beset by most of the worries that confront all of us: money, sickness, taxes, dreams of a better tomorrow. Money comes in and money goes out and, hopefully, somewhere along the line enough of this money may stick to your fingers to allow you to retire someday, in peace.

It is late evening now. You have been on your feet for about ten hours and you are tired. You look at your watch and, like most of us, you forget the time about five seconds later. You know, after looking at the watch, that you will be able to close up shop in a little while. Perhaps you light a cigarette or look at the day's receipts as you mark time, waiting to close. Your feet may hurt, for you have been standing erect for most of the day. In brief, your mind is probably distracted by a thousand and one little problems.

A man comes into the store. He walks to the refrigerator, opens it, takes out a six-pack of beer. Automatically, you know that this six-pack retails for one dollar and, say, twenty-five cents. If you see the man, you see him only as another customer; another face to smile at, another few pennies to add to your net profits for the day.

The man approaches and perhaps he says, "And a package of Camels, too." You turn your back to get the cigarettes from a rack and, when you are facing the man again, he has a pistol pointed at your stomach.

"Give me the money," the man says.

What do you do? What do you think, standing less than two feet away from a man who, with pistol in hand, has just told you to give him ten hours of your hard labor? If you resist, he may shoot you. You have read, somewhere in yesterday's paper, that another little store owner in this city was pistol-whipped and wounded in the arm by such a gunman. If you are able to think at all, while this pistol is trained on your stomach, you will probably think of your wife, your children, the unpaid insurance policy on your life, school for the youngest child, the operation your wife needs . . .

If you think at all, you will think that you do not want to die and better give him the money, the ten hours of your labor, than to lie bleeding and dying on the floor as you pray that the ambulance will arrive in time enough to save your life.

You open the cash register and you give the gunman the money. He stuffs it in his pocket and quickly leaves the store. In all, the whole transaction has taken less than ninety seconds.

You watch the man run down the dark street, see him get into a car or perhaps run around the corner. Then he is gone and you are alone with your empty cash register. You are torn by emotion, enraged that you have been robbed, thoroughly frightened, for you saw death inside the muzzle of that man's pistol—and perhaps that was all you really saw as he stood before you, waiting for you to hand him the money.

You telephone the police and perhaps you garble the message so that the police operator asks you to repeat it several times. Then you sit down, trembling, barely able to control yourself. You may be a little ashamed at how easily you were robbed. You may feel a great sense of relief that you were not pistol-whipped or shot. But, no matter how you feel, you do not feel "normal." You have been through a harrowing experience, something that has never happened to you before, and even as you wait for the police you try to sort your thoughts out, try to calm yourself, for you know that the police will have questions and you must have answers for them.

The police arrive and they *do* have questions. They want to know *your* name, *your* address. They want to know when the holdup took place. What was the exact time? What did the holdup man look like? Color of eyes? Color of hair? Type of clothing worn? Height? Weight? Peculiarities? Kind of gun? What did he say? How did he say it? Did he have a getaway car? Did he handle anything in the store?

Your mind is swimming as you try to make some sense out of these strange, new events. You want to tell the police: "This has never happened to me before; you must give me time to think." But the police, as you can see, are in a hurry. Perhaps one of the patrolmen gives you a few hints. Perhaps he says something that serves as a stimulus to your memory. Perhaps he shows you *his* gun and asks if it is similar to the gun the robber carried.

The police finally leave. You close up the store, trying to remember just what happened. Already, the whole thing seems to be a kind of hallucination. What *did* the holdup man look like? Somehow, you have the impression that he looked something like your younger brother. Or maybe it was Robert Taylor, the movie star, that he resembled. It is so hard to remember; so much happened and the police asked so many questions.

But the police seemed to know what they were doing. This is their job, you tell yourself. They'll get the right man. They'd *better* get the right man; they're civil servants! You pay their wages.

When you get home you tell your wife and your children about what happened to you. Neighbors come over. Everyone has questions to ask you. Perhaps you add a little to the story, for now you may have the idea that you behaved badly in the store, tonight. You didn't put up the kind of fight Humphrey

Bogart would have fought, had he been in your place. You didn't tell the stick-up artist to go to hell. You didn't throw a bottle at him as he ran out of the store with your hard-earned money. You did none of these things and, while you have no right to feel ashamed, you still do.

Three days later the police telephone you. They believe they have the man who did it, they say; just come down to the station house and identify him. Just a formality, they tell you; it is the same man.

You go down to the station house, a little relieved that the police have apprehended the man. Perhaps they recovered the money too. As you hurry to the police station, any doubts you may have had about the holdup man's identity leave you. The police must know what they are doing. Sure! They have the right man. Just like on the television, they always get the right man. You smile and you feel a little proud of your Police Department. You'll have to remember to buy a ticket to the policeman's ball, next year.

Now you are inside the police station, in the line-up room. The detective in charge of the case shows you a photograph of the suspect. He gives you plenty of time to study the features of the man on the photograph, both full face and profile. Yes, it *does* look like the man who held you up. You hand the photograph back to the detective and he tells you that now some men will walk out on the stage in front of you. You will, in turn, tell this detective which of these men was he who held you up.

Six men walk out onto the stage, their features lit up by the blinding white lights set in the ceiling. You scan the faces and you recognize one of these men; it is the same face you just looked at in the picture the detective handed you. No doubt about it!

"That's the man, Officer," you whisper, pointing at one of the men on the stage. "That's the man that held me up."

You leave the line-up room and sign a formal complaint. The police tell you that the suspect has a prior criminal record of some kind or other. While the police may not tell you that the suspect was or was not found with the money from your store, with the pistol that was used in the robbery, or even if he made a confession of guilt, they *have* told you he was an ex-convict and that, to your way of thinking, is enough to satisfy you. Once a criminal, always a criminal.

A trial date is set and you are in court. The district attorney puts you on the witness stand and asks you, in front of the twelve members of the jury, if you have ever seen the accused before.

"I have," you reply.

"When was the first time you saw the accused?"

You have memorized the date and the time of the robbery, as the district attorney, before the trial, had suggested. You state, in a loud and firm voice, the date and time of the robbery. You go on to describe the events that took place perhaps three months ago. You have had time to think, you have seen the suspect in the line-up. The police never make mistakes on things like this, you tell yourself as the district attorney finishes his examination.

The accused is represented by a young man who only this year was admitted to the practice of law. He is a sincere and intelligent young man, but he lacks experience. He does not yet know how a line-up is conducted, how certain thoughts and conclusions may be put into a frightened witness's mind. The young attorney does his best to rattle you, but to no avail. In the end, he excuses you and that is the end of it.

The accused is found guilty. In accordance with the laws of your state, the accused is sentenced to prison for a period of not less than a certain number of years. As you leave the courtroom you tell yourself he was lucky; any man who would pull a stick-up ought to be sent up for life!

As the days pass you forget much of what has happened to you. Perhaps you buy a pistol with the intention of using it on the next person who has the audacity to hold you up. You are regarded as something of a minor celebrity in the neighborhood for a while and then even your neighbors forget about the holdup.

A year passes. One day you receive a letter from the man you helped send to jail. It is a short letter, asking you to search your soul, for he says he is innocent. The letter concludes with a plea to go to the police, tell them that you were mistaken in your identification. For a long moment you stare at the letter, then throw it in the wastebasket. A typical criminal trick, you tell yourself. There he is, stuck in prison for the next five years, trying to lie his way out.

You look at your watch; almost time to close. You go to the door of your shop, and just as you throw the lock the door opens and a man stands before you. He says: "Give me the money, just like last time." He has a gun in his hand and it is pointed at your stomach.

It is the same man who held you up over a year ago. It is not the same man you helped send to prison.

If ever you are called upon to testify in court as an eyewitness, think very carefully before speaking. You may be sending an innocent man to the penitentiary.

INSTANT TRUTH

MAN STARTED SEARCHING for something guaranteed to make his brothers tell the truth about one hour after he learned to lie. Contrary to the opinions of the "experts" who appear to be willing to state, for an appropriate fee, that they can tell with certainty when a man is lying, we still continue to search for the truth. And in spite of today's highly touted truth serums and lie detectors, the truth continues to remain elusive.

Our search for "instant truth" is as random and as unsuccessful as it was during the time of Moses. Each time Science opens a new door, telling us we may expect to find the truth revealed inside, we find only the grinning face of an "expert" armed with the tools of his trade. In the past the "expert" came to us with the rack, the dunking stool, thumbscrews, or a set of red-hot forceps. Lately, they have taken to carrying hypodermic syringes and lie detectors.

Many of these experts would have us believe that a combination of Science and the Almighty have endowed them with the same powers that the old-time "water witches" were supposed to have had as they roamed about barren farmlands, armed with willow switches guaranteed to bend each time the "witch" passed over a hidden pool of water.

Of the two "experts" I prefer the water witch; he was willing to admit that he didn't understand his magical powers. The best of these witches, by the way, would not charge you a cent if they could not find any water. The truth expert, however, will tell you that he finds truth each time he searches for it. Unfortunately, it is usually impossible to verify his results.

History abounds with devices that were, according to the experts, guaranteed to compel a man to tell the truth. Trial by ordeal, as practiced during the various European inquisitions, is probably the best known of these devices. It was assumed, in those days, that if a man was properly tortured for a sufficient period of time, the truth would flow from his lips as wine from a broken jug. The average man, free from the clutches of the torturer, tended to accept evidence obtained from agonizing periods of abuse deep inside the inquisitor's cellars.

Later on, when the experts became too zealous in the performance of their labors and began torturing the wrong people—noblemen and others in positions of power—the people became quick to renounce the experts and their various "truth techniques." Indeed, many of these "experts" were to spend their

last days being subjected to torture by the use of the same imple-
ments they had used on others. In the end the tortured experts,
like those who had gone before them, gladly admitted their com-
plicity in pacts with Satan and other supernatural plots against
the Crown.

Trial by jury of one's peers gradually replaced the torturer's
rack. True, there were some dark intervals when such enlightened citizens as our own Cotton Mather had a tendency to back-
slide toward a return to the old ways. But by and large the
tendency in this country was to think that about the only sure
way the truth of a thing could be finally determined was in a
court of law.

And then came Dr. House.

Dr. House was a Texas obstetrician, a profession not, on the
face of it, related to lie detection. Dr. House also appears to
have been a kindly man, a man who was perplexed and upset
by the anguished cries of women as they went into labor with
child. Sometime during his years of practice in the early 1920s,
Dr. House experimented with his patients in an attempt to ease
their pain. He gave them a drug called scopolamine, a prepara-
tion that relaxed and tranquilized them in somewhat the same
way narcotics tend to relieve pain and suffering.

While his patients were under the influence of scopolamine,
Dr. House discovered that they talked freely, discussing things
they would not normally speak of. So, like many a dedicated
amateur, Dr. House was quick to rush to the newspapers with
his new discovery. The newspapers, in turn, were quick to give
this new drug a name: "truth serum."

There was considerable publicity connected with the use of
scopolamine and similar drugs—sodium amytal and sodium pentothal—for the following years. Then, more level-headed medical
authorities began to investigate Dr. House's discovery. They
concluded that scopolamine and the other "truth drugs" had far
more drawbacks than benefits. For one thing, many persons

under the influence of these drugs continued to tell lies. Other persons tended to repeat whatever the doctor giving them the drug told them to say. And some neurotics, when drugged, would confess to crimes they could not possibly have committed.

In the end, medical authorities agreed that the effect of truth serums could be likened to the impact of five or six tumblers of fine Kentucky bourbon, taken within the space of a few moments. Both of these preparations make talkative persons talk; neither is noted for its ability to make talkative persons tell the truth.

While many psychiatrists in this country employ the use of drugs that could be compared to "truth serums," they recognize that anything the patient may say while under their influence must be carefully evaluated on the basis of the patient's make-up. None of these psychiatrists, by the way, will ever go on record as saying that such a thing as truth serum exists.

Perhaps the greatest and the most unwanted impact of Dr. House's discovery was its criminal application by totalitarian governments. During the 1934 trials in Nazi Germany, following the burning of the Reichstag, or parliament building, the gestapo produced a suspect in the person of one Marinus Van der Lubbe. It was freely acknowledged that Van der Lubbe had been drugged with scopolamine and interrogated for weeks prior to his trial.

At the time of Van der Lubbe's trial journalists pointed out his general appearance and conduct, stating, ". . . the accused was slovenly . . . drooled upon his shirt . . . had to be led many times by the prosecutor . . ."

Van der Lubbe was "tried," found guilty, and shot. His innocence was later established beyond question; Goering had started the fire as a political move to cast discredit upon the opposition. Van der Lubbe? Merely a neurotic, dimwitted petty criminal who would testify that the moon was made of green cheese, while under the influence of "truth serum."

During the Moscow trials in the late 1930s, Russian interro-

gators worked overtime in the basement of the Lubianka
as they pumped suspects full of pentothal, amytal, and s
mine. A few lives were lost due to the overzealous admini
of these drugs, but totalitarian countries have never beer
for their practices of supply economy when dealing with human
lives. A few more mass arrests, another group of "suspects," a liberal supply of "truth serum," and the "guilty" are ready for trial.

Perhaps the disgust felt at the use of these drugs by the police
in America may be explained on the grounds that they are so
often associated with tyranny. As a man is known for his deeds,
so is a dictatorship known by its practices.

The 1920s produced truth serum. During this same era we
also encountered marathon dancing, the Thompson submachine
gun, Prohibition, flagpole sitters, the St. Valentine's Day Massacre, and goldfish swallowers as representative forms of American
self-expression.

It was also during the 1920s that the polygraph, or lie detector,
was first introduced in this country.

The lie detector does not measure truth; proof of this subtle
quality cannot be found by a machine. What the lie detector
does measure are emotions; body responses in the form of pulse,
blood pressure, respiration, and perspiration. The theory behind
the use of the lie detector is that the subject's physical reactions
will betray him when he is asked certain questions. While the
subject's words may be lies, say the experts, his bodily reactions
will shriek out the truth.

If the polygraph were somehow magically endowed to ferret
out the truth we should all probably be the better for it. But this
is not the case. Without an operator the machine can no more
function than can an airplane without a pilot. And here is the
crux of the matter: the operator.

Let us consider, carefully, just what the operator's duties are
in connection with the polygraph. For one thing, this gentleman
must be a highly skilled psychologist, for the questions he will
be asking the subject and the interpretations he will attach to

the subject's answers may very well mean the difference between freedom and years in prison. And in some cases the operator's mistakes could cost the subject his life!

The operator of the polygraph should certainly be a physician, preferably a well-rounded diagnostician who is able to determine if his subject might have certain physical conditions that could wrongfully influence the tests. It would also be a good thing if the operator were a toxicologist or at least a laboratory technician who could, prior to running the tests, take samples of the subject's blood and urine for analysis. It is not uncommon for some persons to drug themselves with tranquilizers or sleeping pills before they take a polygraph test and a person in such a state should certainly not be questioned.

A rather imposing list of qualifications? But I think you will agree that in the interests of justice they are a very necessary set of qualifications. Now, just what are the facts?

You or I or anyone else who had the notion could, with less than a thousand dollars, set up shop as "expert lie detectors." Many police equipment houses sell these devices for about $400; if cash is paid they will also throw in a manual on how to use one. Then, by paying the proper fees and filing the necessary papers, you or I or anyone else could take out advertisements in the newspapers, on television, or over the radio, offering our services to all interested parties. While we might be understandably new to the game of lie detecting it is likely that after we had interrogated a few hundred suspects we might achieve some degree of accuracy. By the time we had been called on to report our findings we would certainly be able to call ourselves "experts." We would have questioned a large number of suspects and no one, looking at the imposing strips of paper we had submitted to our client, would have the vaguest idea of what we were talking about.

That, you see, is the beauty of the lie detection business: we could do our work in private, away from the eyes of physicians, attorneys, and others who could monitor our work. Best of all, no one could challenge our test results, for we were alone with the suspect when the tests were conducted.

How does the lie detector work? How is the subject interrogated? The subject is usually told sometime beforehand that his honesty and his truthfulness have been questioned. This is guaranteed to upset anyone. Then the subject is given a date and a time and he is told to report to the interrogator who will ask him some questions. As the days pass it may be assumed that the subject's state of mind will be anything but tranquil; the subject knows he is a truthful person, but does the expert?

On the appointed day for examination the subject reports to the office of the lie detector operator. Once inside, the first thing the subject sees is a large chair containing straps and belts. Perhaps it is only accidental that this chair looks so much like the electric chair. Surely, the appearance of the chair cannot be designed to frighten or intimidate the subject, for we know that if this were so his reactions to the examiner's questions would be unduly influenced and could be subject to misinterpretation. No, we shall assume that the chair's resemblance to the electric chair is purely circumstantial. We shall assume that the examiner is the most scientific kind of person, one whose sole purpose is to discover, fairly, independently, and objectively, the truth.

The subject is told to seat himself in the chair. The expert is closely studying him because his textbooks have told him that this pre-interrogation period is very important.

"Guilt," the expert's textbooks say, "can often be detected prior to examination by the subject's dry mouth . . . continual yawning . . . unnecessary body movements . . . licking his lips . . . fidgeting . . . scratching . . . protesting that he is uncomfortable . . . complaining that he has another appointment . . . manifesting a bitter attitude . . . making feeble jokes . . ."

This information comes as something of a pleasant surprise to me. I have been searching for a sure-fire way to detect the truth for most of my life. The next time someone "yawns," or "licks his lips," or even "complains he has another appointment," I shall certainly have to conclude that he is lying.

The next phase of the examination begins as the operator straps the subject into the chair, placing various cuffs around his chest and wrists. An air-filled belt is placed around the subject's chest. Changes in the subject's blood pressure will be measured by an inflated cuff placed around his arm. Electrodes placed in the palm of the subject's hand will measure a form of galvanic electricity, for it has been assumed that lying subjects are most often sweating subjects.

And what of a subject who has a natural tendency to perspire freely? Or a subject who has a heart condition t' at tends to interfere with the regularity of his pulse? Or a subject with asthma, bronchitis, or even a missing lung? These conditions are certainly not the concern of the operator, for he is not a physician and he cannot take them into account during the course of the examination. No matter. We have the examiner's word that his machine is "ninety-five per cent accurate, regardless of the subject's physical condition."

The tests will usually begin with a "card trick," designed to impress the subject with the machine's accuracy. The operator will give the subject ten playing cards, ask him to mentally select one, and then return them to the operator. Then the operator will ask the subject if he took the ace of hearts, the king of hearts, and so on. Each time a question is asked the subject will be obliged to answer with a simple No. In this manner the operator will often be able to predict the card the subject took, for when the correct card is mentioned and the subject says No, the various gadgets recording the subject's emotions will probably register more mightily on this occasion than they did on the others.

From card tricks the interrogation will move swiftly to matters more pertinent to the proceedings. If the subject stands accused of some kind of theft he will be questioned about it; he will be questioned about everything he ever took. The operator's questions will take him back to his childhood, then through school and manhood. Again, the subject will be obliged to answer all questions with a Yes or a No.

If the operator has been reading his manual he will, as the interrogation progresses, infer that the subject is not telling the truth. He will accuse the subject of lying to him; he will shake his head sadly as the subject responds to a question. He will try to confuse the subject; he will ask questions that cannot possibly be answered with an affirmative answer or a negative answer. The operator will behave as a policeman, not as a scientist.

The operator will do everything in his power to jolt the subject, to create an atmosphere charged with emotionalism and not the truth.

How accurate is the lie detector when it is used under these conditions? In one case, reactions interpreted by the polygraph strongly suggested that a man had done something wrong in spite of the fact that he steadfastly maintained his innocence. He was given a second test and this time he was cleared by the machine! Why?

In the first test the apparatus that measures breathing showed a distorted pattern. Prior to taking the test the man had told the operator that he had a skin rash on his chest but that he didn't believe this would make a difference. The operator said nothing at that time, perhaps assuming that the subject's comments could be interpreted as: ". . . protesting that he is uncomfortable . . ."

When the second test was taken, the breathing apparatus was moved somewhat lower on the subject's chest, avoiding contact with the area of the rash. And the difference between truth and falsehood—in this case, a skin rash—was shifted by a scant few inches.

In a recent Chicago case, one involving rape, several suspects were questioned by a polygraph operator. All were cleared of the crime. Several weeks later a new suspect was questioned in connection with the rape. The polygraph said he lied. The suspect protested that he was telling the truth. In spite of the suspect's denials of guilt he found himself arrested, indicted, and on his way to court.

Some time after this man had been arrested a second rape was committed in the same neighborhood as the first. The police had a suspect: one of the men who had been questioned and cleared in the first crime. While he was being interrogated this man confessed to *both rapes!* It is hoped that the Chicago authorities now have the right man under arrest.

At this time the findings of a polygraph examination cannot be introduced in court in criminal or civil actions. Evidence obtained from polygraph examination is considered inconclusive. If such evidence *could* be introduced neither the trial lawyer nor any witness he might retain would be able to make sense of the polygraph results. They would simply have to rely on what the operator of this machine told them: that neither force nor threats were used during the course of the examination.

The lie detector may have some value in the years to come. As it stands now it is frequently used by the authorities as a tool to intimidate, to frighten, to confuse the person being interrogated. A product of science, the polygraph is most often used in an unscientific way. It is something like giving a gorilla a fine Swiss watch and a bench of precision tools, and then asking him to repair the watch.

No one need take a polygraph test under any circumstances. One of our most basic rights is the privilege of remaining silent. It is the job of the prosecution to prove that he who stands accused is guilty. The accused, by law, is not required to say one word in his defense. He who allows the prosecution or the suspicious employer to strap him in a chair and conduct examinations that would never be tolerated in a court of law is selling his birthright for a mess of pottage.

Law requires that poison be labeled with a skull and crossbones, so that even a small child may see the danger before him. We ought to have the same kind of law for the lie detector.

Personalities and the Law

MR. DISTRICT ATTORNEY

I CAN THINK of no other particular field of the law that is more popularly misunderstood than that occupied by the prosecutor, the district attorney. Most often, the district attorney is thought of as a heartless, snarling wretch who is continually after the defendant's neck. Such persons exist, of course, and their daily utterances in court, or to members of the press, seem to satisfy the needs of certain deranged citizens in every community. "Murder foul," screams one of these prosecutors, pointing his finger at the defendant, hoping that the jury will subsequently retire and decree that the state practice a little "murder foul" upon the defendant.

Who is the district attorney? Well, he is really *your* representative in court. He speaks for the People and he is charged, by law, to prosecute any and all lawbreakers who come his way. The district attorney is a kind of legalistic policeman, the one ultimately responsible for investigating and subsequently prosecuting him who has broken the law. This job, by the way, can be a great strain upon a man who as district attorney may know that the law is wrong, but has no other choice than to prosecute.

District attorneys are like all of us; they come in varying shapes, sizes, and colors. Of course the district attorney himself does not prosecute all the criminal cases that come into his office unless he is in a very small town. In cities he will have a staff of assistants. Many assistant district attorneys are young men, not long out of law school, and their function is somewhat like that of the intern in medicine; they know theory but they must have "warm bodies" to work on until theory and practice have melded into one. Many of these young men work in the prosecutor's office for a few years and then leave, going into private practice and later, perhaps, politics. The Chief Justice of the United States Supreme Court, Earl Warren, followed such a path, being district attorney of Alameda County, California, many years ago.

The district attorney first comes into a case when a person has violated the law and has been apprehended. I ought to qualify this statement by saying that when it is *assumed* a person has violated the law we immediately impute guilt to him. Because the district attorney's office is not staffed by psychologists, it is difficult for them to appreciate that the offender is a man with a personality and that personality is the result of an interaction between disposition and environment; that the individual act is the reaction of this personality to a definite, external situation. The district attorney, for all his enlightenment, could do nothing save prosecute, even if he knew that the defendant, as a product of disposition and environment, could not avoid the hereditary disposition with which he is equipped any more than he can help the environment into which he was born.

My friends, what the district attorney's office is up against is this: Few human beings have any "free will," as such. They do the best they can with whatever the Almighty and the state have given them, but no criminal code in this country is equipped to deal with the diamondlike facets of each individual offender. How can man be reproached for an action if he cannot be reproached for any of the factors which have determined it? Why do we punish?

The office of the district attorney seeks punishment. The jury determines if punishment should be levied. The court metes out the degree of punishment. In all cases, punishment is first asked by the prosecutor for the oldest and most out-of-date reasons imaginable. It is the prosecutor's theory that by using punishment, we induce the person being punished to abide once more by the law, and by this example—sending some wretch off in chains for a few years—we (the prosecutor, for he is our collective "we") hold up to the members of society, generally, the need for obedience to the law. And when the prosecutor prosecutes, he usually does so with the misconceived notion that the aim of punishment is retribution for the crime, that punishment is really to the benefit of society.

The district attorney, by the laws we have helped make, is truly cast in our own image, for he—like the society we live in—is too much preoccupied with punishment and too little concerned with the causes of social derailment and the subsequent possibilities for social rehabilitation. As we do not punish the whole man for the malignant growth that is eating at his vitals, neither should we punish him who is a victim of hereditary, environmental, and other subtle factors we are still able only to speculate about. But because we refuse to take cognizance of these many and varied circumstances that make up each and every criminal offender, the district attorney has no other choice than to go into court, as prosecutors have been doing for hundreds of years, and demand punishment to the fullest extent of the law.

The defense attorney is most fortunate when he is able to encounter a member of the prosecutor's office who is enlightened enough to realize that the man he is prosecuting is being prosecuted under a bad law. There are many bad laws on our books and most district attorneys are aware of them, though they are powerless to do much about them. In the case of a young man who has been misled by a young girl to believe she is of the "age of consent," this young man could be subject to prosecution on a charge of statutory rape. In spite of the young man's intentions, and with a complete lack of premeditation insofar as his realizing a crime was being committed, many years of his life would automatically be spent in prison and his future, upon leaving prison, would be marred by the stigma of being branded a "sex criminal."

Unless the district attorney is a scrupulously fair person he can, in court, have a powerfully detrimental effect upon the jury. As

I have pointed out, the district attorney is a representative of a sovereignty whose obligation to govern impartially is as compelling as its obligation to govern at all. Theoretically, the district attorney's obligation in a criminal prosecution is not so much that each case be won but that justice be done. As such, he is in a peculiar and very definite sense the servant of the law. The district attorney may prosecute with earnestness and vigor—and, indeed, he should do so—but while he may strike hard blows, he is not at liberty to strike foul ones. It is as much his duty to refrain from improper methods calculated to produce a wrongful conviction as it is to use every legitimate means to bring about a fair one.

And yet this same district attorney, knowing a bad law, knowing that the defendant's guilt is only academic, must do his job to the best of his ability, for to do otherwise, he, too, could be subject to prosecution. What a terrible dilemma!

Imagine that the following case confronted a district attorney. It concerns itself with George Washington, the father of our country and the commander of our first armies. Washington, if a prosecutor were to have held hard to the law, could have been prosecuted for treason; he was a common traitor to his country—England. His crime was successful and he became the emblem of virtue, the example of everything good in American life. And yet when Washington was laboring so mightily against his own, true country—England—he was committing treason. He was not alone in his labors, nor would he have been the only party subject to criminal prosecution. Benjamin Franklin, during Washington's time, was supposed to have said that the leaders of the Revolution would either have to hang together, else be hanged one by one.

Suppose Washington had failed? Surely, he and our other revered leaders would have been hanged as traitors, and today, perhaps, we would be less concerned about our income taxes than about the love life of a princess. It was only by a series of flukes that Washington and Co. were not hanged. Had the British

continued their efforts to bring about our downfall, their equivalent to the district attorney, perhaps with sorrow in his heart,
would have still demanded the extreme penalty for Washington
and the others.

This is what I mean about the inequality of the law, the inequality that our best prosecutors may understand but are powerless to do much about. Away from court, the average district
attorney will readily admit that most people, deep down in their
hearts, have a longing for action and a constant interest in those
who act out what they themselves had only thought of doing.
The so-called good citizen, they know, enjoys reading about the
phenomenon of action, whether by the common sneak thief or
by the murderer, or by the policeman who is permitted to act
out his most aggressive impulses on the "right side" of the law.
Mr. Prosecuting Attorney knows that there is magic in murder;
most men have never killed anyone but they persist in reading
the obituaries with a great deal of interest and pleasure.

I feel a little sorry for the prosecuting attorney. If he is, like
most of us, basically a man good of heart, he must often be
called upon to demand penalties he does not believe in. He must
follow the brutally narrow course of law that is archaic, today,
in a world where we know that the subtle difference between
too much insulin and too little sugar may turn a thinking, coher-
ent, decent man into an automaton. The district attorney, really,
is most often a terrible swift sword in the hands of an outraged
mob; he must cut and slash, though in the end he is the one
steeped in blood, not the mob. He must ask for penalties that
John Q. Public—supposedly the man he serves—would flinch from
asking, were he to know the consequences of his words. Too
often it is the district attorney who must send a man to his death,
then lie awake in the early dawning hours of the morning, waiting, knowing that before the sun has been too long in the sky his
work product will come to fruition and the victim of his prosecution will die. The memory of the victim's death will not soon
leave the district attorney's recollections, though it will be so

much cold news in the mind of the great public, the master the prosecuting attorney must serve.

I could never be a prosecuting attorney, though not because I feel such men are not an honorable breed. But I could never prosecute another man because, if it becomes me to instance myself, I say that there is not the wretch so guilty, so despairing, so torn with avenging furies, so pursued by the law, so fearful of life, so afraid of death—there is no wretch so steeped in all the agonies of vice and crime that I would not have a heart to listen to his cry, and a tongue to speak in his defense, though 'round his head all the wrath of public opinion should gather, and rage, and roar, and roll, as the ocean rolls and beats against the rock.

THE FIRST PUBLIC DEFENDER

IN THEORY, neither the rich nor the poor may loiter on the streets at a late hour of the night without being able to explain their presence properly. In practice, you and I both know that the police will never arrest the rich man, should they find such a person in a comparable situation. By the same token, if you were given full and complete access to the files of your state's penitentiary, you would be most hard pressed to find confined there a prisoner who had once been a man of means. True, the wealthy person does go to prison from time to time; and each time a rich man is sentenced to jail the newspapers herald it on page one, so rare is the occasion.

The wealthy man need not trouble himself, should he run afoul of the law. With his money he will be able to purchase the finest defense attorney available, should his case ever reach court. In this respect the law is exceedingly democratic; when one is able to afford seasoned counsel, each and every one of the defendant's many and varied rights will be scrupulously protected.

But what of the poor man, the class of man who makes up more than 90 per cent of all the defendants in all the criminal actions? While it is true that the law stipulates that all who are brought before the bar of justice may be, and should be, represented by counsel, the fact remains that many of these unfortunate persons "cop a plea" or plead guilty without benefit of ever consulting an attorney. Most tragic of all, I think, is the plight of one who has been in trouble before; recent studies indicate that the recidivist will more often simply plead guilty to whatever charge the People have brought against him. Needless to say, most of these persons are usually unable to secure the services of an attorney or, in their understandable ignorance of the law, have the notion they can represent themselves without benefit of counsel. I do not believe that this is right; when a man stands accused in a court of law he needs as much assistance as is humanly possible, just as a man needs the finest medical facilities available, should he be contemplating major surgery.

Most of my fellow lawyers—especially those of us who are on familiar ground in the criminal courts—take on many cases that are known, in the vernacular, as "charity jobs." If we receive any remuneration for our services it is a token fee, usually a small sum fixed by the court. Like physicians, most of us recognize the obligation foisted upon us from the moment we were admitted to the practice of law: to insure, whenever possible, that a defendant, in spite of his income or his background, receive a fair trial. For, in the final analysis, it is only when the defendant is represented by legal counsel that he truly *can* receive a fair trial in every sense of the word. Without the presence of his lawyer, the defendant finds himself in the loneliest place in the world: the bar of justice. Walking into court without an attorney, the average defendant in a criminal action is lost and frightened by the awful, intimidating majesty of the incomprehensible machinery of Justice.

But even those of us who, in private practice, do our best to represent such indigent defendants as time allows cannot deal with more than a fraction of all the helpless and poverty-stricken defendants that come our way. Fortunately, we have in the United States a system that has gradually become part of our judicial structure simply because of the great numbers of poor who find their way into our criminal courts. These indigent defendants, as a result of the combined pressures of history and the sheer weight of numbers, may avail themselves of the services of the public defender. A lawyer highly trained in defense law and especially retained by the state to insure that each and every defendant, regardless of his circumstances, be given adequate representation when his day in court arrives. Los Angeles, California, was the first municipality in America to formally enact such a concept, in 1916. Today, almost all of our larger cities offer the penniless defendant the services of this skilled professional, the public defender.

To those of you who have automatically assumed that without the services of a "high-powered criminal lawyer" a man did not have a chance, perhaps news of the public defender system will come as something of a surprise. To the others—those who would say America leads the way, as usual—I offer a word of moderation: the public defender system is neither new, nor is it peculiar to America. Like most of the things we live with and often take for granted, the role of the public defender has a long and honorable history.

About seven hundred years ago a man named Ives of Brittany served the poor without either thought or desire for reward. Ives belonged to a noble family and he had had every conceivable educational advantage. In his fourteenth year his parents had sent him to Paris, where for seven years he studied theology and canon law, important religious-legal concepts that heavily tended to guide the courts of that day.

When he concluded his studies in Paris, Ives went to Orléans, France, to study Roman law. At the age of twenty-three he concluded his studies in Orléans and from that time until the day of his death he dedicated himself to the cause of justice as it concerned itself with the poor, the unwanted, the friendless. Without compensation of any kind, Ives of Brittany assisted the widow, the orphan—anyone who was brought into the courts, and came without counsel.

During his later years it is written that Ives was ordained a priest. He did not, however, choose this moment to retire to the relative comfort of a monastery, nor did he, like so many at that time, use his clerical offices to win favor with the Crown, perhaps hoping to build a minor duchy for himself. No, Ives continued his work, alone and unheralded. He was that most rare breed of man: He never worshiped money, giving all he had to the poor. As the years passed, his good works earned him the honorary title of Advocatus Pauperum: the Lawyer of the Poor.

Ives of Brittany died in 1303, and by 1347 the all-powerful Church, as a tribute to the man and the charitable work he had done in his lifetime, canonized him St. Ives. Today, all lawyers know of him; he is our patron saint.

Equal justice for all, I should like to add, is hardly a modern revolutionary concept, nor is it peculiar to America. Although the poor, befuddled defendant who comes to our courts in legion numbers daily may not be able to see him, those of us who are called upon to defend this man—if we stop for a moment before the inexorable wheels of Justice begin to grind—will surely feel, in that courtroom, the presence of St. Ives of Brittany, our first public defender.

PORTRAIT OF AN IMAGE:
MR. JUSTICE HOLMES

WE HAVE always lived with a certain amount of fraud in the land. In the old days we had such personages as Bat Masterson, acknowledged procurer of women, fobbed off as the finest sort of fellow. General George Custer, an incompetent whose greatest blunder was blamed on his subordinate, Major Reno, was another personal fraud whose exploits, as we know today, were so much hokum.

Today liars, windbags, and other perpetrators of verbal swindle are said to have "an image." We are told, for example, that a popular contemporary politician must have a certain kind of "image" before the public, while, in fact, he may do many things that directly refute what he has said. Movie magazines tell the childish—in years and in mentality—of a certain handsome young star in Hollywood who is seen in the company of countless beautiful young women every week. This young man is given an "image" of virility, while the enlightened know better. So does his attorney, who kept the sordid news of his arrest, in the company of other attractive young men, from the newspapers.

Having qualified the long and involved history of verbal fraud, let us now consider the "image" of Mr. Justice Oliver Wendell Holmes . . .

Mr. Justice Holmes has always been thought of as a kind of witty liberal. While today's schoolboy could not pinpoint any one phase of Mr. Holmes's liberalism, he would certainly not be of the opinion that Holmes was a "reactionary." Nor would most people, for that matter, so successful has the "image" been.

This sort of behavior, by the way, always reminds me of that old refrain, "The song is over but the melody lingers on."

Holmes was no more a liberal than President Kennedy is a Moslem. A careful examination of Holmes's record during his period on the bench of the United States Supreme Court discloses that he went along with the majority about ten times more frequently than he dissented.

Mr. Justice Holmes, in the words of a gambler friend of mine, was the kind of man who played it very close to the vest. He relied on small but steady house percentages, never being inclined to take the dice in his own hand and stand away from the crowd. Most important, it is to be noted that Holmes, during his long life, did nothing to change public opinion regarding his alleged "liberalism." To the contrary, he did everything possible to further the myth.

It is my premise that Holmes, as a result of his legalistic barometer readings of public opinion, as a result of his image building, did more to undermine and lay waste to our precious Bill of Rights than *any other judge in our history!* As for proof, I offer the following.

In January, 1932, Holmes read his last opinion before the Supreme Court. As you will recall, 1932 saw the beginning of the end of "The Great Experiment," a piece of legislative stupidity known as the Volstead Act, or Prohibition Law. The case Holmes was concerned with was that of a Mr. James Dunne of Eureka, California.

Defendant Dunne had been found, according to the prosecution, to be in possession of certain potables—liquor—something he had in common with only about 75 per cent of the adult American population. By law, however, Dunne was guilty of a felony. Accordingly, he was tried in California on a three-count indictment.

To backtrack for a moment, it is of interest to examine the three-count indictment. The first count charged Dunne with the crime of keeping liquor for sale. The second count charged him with possessing liquor unlawfully. The third count dotted the *i*'s and crossed the *t*'s by charging Dunne with selling this same liquor.

Someone, it would appear, wanted a slice of Mr. Dunne's hide.

At the conclusion of the trial the jury found Dunne to be not guilty of the second and third counts; unlawful possession and unlawful sale. The jury did, however, somehow find him guilty of *keeping* liquor for sale.

Perhaps mystified by the jury's logic, Dunne appealed his case. The evidence as to the three offenses, it should be noted, was the same in all cases. If Dunne was innocent of unlawfully possessing liquor and innocent of unlawfully selling liquor, how could he possibly be guilty of having this same liquor for sale? No matter. Surely, when this case of mangled justice reached the Supreme Court of the United States of America, the learned members of the court would swiftly see that Dunne had been "done." Surely this august body, after examining the evidence, would readily see that there was simply no case against Dunne. Even someone not connected with the law could, simply by using a little common sense, readily come to the conclusion that Dunne was no more "a little guilty" than is a woman "a little pregnant."

Accordingly, Dunne's case was studied by the Supreme Court. After due deliberation our "great liberal," Mr. Justice Oliver Wendell Holmes, delivered the majority opinion, whereby he spoke for himself as well as the other, concurring justices.

Here is what Mr. Image said:

> Consistency in the verdict is not necessary. Each count in an indictment is regarded as if it was a separate offense. If separate indictments had been presented against the defendant for possession and maintenance of a nuisance, and had been separately tried, the same evidence being offered in support of each, an acquittal on one could not be pleaded as res judicata of the other. Where the offenses are separately charged in the counts of a single indictment the same rule must hold.

Discounting Holmes's peculiar logic for a moment, let us consider the effect his opinion would have upon all of us. The learned Mr. Justice Holmes, in laying down the law on the Dunne case, said that double jeopardy—trying a man twice for the same crime—was hereafter the order of the day. Had Holmes had his way, we would today be living in a police state more cruel and vicious than any of us can imagine.

Possession of liquor, in the Dunne case, was an included offense in the count charging him with keeping liquor for sale. Under the Prohibition Law—or any other law—it simply defies the imagination to understand how a person can keep liquor for sale without possessing it. A first-year law student knows this much and if he were to parrot Holmes he would surely be thrown out of school on his ear!

I must conclude, after studying the Dunne case, that Holmes either had no common sense, absolutely no knowledge of the law, or . . . he rather cynically went along with the times. Either the "great liberal's" intellect was asleep, I must conclude, or he, like so many others, did not want to "rock the boat."

A broad and comprehensive examination of Holmes's long career discloses that, except for manufacturing cute sayings and beaming widely each time he was touted to be a liberal, the man was no liberal at all. When the chips were down, Holmes was quick to retreat. He was a man born to cut bait where the braver did all the fishing.

If the liberals must have an idol, one who was honest in both judgment and purpose, they would do well to consider Justice Pierce Butler, a man more concerned with truth than image. Curiously, Butler's "image" was poison to the liberal element. Perhaps this able jurist was more concerned with keeping our Bill of Rights intact than with whitewashing the public's opinion of his personal affairs.

Here is what Justice Butler had to say in the same case:

> Excluding the possession negatived by the finding of the second count, there is nothing of substance left in the first count,

for its specifications were limited to the keeping for sale of the identical drinks alleged in the second count to have been unlawfully possessed. . . . The evidence having been found insufficient to establish such possession, it cannot be held adequate to warrant conviction under the first count. The finding of not guilty is a final determination that possession, the gravamen of both counts, was not proved.

Judge Butler, concerned more with the law than with his image, saw not only the inconsistency of Dunne's "partial guilt" but, further, was aware of the effect Holmes's decision could have upon all of us, for Holmes had quite plainly said that if one jury acquitted Dunne he could still be subsequently tried until such time as some jury, somewhere, would find him guilty.

It seems strange that Holmes could have been such a poor lawyer. Not only did he prove himself to be illogical but he was completely ignorant of the doctrine of included offenses, in the bargain. Hardly a liberal, Holmes was a lawyer only by sufferance.

But that may be explained, too. The law does not require that a justice of the United States Supreme Court be a lawyer! Justice, anyone?

WHAT'S IN A NAME?

THE FOLLOWING appeared recently in a local newspaper:

> Eugene Weingand, 29, a Los Angeles real estate salesman, looks like Peter Lorre and talks like Peter Lorre. But now he wants to be Peter Lorre, and the 59-year-old actor is not sympathetic.
>
> Lorre's lawyer told Judge Philbrick McCoy yesterday that the actor is vigorously opposed to Weingand's petition to change his name—to Peter Lorre.
>
> The judge set a hearing for October 3.

All of us, after showing proper cause, may legally change our names. While laws tend to vary from one state to the next, it is usually the rule that a petitioner must take out a small advertisement in the "Vital Statistics" section of the local newspaper, stating his intention to change his name. For those who want to kill a few hours, a study of the Vital Statistics section will often reveal some fascinating trivia in the form of petitions to have a name changed. It seems not so long ago that I recall seeing a certain lady's name being changed from Evelyn West to Evelyn $50,000 Treasure Chest West. Miss West is a stripper and such a name would, I suppose, be in keeping with her occupation. However, it is well that the day of Captain Kidd and other, assorted nefarious pirates has passed.

As to the matter of taking another's name, however, I could paraphrase Iago: ". . . who steals my good name steals my life." Names, of course, are our life. We are stuck with them at birth and although Willie Stinchfield, upon reaching legal age, may change his name to William Stine, he will always be known to his childhood friends as Stinky. No matter where Mr. Stine may go, every time someone yells Stinky, he will turn around, if only for a moment. His name changed and money in his pocket, he will still be Stinky of old.

I am not surprised that Mr. Lorre "vigorously opposed" petitioner's move to change his name from Weingand to Lorre. Let us consider the years Mr. Lorre has spent assiduously building his character so that even the young among us will instantly recognize it. True, Mr. Lorre has never been a "star" in the strictest sense of the word; he has been more. He has been the spice, on many occasions, that has made a Hollywood turkey edible. Laboring long and hard in the vineyards of Southern California, Mr. Lorre has systematically made his name synonymous with villainy, chicanery, and other nefarious cinematic doings. From his first film, *M*, to the long series he made for Warner Brothers in the 1940s, who can forget his menacing performances? It seems only yesterday that he was selling Clark

Gable down the river in *Strange Cargo*. And who can forget his machinations in *Maltese Falcon* as he did his best to swindle Humphrey Bogart and Sidney Greenstreet out of the big black bird?

The newspaper article further states that petitioner Weingand is a realtor, a professional calling sometimes associated with the early activities of Jim Fiske. Now, I wonder just what purpose Mr. Weingand has in mind, wanting to change his name to Peter Lorre? Is he hoping to intimidate a little old couple from Southgate into selling him their home at below market value? Is he planning on peddling an old, abandoned house with the stipulation that buried treasure is hidden beneath the floor boards, along with a body he planted there in some now long-forgotten assassination?

History has been most unkind to those who, legally or otherwise, took the good name of another, for whatever reason. Before we had social security numbers, fingerprint identification, and other modern means of continually establishing character through established data, a man's name was his passport.

Traditionally, names have been associated with one's occupation. Carter, for example, is an old English name that is associated with one who operated a cart; Johnson, the son of John. While I do not know the origin of Mr. Lorre's name, we all do know what it is associated with; it is his fortune and he has earned many times over any recognition he receives from it.

If Mr. Weingand wants a name associated with notoriety, why not John Dillinger? If he would prefer to be only a minor celebrity, he could start out with Pretty Boy Floyd, gradually working his way up to Mad Dog Coll, thence to Abe "Kid Twist" Reles. After five or six years he could make a final appearance in court and petition to have his name changed from Reles to Alphonse Capone. With the current boom in things smacking of the Roaring Twenties, his fortune would surely be made. Unless, of course, a few old-time Capone antagonists still existed.

I cannot predict the outcome of Mr. Weingand's date in court.

I truly hope that his petition will not be granted; one Peter Lorre is enough. With two of them in circulation, I am sure Mr. J. E. Hoover would go before Congress and demand another million dollars of the taxpayers' money to guard us against a double menace.

FINE PRINT

HISTORIANS would be hard pressed to find an example of sophisticated hatred rivaling that which Aaron Burr and Alexander Hamilton felt for each other.

Many and varied were the reasons that caused Burr to loathe Hamilton and Hamilton to detest Burr, but in each instance an essential element proved to be either money or power.

The backgrounds and characters of these early American giants were strikingly similar, and therein lies the probable answer for the intense mutual hatred. It is a basic law of physics that like poles of two magnets will forever repel one another. Descriptive words, such as well-bred, learned, industrious, ambitious, etc., suited one as well as the other, but many men with those attributes make their way through life without gaining the animosity of a Burr or a Hamilton.

Add greed and jealousy to the list, however, and you discover why these two battled from the day of their first meeting until the day, in 1804, when Hamilton fell fatally wounded during a pistol duel with Burr.

The roles they played in the Revolutionary War enabled Burr and Hamilton to gain considerable wealth and political power, and, like most ambitious men, the more they acquired the more they desired. Fate threw them together on many occasions during the long climb up the ladder of success. It is natural that each hoped the other would fall in order that his own journey might be swifter and surer.

During the 1790s, Burr made several attempts to establish a banking concern in his native New York City. On each occasion the move was blocked by the state legislature at the behest of Hamilton. At the time there were only two banks in New York. One was a branch of the Bank of the United States. The other was the Bank of New York, an institution of finance owned by one Alexander Hamilton.

In 1797, after serving six years in the United States Senate, Burr was elected to the New York State Assembly. Hamilton feared the move a preamble to an attempt to acquire a bank charter, but Burr seemed content, during the 1798 session, to occupy himself with bills to establish a state bankruptcy law, to abolish imprisonment for debt, to impose a tax on woodland and unproductive property, in addition to a proposal to do away with slavery in New York.

Burr proved such a willing and able legislator that his re-election the following year was accomplished with ease. And while Hamilton was convinced that Burr was up to something, the legislators who had toiled alongside Burr scoffed at the idea.

On April 2, 1799, Burr pushed through the legislature a bill granting him the right to supply the City of New York with pure and wholesome water.

New York, during the summer of 1798, had been visited by one of the most virulent of those epidemics of yellow fever which so frequently set the inhabitants of New York, Philadelphia, and other large cities to burning niter in the streets, firing horse pistols at the bedsides of sufferers, wearing cloves of garlic in their shoes and bags of camphor around their necks, and liberally dousing themselves with Harlem Oil, Essence of Aloes, and Vinegar of the Four Thieves.

The epidemic of '98 caused a panic in New York, for everyone remembered a similar plague in Philadelphia, in 1795, that re-

sulted in a stoppage of commerce and supply, since few desired
to enter a contaminated city. The panic was justified, for New
York became a place of horror and death. Whole streets were
barricaded or burned. Pest houses were established which sur-
passed in filth and misery anything conceivable. A system of
inspection was initiated, with rewards for informers, which
quickly became the instrument of countless personal vengeances.
The dead numbered in the thousands.

The epidemic was due to the disease-laden ships that tied up
at the New York wharves; it was due to the filth and dead horses,
pigs, and dogs that lay in the streets.

Few of New York's populace knew this. Instead, the plague
was blamed on the brackish water that offended their taste.
Obviously, anyone who promised a regular supply of pure and
wholesome water would gain the support of the people.

With this in mind, among other things, Aaron Burr bestirred
himself to Albany for the 1799 session of the Assembly and,
during the closing days of the legislature, when the members
scarcely had time to read it, brought about the passage of his
water bill, fixing the capital of the company at two million
dollars.

The capital was quickly subscribed and a well was dug during
the following summer, followed by the laying of a pipe line to
convey the water.

The real purpose of the company, however, was made evident
through the opening, at 40 Wall Street, of the Manhattan Company Bank, an occurrence that puzzled, to say the very least,
Alexander Hamilton, since he owned the only bank charter other
than that of the branch of the Bank of the United States.

Hamilton dispatched his lawyers to investigate and they had
little trouble determining the answer. Tucked away among the
clauses of Burr's water charter was a paragraph stating that the
surplus capital might be employed in any way not inconsistent
with the laws and Constitution of the United States or the State
of New York.

Hamilton protested, accusing Burr of chicanery in securing passage of his bill. But nothing could be done and Burr had fulfilled his ambition to become a banker.

Actually, Governor Jay, who had signed the bill granting the water charter, was warned beforehand by one who had read it that there was more than pure and wholesome water in that paragraph. There was, indeed.

The Manhattan Company Bank operates today under the original charter. In 1955, when it merged with the Chase National Bank of New York, the intent was to have Chase be the surviving corporation. But the lawyers found that Burr's charter required any sale of the bank to be approved by every single stockholder, which meant that almost anyone could prevent the merger. So the Manhattan Company Bank bought Chase instead, and the Chase Manhattan Bank is the present-day form of the water company and banking business that Aaron Burr started in spite of Alexander Hamilton.

HONESTY

THE CYNICAL GREEK philosopher Diogenes spent a great many of his eighty-nine years walking the streets of Athens in search of an honest man.

There is no record that he found one.

It is possible Diogenes was unsure of the shape he stalked. Honesty is, to say the least, a complicated quality. The word itself implies many things to many people, but one thing is certain; it is something each of us looks for in others if not ourselves.

When a man acquires the label of honesty he has achieved a

mark of highest respect. To earn such recognition, the man must
be straightforward in conduct, thought, and speech. The honest
man must be equitable in his dealings, sincere in his relations
with others, and free from duplicity.

To say of a man that he is honest is to pay him the greatest
honor.

Over the years there has been concern as to the honesty of
some members of the legal profession. Of course, such concern
is unfounded in fact and scurrilous in intent. No less an authority
than the American Bar Association states unhesitatingly that
attorneys always have been and always will be honest men.

A New York attorney of the 1840s, named Scheuster, was just
an honest lawyer. Unfortunately, most of his clients did not
recognize this and were most critical of his methods. Their actions
can be excused since they must have been poorly educated, for
they insisted on pronouncing his name as Shyster.

To those still wary of the legal profession, may I cite this
example of obtaining the services of an honorable attorney.

Recently, a moneylender wrote a letter to the postmaster of a
small town, asking for the name of an honest lawyer in that town
who would undertake to collect a claim against a borrower who
had failed and refused to repay his loan. The reply he received
was an honest one. There was no equivocation or mental reserva-
tion in the mind of the postmaster, who answered:

> . . . I received your letter this morning. In addition to being
> postmaster of this community, I am also an honest lawyer, and
> would not hesitate to undertake to collect a just claim against a
> debtor who refused to pay it. I also happen to be the person to
> whom you made the usurious loan that you are trying to collect.
> I received your demand to pay and I refuse to pay it. I am also
> the banker to whom you tried to discount my note, and who
> refused to buy it because as the borrower I had refused to repay
> the loan. And if I was not for the time being acting in the
> capacity of pastor filling the pulpit of my church, I would tell
> you where you could go with your claim.

LUCIUS BEEBE

MY GOOD FRIEND and erstwhile client Lucius Beebe, renowned author, editor, and publisher, is a man who doesn't mince words.

In a recent editorial column commenting on crime and capital punishment, Lucius penned this opinion:

> . . . A nice point for the consideration of social ethics would be the possible execution of lawyers knowingly engaged in the defense of persons found guilty of murder. In most communities, the accessory to the crime of murder, the lookout, the gun carrier, the active participant at whatever degree removed, is considered equally guilty with the principal participant in the crime. Is a lawyer who defends a man he knows to be guilty of murder and so allies himself against society itself not an accessory after the fact? Is not a proven false witness in the defense of a murderer an accessory . . . ?

You have forgotten, sir, that our law provides that every man is presumed to be innocent until the contrary is proved to a moral certainty and beyond a reasonable doubt.

Mr. Beebe is a gentleman and a scholar, but for all his education he has apparently never come across a basic principle: The trial lawyer does not defend the charge, he defends the man.

Who can evaluate how or why the mental wheels, in their turning, generate the spark resulting in the annihilation of a human being? It is easy to condemn. But who among us can dismantle the mechanism of man's mind and explain the hidden and powerful compulsive drive of the murderer? Could it be that civilization itself creates a killer? This is a question that cannot be answered with denial or affirmation; it is unanswerable.

While some effort has been made to rid it of its worst absurd-

ities, law has advanced little since the days of William Blackstone. If medicine had remained as backward, the chief remedial
aid of today's doctor would be bloodletting.

Man aims gropingly for perfection, but owing to ignorance,
prejudice, weakness, disease, passion, or the complexities of the
world, he often produces near disaster for himself and for others.
In attempting to explain criminal behavior, man is faced with a
network of facts so minute that his lack of understanding must
always far outweigh his knowledge and his judgment.

We cannot help the hereditary dispositions with which we
are equipped, nor can we help the environment into which we
are born. How can we be reproached for any action if we cannot
be reproached for any of the factors which have determined it?
Some are born with mental and physical strength; others are
mentally or physically handicapped. Some are born rich and need
not concern themselves with earning a living; some fight for
existence day by day. Some have fine intellect and some are
idiots. Some have the capacity to learn; others cannot absorb
elementary problems or meet them.

Man is a strange animal; he loves to punish. There is the attitude that the aim of punishment is to be measured in terms of
its benefits to society. Punishment is used not only to induce the
person punished to abide once more by the law, but also to
hold up to the members of society generally the need for
obedience to the law. In the sphere of religion, there is the doctrine of predestination, which declares that some have been
chosen by God from everlasting to enjoy salvation, while others
are doomed.

Since the Law, in its majestic equality, forbids the rich as well
as the poor to sleep under bridges, to get in the streets, and to
steal bread, it is not strange that the murder trial is the most
interesting of the conflicts between man and the state. The public
enjoys the murder trial and its aura of mystery, for strangely,
many good people, nice people, law-abiding people topple from
the emotional plateau and kill.

Murder is a seed in man's soul nurtured by negative emotions —from fear and hatred, from anger and anxiety, from jealousy and greed, from humiliation and spite, from repression and resentment. The seed bears fruit only in rare instances, sprouting only when conscience or consciousness have abandoned man's mind.

The public finds emotional outlet for its own soul-bound seed in following the daily outbursts of others. There is magic in murder.

The role of the lawyer in such circumstances is seemingly difficult to comprehend for such as Lucius Beebe. The Law is established for all men, the lawyer for those who seek him out. In any court, criminal or civil, the lawyer supports his client only within the limits prescribed by personal and professional ethics. He is neither the judge nor the jury, with the obligation of determining right or wrong, guilt or innocence. His function is merely to present his client's case.

If a lawyer refuses to defend, either from what he may think of the defendant, the charge, or the offense, he assumes the position of judge and jury even before the hour of judgment and, in proportion to his rank and reputation, puts heavy influence or perhaps a mistaken opinion into the scale against the accused.

Can anyone question that it is better for our civilization that a hundred guilty persons should escape the punishment of death than one innocent person should be executed? A man must be given the opportunity to present his defense. Even God did not pass judgment upon Adam before allowing him to present his defense. *Adam* (said God) *hast thou eaten of the tree whereof I commanded thee that thou shouldest not eat?*

Does the Punishment
Fit the Crime?

NIGGER JACK

THE HISTORY of capital punishment indicates man has been put to death by his fellow man in a variety of ways. Hanging has been the most popular mode, but executioners have never relied solely on the noose. On occasion the convicted has been shot, starved, drowned, electrocuted, gassed, poisoned, crucified, guillotined, stoned, or burned at the stake.

Despite a suggestion of acceptance in the Old Testament, burning became too closely associated with the deaths of religious martyrs and lost favor in the western world. It can be supposed some credit for such feeling is due England's Queen Mary I, who put to the torch three hundred stubborn Protestants. Following her reign, the legal burning of a human being was an infrequent occurrence.

But while such method of execution was practically non-existent, the statutes which allowed it were not always stricken from the tomes of justice. In South Carolina, as late as 1825, an inferior court of two magistrates and five freeholders tried a man called Nigger Jack for the double crime of rape and murder. Deciding to make of Nigger Jack a dreadful example, the court sentenced him to be chained to a stake, soaked in turpentine, and burned alive.

The story of Nigger Jack is preserved in the Miscellaneous Records of South Carolina. As a historical document, the statement of account from the constable to the state treasurer for services rendered is evidence of the executioner's impassiveness concerning his duties.

DUE Thomas Goodman, Constable:

To Summons five freeholders at 54	2.70
To Summons one Magistrate	.54
Guarding of Nigger Jack four days & nights at 1.50	6.00
Feeding Nigger Jack four days	.50
Two waggons & teams one day a-getting of lightwood for to burn Jack	6.00
Four hands one day extra of the driving for the waggons	2.00
Paid Black Smyth for ironing of Jack	2.50
Two bottles of Spirits Turpentine at 56–1/4	1.12–1/2
Chains for to confine Jack when burnt	3.00
Executing of Nigger Jack	3.00
	27.36–1/2

South Carolina
Abbeville District

I John C. McGhee one of the Justices of the peace for Abbeville District hereby Certify that Thomas Goodman is a constable for this District Regularly appointed, that I believe the charges in the above account are just and reasonable.

22nd Nov. 1825   JOHN C. McGHEE, J. P.

The law was changed. The South Carolina legislature amended the slave code of the state to read: On the conviction of a slave or free person of color for a capital offense, the punishment shall be by hanging and not otherwise.

But Nigger Jack burned.

IT'S THE LAW—BUT DON'T
YOU BELIEVE IT

UNITED STATES SENATOR John L. McClellan of Arkansas has
written a book—*Crime Without Punishment*. In it he has given
the reader a report on the work of his committee. McClellan's
years of experience in both the House and Senate have fitted
him well for the chairmanship of the Rackets Committee of the
United States Senate. The book is a great record of trial without
benefit of defense.

McClellan is a determined man. After his election to Congress
in 1938, he ran against Mrs. Hattie Caraway for the Senate. He
was defeated. He tried again in 1942 and won, and is now serving his fourth term as United States Senator.

The Senator's book is a review of the testimony given in the
many cases investigated by his committee, and sets forth some
of the more important aspects of the evidence on the alleged
improper activities of Labor and Management alike. Of course,
no one appearing before the Senator's committee had a lawyer
to advise what course to follow.

The Spanish Inquisition spilled more blood it is true, but these
congressional committees have ruined more families without
one thought concerning their constitutional rights. This is something new in America. We fought against England because of
the Star Chamber proceedings which destroyed men without
benefit of trial by jury, but now we have opened the doors wide
for congressional committees to run wild and to destroy man
without benefit of the right to a defense—right or wrong.

The only important chapter in the Senator's book is titled
"I Decline to Answer"—and here the Senator gives us his

thoughts about the Fifth Amendment to our Constitution. He writes that about 22 per cent of the witnesses who appeared before the committee took the Fifth Amendment. The Senator does not approve of the use of the Fifth because, as he says, "many of the witnesses would tell only their names and addresses and would then decline to answer any further questions . . . many of these un-cooperative ones were obviously attempting to hinder and obstruct the Committee in its efforts to get at the truth, more so than they were seeking to protect themselves against self-incrimination. . . ."

The Senator, in attempting to justify his destruction of the rights guaranteed by the Fifth, is blind to the fact that this amendment is part of our United States Constitution. The words mean what they say: ". . . *nor shall be compelled in any criminal case to be a witness against himself.* . . ." The United States Supreme Court through the years has ruled that even in civil cases a witness may refuse to answer any question his answer to which might be used against him in any criminal proceeding.

I disagree with the Senator and his thinking. While the Fifth has protected some criminals, it also protects the innocent. I am informed the Senator is a lawyer. I ask him what would be his advice to his client if he were for the defense; if he were alone fighting for some man who had faith in him and in his judgment.

The Senator writes that "most of our citizens have little to do with Congressional hearings and with courts and judicial proceedings, and therefore they do not always have a clear understanding of the Fifth Amendment, nor do they know its wording, its history, and the broad concept of freedom and justice that it projects. . . ." Well, Senator, it is time that you took notice of the broad concept of freedom and justice the Fifth Amendment guarantees to all men.

The Senator continues:

> . . . the Amendment was submitted to the people with nine other Amendments at the first session of the first Congress to convene under the new Constitution (all of the ten were adopted and

came into effect on December 15, 1791). Its provisions go to the
heart of Anglo-Saxon justice as it developed in Britain during
centuries of struggle by brave men against their oppressive rulers
—rulers who grossly misused the great powers of nobility and
government which they possessed. Its ideals crossed the seas with
our ancestors who settled this land, and the principles it declares
and vouchsafes to us are now an integral part of our heritage. Its
safeguards are the proud possession of free men—they were designed and developed to protect freedom. . . .

I agree with Senator McClellan that the language has a
splendid dignity, and I point out to him that its meanings are
as clear and appropriate today as they were in 1791. This nation
stands in glory upon its Constitution. The efficacy and grandeur
of that sacred document should be, by resolute purpose and
dedication, steadfastly strengthened and preserved, and not whit-
tled or hacked away by expedient interpretation of congressional
committees seeking publicity or by reckless tinkering and ir-
reverence.

These fourteen words, *"nor shall be compelled in any criminal
case to be a witness against himself,"* mean exactly what they
say. If we as a nation believe their usefulness at an end, then let
us lawfully abolish the Fifth by amending the Constitution of the
United States.

Individual liberties in America are declining, in the view of
Associate Justice William O. Douglas of the Supreme Court.
Expanding on a theme he developed in a recent booklet, *Freedom
of the Mind,* Justice Douglas cited these examples in a TV
interview.

The Fifth Amendment "has become a slur" because of improper conduct of congressional investigations. "The Fifth
Amendment is one of the greatest heritages we have. . . . It was
designed to protect the innocent as well as the guilty. The design
was to make Government produce evidence . . . rather than
putting a man or a woman on the rack and squeezing out of him
or her the stuff to convict them. . . ."

I pray God that someday—*soon*—we will hear voice after voice of the American people reiterating Mr. Justice Douglas. Perhaps if we keep the right thought, even McClellan may become a worker in the field of law and not the inquisitor who is destroying our heritage of liberty. The Senator may become a convert to a religious belief in our Constitution and in the rights of man. But, I say "may"—only God knows and he doesn't talk to McClellan.

Every judge, every lawyer, and every citizen must condemn the practice of imputing a sinister meaning to the exercise of a person's constitutional right under the Fifth Amendment, nor dare anyone permit any inference of wrongdoing to flow from the invocation of a constitutional right.

I do not argue the cause of law violation, but I shall fight to the death for the rights my forefathers bled and died for. If this be wrong, my license to practice law and that of every other lawyer should be taken away . . . including your license, Senator.

ORGANIZED CRIME

I HAVE JUST CONCLUDED reading a book on organized crime. Some of us who have tried criminal cases and are interested in the cause of crime do not find, from either observation or experience, the fearful amount of organized crime that our investigating committees would have us believe exist.

The Committee on Mercenary Crime of the American Bar Association reported some thirty years ago that "the gangster flourishes because of the conditions, laws, and customs which make his business profitable, and because of a large popular demand for the products of his illegal business." He will doubtless continue to flourish as long as crime continues to pay such large dividends and there is such a remarkable demand for his wares.

We, the people, demand that some so-called organized crime exist and flourish to the profit of certain groups, organized or unorganized. The clearest example, and the one nearest to us all, is the horse-race bookie, who is found in every city and hamlet. Look carefully at this organized crime. Here is what is really happening, the late Senator Estes Kefauver to the contrary notwithstanding.

Horse racing is legal in many states. We permit citizens of all walks of life to attend race tracks and bet their fool heads off. This is lawful. From the bottom of our society straight to the top, no one is molested, degraded, or called a criminal so long as he bets at the race track. Of course, he must have the time to go to the track.

There are others of our citizens who also enjoy the thrill of a bet on a race horse but cannot take the time to go to the track, and so you have the bookie around the corner who will take a bet and absorb it if the bettor loses, or pay track odds if the bettor wins. This bookie is a criminal. The person betting with the bookie is also a criminal because he and the bookie have conspired to violate the law which specifically provides that you can bet all you please at the track but not elsewhere.

Now go a step further. The bettor wants to bet on a horse running at a Florida or New York track but unfortunately cannot travel to these tracks, so he places his bet with the bookie. Having made this wager he wants to be sure that he will not be cheated if he wins, so he buys, the pure, moralistic, holier-than-thou morning or afternoon papers to read the race results from those far-off places. There is a whole page given to this important information. The newspapers, on this page, recommend which horses to bet on, and boast daily on their exactness in picking winners. In addition there are newspapers given over entirely to race track results and to race horses. These papers are transmitted by our holy Post Office Department and distributed over all the United States.

The people telegraphing this information to the newspapers also make it available to the bookie. All this to fill the demand of our citizens.

Yet another thing. If you are just inside the wire fence of the race track and place a bet, it is all pure and legal. If you do the same thing six inches away, but outside the wire fence, you have become an aider and abettor of organized crime. Who is kidding whom?

You can't legislate against man's will.

IN THE MIDST OF LIFE . . .

THE LATE ERNEST HEMINGWAY once wrote of "men dying well." I have seen men die and none of them did it well. At best a man is felled swiftly and is denied the months of agony that many victims of slow and insidious terminal illnesses are forced to bear.

But of all who die, perhaps it is hardest for those who die as a result of no accident, no prolonged illness. Perhaps it is hardest for those to die who know, months in advance, the day and hour they will be killed.

Even Hemingway, had he been compelled to witness a state-sponsored murder, might have rewritten his lines about men dying well.

Our whole life is a sort of training period for the business of dying, much as maneuvers are a training period for a soldier who will someday face combat. Like the soldier, none of us can tell how we will react when the warm summer of maneuvers has passed and we are left to stand alone and frightened in a barren country, about to face an enemy we have never met.

I have received a letter from a man who is in training to die.

This man wrote me from condemned row, San Quentin State Prison. I do not know this man, nor can I truly imagine what was going on inside his head as the date of his execution approached. I cannot imagine his thoughts or his feelings as he watched others being led from their pens, down the corridor, never to return.

I cannot imagine this man's torment on the day when impassive guards will come for him and bear him to the lethal gas chamber where, in compliance with the will of the People of the State of California, the executioner will cause lethal hydrocyanic gas to choke the life out of him.

This man's letter speaks for itself. It is a letter from a man possessed of a subtle terror. It is a letter from a man who does not want to die, who is pleading for his life in the only way he knows.

In his place, what kind of a letter would you write?

My Dear Mr. Ehrlich:

I am in a predicament that forces me to look forward to having that pill of Cyanide dropped, with me as its victim. The most harrowing aspects of the predicament is the fact that I am innocent of the crime which I am accused of— The crime: MURDER; killing a police officer, which at the time was performing his duty. The co-defendant in this case has confessed to the killing, implicating me by stating the initial shot, the shot that supposedly killed the officer, was fired by himself, and further stated that I too fired shots into the officer's body.

The facts are contrary to those statements signed by the co-defendant in this case.

I am certain that your knowledge of how the people, in their clammoring for justice, force the prosecution to extract blood for blood! And, as in all cases concerning the death of a police officer, the more blood, the better. Picture, if you will, just how much consideration my word will receive in denying the allegations set forth by the co-defendant!

I cannot help but feel that the co-defendant and the prosecution are conspiring to take my life. My situation is so complicated that only the best legal mind in the country can possibly save my life. . . .

I admit to being a thief, a social outcast, and immoral according to the standards of the people, but I am not a murderer and abhor violence in any form.

What I am asking you to do, Mr. Ehrlich, is save my life.

No one knows where the true balance of justice lies, and the laws of Polarity have always puzzled my mind. Good and evil, right or wrong, rich or poor, hungry and insatiated; what human being has the power to put all these seemingly contradictions in their proper perspective? If I am to die for a murder I did not commit, I would like to believe that it is the will of God, rather than that of the people . . . to distinguish the will of God from the will of the people is a purely personal thing, yet I feel certain that you will understand what I am trying so desperately to convey.

If you defend me, Mr. Ehrlich, and I am found guilty, then I will die peacefully and courageously. For then I will feel that God has redeemed a lost soul from a world of chaos and misery, otherwise I will feel that the forces of evil have, through the people, destroyed my soul, and will walk laughingly at the funeral, jeering at the dignity of innocence. One more life perhaps doesn't mean anything to the persons whose work consists of legally killing another person. Compassion for the condemned is something foreign to the principles that life has taught him in our society. But, knowing that your understanding transcends that of the average man, I believe that through various forms of abstractions that you know the value of life, that a human life is neither immaterial nor irrevelent; that no matter what his station in life may be, he also deserves to live.

Punishment by death is lawful, and I understand that it exists: to die for having committed a capital crime would never make me shrink under the hands of the executioner, for I well understand the intricate implications involving crime and its punishments. But, to die for something that I am innocent of, even though the possibility exists, is not my idea of propriety.

God does not endow men with exceptional gifts unless he has chosen to use them as an instrument of his benevolence . . . I hope and pray that you recognize this urgent need and decide that this life too is worthy of his grace. God is not a respector of persons only, but through one righteous soul he bringeth forth good fruits of abundance upon the multitudes . . . So, in essence, though I knowingly will benefit from it, it is not just myself who will reap the bounty of your understanding.

With death seeming so imminent, it turns the vision inward; I have stripped my soul to nakedness—I do not like what I see. The truth is not very pleasant, except for the fact that I have learned the truth about myself. But, one fact still must remain; I am not a murderer and should not have to face the possibility of dieing as one!

With overwhelming humility and preponderance of humbleness, I pray that you have enough compassion to save an innocent man's life so as to give him the opportunity to save his soul.

Respectfully,

ENTRAPMENT

———

THE LIBRARIES of our scholarly nation are stocked with countless treatises dealing with the hows, whys, and wherefores of the criminal mind.

The subject is as popular as motherhood and patriotism. Philosophers and historians, policemen and prosecutors, theologians and lawyers, social workers and psychiatrists—all have sought to explain the mental make-up of the criminal as though he were a mathematical problem subject to exact proof.

Possibly there has been too academic an approach to the subject.

Not so long ago a criminal was born. It wasn't immediately apparent. He was an obedient and respectful child and emerged into adulthood a seemingly honest and trustworthy member of society.

When employment beckoned he did not balk; in fact he chose to become a policeman, assuming the duty of protecting his fellow citizen and his community.

On the surface he was a God-fearing man. He attended church regularly, and upon entering or leaving the place of worship his uppermost thought was the welfare of his brethren.

Despite his background, his honest purpose in life, his desire to be a model member of mankind, he left the straight and narrow path of lawful life and entered the hall of crime.

He was a member of a large Police Department in a metropolis in that portion of our nation known as the East. The department itself was no better, no worse than most.

On a particular day a well-known gangster was given his just desserts through a shotgun employed by a fellow hoodlum. When considerable time had elapsed and the killing remained unsolved, the citizenry, goaded by the press, demanded a reform in the Police Department.

Our hero, and his fellow bluecoats, responded by launching an intensive crackdown on crime of all sorts, but mostly misdemeanors, violating obscure, long-ignored, microscopically minor city ordinances.

In his pursut of righteousness the officer learned a certain grocery delivery boy was carrying a supply of tobacco on his motorbike, for the convenience of his customers, and was dispensing cigars and cigarettes without the benefit of a city license, thus violating an ordinance that had been on the books for more than a century. The act was obviously a most heinous offense, and the officer made plans to trap this public enemy.

The plot came to the attention of an old-timer on the force. Being a sympathetic sort, and wise in the ways of the world, he tipped off the grocery boy and had him hustle down to City Hall and obtain a tobacco permit.

On the day following, our police officer hailed the youth and asked to purchase a package of cigarettes.

"All out," answered the boy, "but I got cigars."

"Okay, give me a cigar," said the policeman.

"Only sell them in boxes. Ten dollars a box," said the boy.

Eager to reduce the crime rate, the officer handed over ten dollars, and immediately demanded to see the boy's tobacco license.

"Right here," said the youth, pulling the permit from a pocket and leaving our officer, who himself didn't smoke, with a box of unwanted cigars.

Then the officer had an idea. "You're a good lad. How about buying them back?"

"Sure," said the boy, "for five bucks."

The policeman was almost apoplectic with the knowledge that he had been had, but made the exchange anyway.

Whereupon the boy rode straight to the office of the district attorney and swore out a complaint against the officer.

The charge: Selling tobacco without a license.

CRUEL AND UNUSUAL PUNISHMENT

THE EIGHTEENTH CENTURY in England was hardly an age of enlightenment in the field of punishment for crime. The list of felonies had been greatly enlarged by statute and every felony was punishable by death. Pressing to death—the *peine forte et dure*—was not abolished until 1772, nor was burning at the stake, as a punishment for women convicted of petty treason—killing a husband—until 1790.

Flogging in the British military and naval services was carried to such barbarous extremes that its execution, while savage in its cruelty to the subject, was demoralizing to those who inflicted and who witnessed it. Judged by contemporary British standards, the Continental Army's limiting of corporal punishment to one hundred lashes may be viewed as indeed humane. A proposal to raise this limitation to five hundred lashes was rejected by Congress in 1781. One hundred lashes was the Navy maximum.

In the American Army, desertion was at first a capital offense. Not until 1830 was it made noncapital in time of peace; and soldiers were regularly executed for deserting. Sometimes death sentences were commuted, but this was rare.

In a letter from a Colonel Hamtrack to the Commanding General, December 5, 1794, on soldiers convicted of larceny, the colonel writes, ". . . I have flogged them till I am tired. The economic allowance of one hundred lashes allowed by government, does not appear a sufficient inducement for a rascal to act the part of an honest man. . . ."

Years ago the U.S. Army directed that whenever ball-and-chain is imposed as the sentence it should state the weight of the ball, the length of the chain, and how it is to be attached. In practice, the military court generally fixed the weight of the ball at from six to forty pounds—most frequently, perhaps, twenty-four—and the length of the chain from three to six feet, and specified that the latter should be attached sometimes to the right leg or ankle and sometimes to the left. In an early instance, a part of the sentence read: ". . . to wear a ball and chain attached to his neck for two weeks."

This punishment, though very frequently imposed in the earlier days of our history, was later by direction of the Judge Advocate General not a penalty to be resorted to except in aggravated cases, and was usually remitted except where the offender was shown to be a violent person, or where attempts to escape were to be expected and he could not otherwise be secured.

In the early English Articles and the contemporary German Code of Gustavus Adolphus there is worse prescribed as sundry punishments, such as decimation—where regiments were discerned in misbehavior before the enemy; beheading; being drawn and quartered in connection with the death penalty; being drowned or buried, bound to the person killed, in punishment for homicide; having the tongue perforated with a red-hot iron for blasphemy; losing the right hand; losing an ear; being dunked in the sea; and having to perform the duty of scavenger.

Our original Military Code of 1775 enumerates the punishments authorized to be imposed by courts-martial—whipping, not exceeding thirty-nine lashes; and certain offenses were declared punishable with not less than fifteen or twenty, nor more than thirty-nine, lashes.

In 1790 public whipping was authorized by statute as punishment for sundry civil offenses such as larceny, embezzlement, etc., the limit being fixed at thirty-nine stripes, and by statute in 1799, forty lashes for robbing the mail. It was finally abolished as a punishment for civil offenses by an Act of Congress in 1839.

The Military Code of 1806 fixed the maximum of this punishment at fifty lashes; but a few years later, Congress repealed this provision, and whipping or flogging was done away with. Later, however, in 1833, this form of discipline was revived for deserters. At length, at the beginning of the Civil War, by an 1861 statute, flogging as a punishment in the Army was abolished.

Flogging came into disrepute because this punishment had failed, due in great part to the fact that in the British service it was carried to a brutal and perilous extreme. Five hundred lashes was not an uncommon sentence; one thousand were imposed in repeated recorded cases; and fifteen hundred and even two thousand were sometimes reached.

The offender being secured in an unnatural position, the lashes were applied by an enlisted man . . . right-and-left-handed drummer being preferred . . . with the . . . cat . . . its thongs sometimes steeped in brine or salt and water . . . upon the bare back and shoulders, which soon became flayed and raw. The victim was not relieved till the surgeon pronounced that he had endured as much as could safely be inflicted for the time. He was then removed to the hospital, to be brought out again, when his wounds were partially healed, for a second installment of the punishment, and this process was repeated till the whole number of lashes had been administered. The sufferer, however, sometimes perished under the blows, or in consequence of the injuries received, before the law had been fully vindicated.

In the American service, after the Revolution, comparatively few sentences of flogging were adjudged until after the punishment had been revived for deserters in 1833, when it was frequently resorted to, especially during the period of the Mexican War.

An instance of a sentence approved, of fifty lashes, is found in a general order in 1861 and in February, 1862—the last case of the kind that I have discovered.

Marking of deserters with the letter *D* dates from the Roman law. This also was authorized by the British Mutiny Act, under which the offenders were marked with the letters *B. C.*—bad character—if discharged with ignominy.

In our service this punishment has been carried considerably further, additional forms of it having been sanctioned by usage. Soldiers have been sentenced to be branded, as well as marked, with *D*, both for desertion and for drunkenness. The mark was commonly on the hip, but sentences to be branded on the cheek and on the forehead have been adjudged and carried out. Other markings imposed by our courts-martial have been *H. D.*, for habitual drunkard, *M*, for mutineer, *W*, for worthlessness, *C*, for cowardice, *I*, for insubordination, *R*, for robbery, *T*, for thief.

Sometimes, also, entire words were marked, such as *Deserter*, *Habitual Drunkard*, and *Mutineer*, or *Swindler*. The branding was done with a hand iron; the marking with India ink or gunpowder, usually pricked into the skin or tattooed. Congress ultimately prohibited such punishment.

Among the more unusual punishments was the carrying of weights, which consisted mostly in marching for a certain time in front of the guardhouse or on the parade ground carrying a knapsack loaded with brick, sand, or other articles, weighing from twenty-five to thirty pounds.

Some of our easier and lighter penalties were standing or marching for a certain time and bearing a placard or label inscribed with the name of the offense, such as DESERTER,

COWARD, MUTINEER, MARAUDER, PILLAGER, THIEF, or HABITUAL DRUNKARD. In some cases the inscriptions were more extended, such as DESERTER, SKULKED THROUGH THIS WAR; CHICKEN-THIEF; FOR SELLING LIQUOR TO RECRUITS; I FORGED LIQUOR ORDERS; I PRESENTED A FORGED ORDER FOR LIQUOR AND GOT CAUGHT AT IT; I STRUCK A NON-COMMISSIONED OFFICER; I ROBBED THE MAIL.

Soldiers have been sentenced, for minor offenses, to stand on the head of a barrel for certain periods, sometimes also bearing a placard. Another punishment with the use of a barrel was for a soldier to carry a barrel with his head through a hole in one end, the barrel resting on his shoulders.

Less usual were such punishments as riding the wooden horse . . . sometimes with hands tied behind the person, or a musket tied to each foot; wearing a wooden jacket; wearing an iron collar or yoke; marching with coat turned wrong side out; being tarred and feathered; the pillory; the stocks; being gagged; being tied up by the thumbs.

But none of this today. We have become civilized and humane. We put a man in solitary confinement on bread and water for month after month. We make him compress himself into a coffin-sized box for months on end. We sometimes have mercy and either gas him, hang him, or shoot him. You will agree that we have progressed.

Lawyers, Judges, and Juries

ARE LAWYERS NECESSARY?

=

IF HENRY III had had his way the ancient profession known as the Law might have withered and died during his fifty-six years as ruler of England.

King Henry distrusted lawyers and feared their knowledge. He knew of their popularity among the commoners. Possibly he saw them as a threat to his shaky status as monarch.

Whatever the reason, his feelings became evident when he banished schools of law from the City of London.

Lawyers, however, are a hardy lot, and King Henry's edict amounted to little more than an inconvenience. Teaching was transferred to the banks of the Thames and the schools turned out more fledgling barristers than before.

Little has changed in the seven hundred years that have followed the reign of Henry III. Among the ruling class there is still a distrust of lawyers. The common man still looks with awe and admiration at the attorney who counsels him. And schools of law continue to discharge new practitioners in ever-increasing numbers.

Joseph Hodges Choate was as well known for his oratory at the banquet table as he was for his oratory in the courtroom. In 1880 he was invited to address the New York State Chamber of Commerce. After a flattering introduction Choate spoke these words:

> I rise with unprecedented embarrassment in this presence and at this hour to respond to this sentiment, so flattering to the feelings of all the members of the Bench and Bar, to say nothing

97

of that shrinking modesty inherent in the breast of every lawyer and which the longer he practices seems to grow stronger and stronger.

At an hour like this, merchants like witnesses are to be weighed as well as counted. And when I compare your appearance at this moment with what it was when you entered this room, when I look around upon these swollen girths and these expanded countenances, when I see that each individual member of the Chamber has increased his avoirdupois by at least ten pounds since he took his seat at the table, why, the total weight of the aggregate body must be startling indeed, and as I suppose you believe in the resurrection from this long session, as you undoubtably hope to rise again from these chairs, to which you have been glued so long, I should be the last person to add a feather's weight to what has been so heavily heaped upon you.

Mr. Blaine, freighted with wisdom from the floor of the State House and from long study of American institutions, has deplored the low condition of the carrying trade. Now for our part, as representing one of the institutions which does its full share of the carrying trade. I repudiate the idea. We undoubtably are still prepared to carry all that can be heaped upon us.

Lord Bacon, who was thought the greatest lawyer of his age, has said that every man owes a duty to his profession; but I think that can be amended by saying, in reference to the law, that every man in the community owes a duty to our profession; and somewhere, at some time, somewhere between the cradle and the grave, he must acknowledge the liability and pay the debt. Why, gentlemen, you cannot live without the lawyers, and certainly you cannot die without them.

It was one of the brightest members of the profession, you remember, who had taken his passage for Europe to spend his summer vacation on the other side, and failed to go; and when called upon for an explanation, he said—why, yes, he had taken his passage, and had intended to go, but one of his rich clients died, and he was afraid if he had gone across the Atlantic, the heirs would have got all of the property.

When I look around me in this solid body of merchants, all this heaped-up and idle capital, all these great representatives of immense railroad, steamship and other interests under the face of the sun, I believe that the fortunes of the Bar are yet at their beginning.

Gentlemen, the future is all before us. We have no sympathy

with communism, but like Communists we have everything to gain and nothing to lose.

The Chamber offered no rebuttal.

THE CRIMINAL TRIAL LAWYER AND THE ADMINISTRATION OF JUSTICE

THE CITIZENS OF OUR COUNTRY would not adopt the Constitution of the United States until a series of amendments were added which have for their purpose the protection of the rights of the people in those areas where individual liberties are concerned. Of the ten amendments adopted, three stand perpetual guard: the Fourth, Fifth, and Sixth.

The Fourth Amendment guarantees that the people be secure in their persons, houses, papers, and effects against unreasonable searches and seizures, and further that no warrant shall issue but upon probable cause supported by oath or affirmation.

The Fifth Amendment provides that no civilian shall be held to answer for a capital or otherwise infamous crime unless upon presentment or indictment of the Grand Jury, nor that any person for the same offense be twice put in jeopardy of life or limb, nor that any person shall be compelled in any criminal case to be a witness against himself, nor that any person be deprived of life, liberty, or property without due process of law.

The Sixth Amendment provides that in all criminal prosecutions the accused shall enjoy the right to a speedy and public trial by an impartial jury, and that the person be first confronted with any witnesses against him, and that he have the assistance of counsel for his defense.

To guarantee that these rights be accorded to all men, the

criminal trial lawyer stands as guardian and defender. Without him, these rights would be nonexistent and unenforceable.

As a nation, we pride ourselves that no one, whatever the crime, can be compelled to stand trial in an American court without a lawyer to aid him in his defense.

This man who stands beside the defendant is commonly called a criminal lawyer, and those living in ivory towers, as well as the moral hypocrite, look upon him as a professional outcast. It perhaps has never occurred to them, nor to some of our holier-than-thou citizens, that a man's life or liberty is more important than his money.

We have always provided men who are willing to defend those accused of crime, no matter how offensive or terrible the crime. More often than not the only reward received by the criminal trial lawyer is the satisfaction that he has rendered a service not only to the individual defendant, but to every man.

While our law schools pay little, if any, attention to criminal law, and while they spend very little time teaching this important subject, it is heart-warming and assuring to know that the criminal lawyer himself has rededicated his profession to the service and the protection of his fellow man.

Great men in our history have thrown away the fears of our legal fraternity and have involved themselves with the most explosive cases of our time. These lawyers courageously accepted the unpopular case, knowing all too well that in so doing they faced a very real threat, a financial loss, social ostracism, and political extinction.

Hamilton in his defense of John Peter Zenger in 1735 anticipated our First Amendment and guaranteed the freedom of the press. In 1770 John Adams, who was to become our second President, volunteered to defend the soldiers in the historic Boston Massacre, and this at a time when the British were the most unpopular of all humans on this continent.

In 1846 William Henry Seward defended William Freeman, a demented Negro whose civil rights were in grave danger of being violated by a bestial and frightened community. It was

William Henry Seward who on January 1, 1863, brought to Lincoln for his signature the Emancipation Proclamation, in which the President said, "I do order and declare that all persons held as slaves are and henceforth shall be free," and thus this same lawyer, Seward, seventeen years earlier had decided for himself that slavery ought not to exist and anticipated the Thirteenth Amendment.

There are so many examples of the moral and mental courage shown by lawyers in the defense of the rights of the people that to enumerate each case would fill volumes.

The criminal trial lawyer renders services which cannot be lowered into the class of civil litigation. To him life or liberty is the pawn; to the civil trial lawyer the issue is always the entries in the ledgers of accountants.

It wasn't too long ago that Judge Charles W. Fricke appointed the late Jack Hardy, a great criminal lawyer, who had entered the judge's court that morning on other business, to defend the notorious Barbara Graham.

Jack Hardy stopped everything and went to work on the defense. He spent months and much money in the defense. He permitted his own business to stagnate. He later applied for a five-thousand-dollar fee and a grateful community paid him nothing. Today, at last, a court may order lawyers' fees paid when they are conscripted for this service.

It is the defense lawyer—the criminal trial lawyer—who day in and day out labors to help those against whom evidence has been obtained illegally; he fights against illegal and unreasonable searches and seizures; he fights to secure every right for the citizen which is guaranteed him by the Constitution and its amendments.

Before our government was created, a defendant had to prove himself innocent, instead of its being the duty of the prosecution to prove his guilt to a moral certainty and beyond a reasonable doubt. How would you enjoy living in such a society and under such government?

It is the criminal lawyer who insists that the citizen be unmolested in the accomplishment of his duties and obligations. It is the criminal trial lawyer who has made it possible for me to write this article. Without him, I would have feared the consequences of an enraged authority.

It is the criminal trial lawyer who stands guard while from the houses of worship are heard the words of the Holy Scriptures: "But as for thee, stand here by me, and I will speak unto thee all the commandments . . . that they may do them. . . ."

Thank your God that there is such a defender of the rights of man.

JUSTICE DISPENSED WITH HERE

LET US TAKE a brief trip, down the street and into the corner drugstore. Further, let us assume we have a chronic heart condition and we are headed, as rapidly as possible, to purchase some medicine for this heart condition. Now, to really give this little scene some meaning, let us assume that if we do not get the right medicine it may cost us our lives.

We arrive in the drugstore; it is empty. The druggist is gone, the counter is bare. Our breath quickens; we are in a great hurry. With trembling fingers we unwrap the prescription form the doctor has given us and try and make some sense of the writing on the form. No use; the symbols are meaningless. Without the druggist, we are lost.

Enter two young gentlemen, neatly dressed, carrying brief cases. They engage us in conversation, learn of our plight. Nothing easier, they tell us as they study the prescription form; they know how to fill the order and send us on our way, our heart again beating regularly. Both of these young men go behind the counter and don druggists' gowns. But at this point, something goes wrong; the two men begin bickering over just what the prescription means. One maintains that the medicine contains ten grains of a thing and the other says that such a dosage would surely kill the patient.

We stand on our side of the counter, watching these two young men. They approach us and argue the merits of their respective cases. We are confused, knowing little or nothing of pharmacology. And to compound our confusion, we must make a decision, for it is time to take the medicine. What will we do? Whom will we trust?

This little vignette could, and often does, illustrate the plight of the trial judge during any particular case that is before him. He is daily being confronted by two attorneys, each with a different viewpoint, each trying to sell him—along with the jury, should one be present—on the particular merits of the "heart medicine" that is at issue. The judge must often pick a particular brand of medicine, and make a decision. Often he knows no more about the validity of this decision than you or I, if we were called upon to choose a prescription down at the corner pharmacy.

What is a judge? Well, unless he is a member of either our highest or our most modest level of the judiciary—the State Supreme Court or the local justice of the peace—the law requires that he be a lawyer. Many of our judges have years of practical trial experience behind them before they go to the bench, and they have learned much of the law; others, with as many years' experience, have not learned much more than the rudiments.

Like medicine, judges come in a multitude of sizes and shapes, and have as many individual characteristics. Some of these gentlemen are harsh, captious, and are quick to convict. Many of these persons have a special peeve, often limited to a certain kind of crime, and woe unto him who appears before the judge who, say, has an especial loathing for wife beaters.

Many of these judges may have worked for years in the district attorney's office prior to donning the black robes and they have never quite gotten over their prosecution orientation, silently (and sometimes not so silently) rooting for the prosecution during every criminal action that is brought before them.

Other judges tend to be as sympathetic with the defense, as the law—and the skill of defense counsel—may allow. Perhaps some of these judges, themselves, have worked for the district attorney in the past and, instead of becoming embittered, have come to understand that no two cases are alike, and it could be that the man standing before him, accused of beating his wife, hit her because she was chasing him with a butcher knife.

The judge mounts the bench with any or all of the problems that beset the average man in the street, if such a creature may be said to exist. Perhaps the learned judge listens to a case, his mind distracted with the knowledge that his wife must undergo an operation a half hour thence. Another jurist may suffer terribly from arthritis and it will be his job to try and keep his face as free of grimaces and expressions of pain as possible, as he referees the proceedings before him.

It goes without saying that a judge must know the law, if nothing else. What kind of man he personally may be is a matter between him and his conscience. The best judges in our land will admit that they have not always been free of prejudice. This quality—prejudice—is as much a part of us as the very head that rests upon our shoulders. He who comes to me and says he is free of prejudice I immediately dismiss as being either a liar or a fool; in no instance would I want such a person sitting on the bench in a case I was trying. While I recognize that all of us have prejudice, I cannot abide by the man who tries to deny it. Prejudice is a heritage all of us must share for a few thousand more years; if we recognize it as such, we can do no more.

One of the hardest tasks that can confront a judge is that of having to make a ruling or a decision that he personally knows to be wrong. Many judges, for example, are compelled to send a man to his death, themselves not believing for one moment in capital punishment. But if the jury has found a defendant in a murder trial guilty, and the law so dictates, the judge can do no more than pass a sentence that is harsh and unyielding. Such a judge may be heartsick for days after passing a death sentence and no one may realize it, such are the complexities of human nature. This may be a terribly difficult thing for some people to comprehend, this fact that many times the judge has no discretion in a case; the law he must support is not his, but the people's.

I think that the best qualification a man may have for becoming a judge is that he has heeded that old admonition: "Know thyself." While none of us were created perfect, the best we can do is to recognize our own imperfections; in so doing, we will be the more understanding of the imperfections we find in our fellows. None of us has led such a lily-white life that our dossier could stand to be scrutinized with the thought of criminal prosecution in mind. And for those who tell me they have committed no crimes during their brief time on earth, I say this: Your crime has been one of the gravest; you did not learn to know yourself and, as a result, you have never learned to know others.

Perhaps it is true that passing judgment upon others may be easier than passing judgment upon ourselves. While we may sometimes tend to rationalize our mistakes, our stupidity, our weakness, we still must arise each morning and stand before the bathroom mirror, if only for a moment, and see that which some call "the inner man." We sometimes spend restless and sleepless nights with the knowledge that we have sat in judgment on something we have done and we were compelled to find ourselves guilty.

As the best trial judges often have a kind of instinct for the direction justice lies in, we too have this instinct, at least as far as it applies to judging ourselves. We know when we have done a truly wrong thing and we do not need a lawbook to point out our crimes. Although some, like the judge in pain with arthritis, may not show the world the face of guilt, it is there, inside their breast, and if it only comes out during the terror of a nightmare, it *has* come out. And will continue to come out for as long as such a person continues to deny that he or she was wrong, in one way or another.

When we judge ourselves, we have our conscience to suffer; when we judge others, we have *two* consciences to plague us, for we may have done two persons an injustice instead of only one.

Let us each be kind to the man who is passing judgment upon another; it may be his turn next.

THE BAR OF JUSTICE

JURY DUTY, like the Olympic games, has come to require that participants be of amateur status.

There is no place in the jury box for a professional peer. The responsibility of sitting in judgment on your fellow man, whether it be in a civil or criminal case, is a matter of obligation, not a matter of choice.

A juror must take his place among the other eleven with a feeling of awe. He must weigh each point as if it were the heaviest burden in existence. He must reach a verdict only after careful consideration of the facts. And he must finally leave the courtroom thankful his servitude has ended.

There is little chance that professional jurors could come to be, under a democratic system of justice. No matter how a juror decides, he forever carries a courtroom label that tells the prosecution and defense his decision in the previous case. It is reasonable to assume that few prosecutors would pass a prospective juror who once voted for acquittal, or that the attorney for the defense would not challenge a prospective juror who once had balloted guilty.

Further, jury duty, particularly during the period of deliberation, is an unpleasant task. It means separation from loved ones, poor pay, personal inconvenience, and confinement.

Under old English law, jurors were required to be kept without meat or drink, fire or candle, until they agreed.

Things are somewhat better today. The law directs that jurors be provided with suitable and sufficient food and lodging during their deliberations.

In 1880 in a California community, one Clarence Gray took objection to a political opinion offered by one Theodore Glancey. An argument flared into a quarrel climaxed by the discharge of a six-gun.

Theodore Glancey fell to the ground mortally wounded.

In due time, Gray was brought to trial. He contended the weapon went off by accident, but this defense was to no avail. The jury found him guilty of murder.

There is nothing unusual in the fact that the verdict was appealed. The decision of the Supreme Court of California is something else again.

The court was asked to judge the appeal on the basis of a motion charging misconduct of the jury, by which a fair and due consideration of the case was prevented.

The court, summing up its reasoning, ruled:

> . . . The jury was fully impaneled on the evening of the third of June. As soon as the jury was complete, they were, by order of the Court, placed in the charge of the Sheriff—instructed as to their duties, and thus remained in the charge of the Sheriff, not being allowed to separate until they were discharged on the morning of the twelfth. After the jury was complete, and before the cause was submitted to them on the afternoon of the eleventh of June, a period of about eight days, four five-gallon kegs of beer were brought into the room at the Tremont House, where the jury was kept by the Sheriff, of which about seventeen and a half gallons [of the beer] were drunk by them;

That during the same period some of the jurors drank claret wine, amounting to three bottles, at their meals, while some of them drank whiskey;

That all this drinking was done before the cause was submitted to them on the afternoon of the eleventh of June;

That on this day, during the noon recess, two of the jurors procured each a flask of whiskey;

That one of the jurors [Price, the foreman] drank nothing.

That all the drinking by the jurors was without the permission of the Court, or the consent of the defendant, or of the counsel engaged in the cause, and in fact without the knowledge of either of them;

That all the beer, wine and whiskey was procured by such of the jurors as desired it of their own motion and at their own expense.

Further, the evidence affords strong reason to suspect that one of the jurors drank so much while deliberating on the verdict as to unfit him for the proper discharge of his duty.

The decisions as to how far drinking by a juror while in the discharge of his duties as such, at his own expense, without the permission of the Court, or the consent of the party, is such misbehavior that the verdict should be set aside and a new trial granted, are not uniform.

When, in the course of the trial, a juror has in any way come under the influence of the party who afterwards has the verdict, or there is reason to suspect that he has drunk so much, at his own expense, as to unfit him for the proper discharge of his duty, or where he has so grossly misbehaved himself in any other respect as to show that he had no just sense of the responsibility of his station, the verdict ought not to stand.

The introduction of ardent spirits into the jury room while the jury were deliberating upon their verdict constituted misconduct per se. The Sheriff was authorized to provide the jury with suitable and sufficient food and lodging. This is a modification of the old rule which required that they should be kept without meat or drink, fire or candle, until they agreed.

It should be added here that if it is necessary that intoxicating liquors of any kind should be drunk by a juror, application for leave to do so should be made to the Court, who can make such allowances as will be proper. Jurors should not be allowed to judge for themselves in this matter. A defendant in a criminal case should not be called on to consent; and in any case where the party consents, if the juror becomes intoxicated, the verdict should not stand.

The purity and correctness of the verdict should be guarded in every way, that the administration of justice should not be subjected to scandal and distrust. For the reason above indicated, the judgment and order are reversed and the cause remanded for a new trial. . . .

The second trial produced no evidence not introduced at the first trial. But Gray was acquitted. It is presumed that the second judgment was a sober one.

A DOZEN ISN'T ALWAYS EGGS

THE CASINOS OF NEVADA cannot hold a candle to the courtrooms of California when it comes to gambling for high stakes. There is no comparison between betting a fortune on the turn of a card and betting a life on the verdict of a jury.

Choosing a jury is a dangerous business. At best, the trial lawyer approaches the selection of a jury the same way a demolitions expert approaches a buried, five-thousand-pound bomb. Like the demolitions expert, the trial lawyer is armed with a working knowledge of juries. The lawyer applies his stethoscope of knowledge to the side of this ticking bomb and if he is lucky—and if he has remembered what he was taught in demolitions school—the bomb will be reduced to a harmless canister. If not, there will be an explosion that will reduce his client, and himself, to a large, smoking hole in the ground.

I have been in the business of disarming jury bombs for over forty years. In addition to innumerable civil jury trials I have, on more than a hundred occasions in my career, been called upon to defend men and women charged with murder. Each case had one thing in common: each defendant faced the possibility of being executed in the name of the law.

Like the doctor, a lawyer cannot afford even a small mistake when he has the exposed and gaping corpus of a jury facing him. And while not one of us is perfect and all of us make an occasional mistake, we dare not make any mistakes when it comes to selecting a jury.

Now, just what *is* a jury? Well, it is supposed to be a group of the defendant's peers, his alleged equals. Obviously, to find twelve men or women or combination thereof that are the defendant's—or the plaintiff's—equals in all respects would be an impossible task. Even the highly touted computers the government has put to work selecting likely candidates for a trip to the moon would be exceedingly hard pressed to find twelve persons that in every way matched up to the litigant's personality, race, creed, and financial circumstances.

What we have today is a modified system that has been in existence for thousands of years. In these thousands of years, it would seem to me that we should have learned all there is to learn about selecting a jury. But our jury system has all the imperfections that any one man has, save that they are multiplied by twelve. Be that as it may, it is the best system we have yet devised and I would rather take my chances with a jury than try to direct an argument to the subtleties of a digital computer.

Today the jury is the only defense against arbitrary laws, the only defense against arbitrary judges, the only defense against persecution, and the only defense against our government. In short, our jury system is the only defense man has against himself.

In my own experience in the practice of the law, I have always tried to operate along the lines of a commanding general planning an attack. As anyone who has served in the Armed Forces knows, the attack is not a spontaneous effort that is launched on a whim. To the contrary, it is often a "hurry up and wait" affair that is months in the planning. Well, choosing a jury can be

similar to a military attack and not even the Almi_
the lawyer who goes into court with no clear idea o_
alities that will be sitting before him on the jury.

Of the greatest importance to a lawyer when he wa_
court will be knowledge of the persons who will compri_
jury. Jury lists are available to counsel and if the case warra_
it—and *all* of them warrant it, to my way of thinking—the lawye_
should avail himself of a jury list. He should study the names on
that list. If necessary, he should look up these names in Polk's
Directory, learn where these people work, in what neighborhood
they live. If he feels the need for greater investigation, he should
call upon an expert investigator for assistance. For when he starts
asking these prospective jurors questions as to their acceptability
to serve on a jury, he will not only have to know *what* questions
to ask, he will also have to know when he is getting truthful
answers! And, believe me, there is no short-cut way to determine
when a prospective juror is telling the truth. Only pre-trial investigation of the juror's background will give the trial lawyer
enough upon which to frame his questions.

I am now going to describe the way I, personally, take my
bombs—the jury—apart. The lessons I have learned have been
hard bought, and they are, of course, *my* lessons. They are not
guaranteed to be sure-fire, for only life, death, and taxes, as Ben
Franklin remarked, *are* sure-fire.

I have chosen thousands of men and women to sit on civil
juries as well as in judgment of hundreds of men and women
charged with a variety of crimes. And even when I have been
armed with the results of a pre-trial investigation of my prospective jurors, I have always noted that what constitutes an acceptable juror—insofar as the defense is concerned—is always a
conclusion based upon little or no facts.

Some trial lawyers never select anyone with an obviously
serious, somber, or sour disposition. Instead, they prefer smiles.
This is an obvious conclusion and it is frequently correct. However, a lawyer must take pains in his examination to determine

that this dour juror is *really* what his expression indicates he is. Perhaps he is sad *because* the defendant is on trial for his life. Then again, perhaps he is sour because his back has been injured by an automobile collision. Perhaps the case before him—if the lawyer is counsel for plaintiff—resembles a case in which *he* was the plaintiff!

Other attorneys are wary of persons whose forebears were English, German, or Scandinavian. These persons tend to believe in absolute law enforcement and severe punishment for anyone who runs afoul of the law. Such persons are ultraconservative, bull-headed, and usually have their minds made up—in favor of the prosecution—at the outset of the trial.

The outdoor or athletic type can take either side and if you can convince him, he will espouse your cause till hell freezes over.

But what do you do with a weight lifter whose name is Harry Brown, whose mother was German? There are no hard-and-fast rules on this. Just pray that your pre-trial investigation has been adequate, for if it has you may be able to throw some of these rules in the wastebasket and make a few of your own!

Jews are acceptable only if the crime is a minor one. The Jew is severe if the crime is one of violence. A brief examination of the cultural background of the Jew will explain his reasons for being severely opposed to violence. However, if the Jew is a man who is making his living as a bouncer in an East Oakland bar, you may do well to consider him as a favorable juror in an assault and battery case.

One hard-and-fast rule that has served me well is this: Never accept a wealthy person if the client is poor, nor a poor person if the client is wealthy. The gap between client and juror simply cannot be bridged and if you choose a wealthy juror who reads liberal periodicals you will *still* be gambling heavily. This a lawyer cannot afford to do, for he is not gambling with his client's money; he is gambling with years of his client's life, if not with *all* of his client's life!

A businessman is not the best juror if the client is a labor official, nor is the person who is in debt a good juror if the client is a banker or an official with a loan company.

A Southerner is often a good juror if the client is a Negro, because the Southerner will often best understand the Negro's problems.

Actors and salesmen are almost always desirable; they have seen all sides of life and know the meaning of misfortune and suffering. By the same token, writers and artists would also qualify as good jurors. And, of course, so would older men; the older man is more charitable, more understanding and forgiving than the young man.

Minor officials, functionaries, religious zealots, super-Americans, and the like tend to take the words of the prosecutor as if they came from God. Such persons have spent years in slavish obedience to authority of one sort or the other and naturally they have come to identify strongly with authority. To such persons the very fact that the client is in court is enough. In their minds he is guilty.

Finally, married men are more understanding and tolerant than bachelors. Women, of course, have always been—and always will be—a complete mystery.

These are some of my own, personal thoughts on types and traits that make good or bad jurors. Professional groups all over the country have made exhaustive studies of jury personalities and have come up with their own results. A group from Fairleigh Dickinson University in New Jersey recently polled some five hundred persons of every imaginable background in a highly specific test designed to reveal the taint of prejudice, regardless of a person's race, creed, or color. Their results are extremely interesting.

For example, this poll concluded that there is a very small amount of pure-and-simple anti-Negro prejudice in today's juries. Generally speaking, the colored juror tends to resent, slightly, the successful defendant. By the same token, the Negro is more sympathetic toward youth, the out-of-work, and the poor. Again, do not let these facts blind you. A colored banker would be a most dangerous juror if the defendant happened to be an indigent Negro who was charged with robbing a pawnshop.

The five hundred who were tested showed little prejudice against the established religions such as Roman Catholicism, Judaism, or the many Protestant sects. There *was* prejudice felt toward some of the newer sects, especially the Seventh Day Adventists. Based upon these findings, perhaps it would be a good idea for the lawyer to advise the client to leave his copies of *The Watchtower* at home, should the defendant be on trial for a crime.

Certain occupational groups, according to the survey, cause the juror to bristle when he encounters them. Those toward whom the prospective juror is especially prejudiced are labor union officials and government functionaries. On the other hand, the study found that salesmen seem to be prejudiced against the unemployed as well as people of Latin and Middle European backgrounds. According to these studies, the salesman-juror tends to be favorably prejudiced toward the female defendant or plaintiff.

Oddly enough, a man stands a better chance of getting a fair shake from a jury than does a woman. According to Fairleigh Dickinson University's poll, men earning less than five thousand dollars a year—and women—are both strongly prejudiced against women.

As to national origins, most prospective jurors feel most strongly prejudiced against persons of Rumanian/Hungarian ancestry. On the face of it, the existence of such prejudice would usually be accepted, if we are to believe the reports of the study. But these facts should not be taken too literally. Consider the De Kaplany case, recently tried in Santa Clara County. The defendant was admittedly guilty of a most heinous mutilation killing, was a Hungarian national, yet somehow escaped with his life while seemingly the odds dictated the gas chamber. Perhaps his economic circumstances had something to do with the sentencing, I don't know. I *do* know that a lawyer can *never* arrive at an absolute set of values when picking a jury.

How much can a lawyer learn from a juror, based upon what he says and how he presents himself? Well, of course not one of them will admit that he has carefully followed the proceedings in the newspapers. On the contrary, the answer the prospective juror will give when asked about his familiarity with the case is: "Well, sir, about all I have done is glance quickly at the headlines." After a lawyer has heard this over a period of years, he will be tempted to add under his breath: "Yes, but you surely took your time reading that *fine print*. . . ."

It has been said that the face is the mirror of our soul. This is not always true. Eichmann looked like a villain, yes, but his chief, Himmler, looked like a man who could not even form the intent to commit crime.

A lawyer must go further when he physically as well as orally examines the prospective juror. He must consider such factors as the juror's mode of dress. Is this man, for example, wearing what appears to be his only suit, and a threadbare one at that? He might be a good juror if the defendant is a poor man. He will be a bad juror if the client is a wealthy one.

Does the prospective juror's face, hands, or other visible body surface appear scarred? Has he been in an accident at one time or the other? Would he be sympathetic if the client is asking damages for pain and suffering? Is this juror old and infirm? Does he or she wear a brace, arch supports? While we are not gifted, as is Superman, with X-ray vision, our eyes can tell us much by the way a person carries himself, how he moves his hands and arms.

Is this juror nervous and flighty? Does he wipe his lips frequently? Does he bite his fingernails? Does he pluck at his cuffs, or, if the juror is a woman, does she pick at her nail polish? If so, here is a flighty mind at work—a mind that will be hard pressed to follow the case. And what about ornaments? What about lodge rings, lapel decorations and ornaments?

These are some of the things that only experience can teach a lawyer, but they are small details that cannot be ignored. If the client never saw military service and is charged with the crime of assault, the lawyer would do well to disqualify that juror who is frowning, whose name is MacPherson, and who wears a miniature Silver Star decoration in his lapel buttonhole.

No matter how many cases a lawyer may try, it is always hard for him to keep calm and unruffled when he begins to examine the prospective jurors. A jury trial is dramatic and complex and the successful trial lawyer must not only keep his wits about him at all times, but must also be one who knows the rules. The successful trial lawyer is keen and vital; he understands something of men and their motives. He knows that the litigants have reverted to their most primitive instincts and are now fighting like primordial animals, eager for victory, asking—and giving—no quarter.

From the moment the trial lawyer lays his papers on the counsel table his every act and word means something to the jurors. They will watch him like a hawk. If he conducts himself properly, they will continue watching him, and listening to his every word, when he begins to sum up.

In his questions directed toward the prospective juror, the good trial lawyer will attempt to discover all he can about each juror and he will often use what he has discovered to alert the juror to his, the lawyer's, theories about the case. The good trial lawyer will not make the mistake of thinking that one theory will suffice for all twelve jurors. It will not, no more than one line of reasoning will allow a parent to govern seven different youngsters. In the examination of the prospective juror, each and every question must mean something, either providing information for judging the juror or enabling the lawyer at this early stage of the trial to lay the foundation for his case.

A trial lawyer should never make it necessary for the juror to say he does not hear the question. If the juror is wearing a hearing aid or similar device, it is not necessary to shout at him. The lawyer should speak firmly and slowly, if necessary, but he should not make this kind of juror feel either that he is unimportant or that the lawyer is obviously patronizing him. As a matter of fact, if the juror *is* hard of hearing and he discerns that the lawyer is taking special care to be understood—without making a great show of such an elementary kindness—the juror will respect the lawyer for it.

In *all* cases, the lawyer should speak clearly and distinctly. Most laymen believe that the lawyer is a cultured and educated person. They are not in court to hear and see the same things they see during their average, workaday life. They are in court to see *lawyers* and they have their own ideas of what a lawyer should be, how a lawyer should act. If a lawyer disappoints them he is halfway toward losing them.

When we are about to meet someone important we are always on our best behavior. This is how it should be when a lawyer first meets his prospective jury. He may never see any of these people again—that is of no importance. Right now these jurors are the most important people in his life, doubly important, for his client has entrusted his cause to him. When you have another's responsibilities to handle they must always be more important than your own. This, fundamentally, is what being a lawyer is all about.

The lawyer's questions should be framed as questions and not as assertions, even if he knows the answers in advance. All of his questions should be concise and certain. They must never be argumentative. They must avoid assumptions and must in all cases call for direct answers.

Juries like to feel that their winning lawyer is made of the same stuff as they. Therefore, it is unwise for a lawyer to be *too* brilliant, too overtly. He should never, by a word or by an act, permit the jury to feel that he thinks he is better than they. In keeping with this, no great lawyer ever memorizes an argument; he frames his speech to the jury in such a way that it will not clash with the court. Most juries believe that judges are wise umpires and the losing lawyer in a controversy destroys—in the jury's eyes—the effect he has planned.

A lawyer should use simple and plain English when addressing the jury. We live in a complex and confusing world and the juror is keenly aware of this. A lawyer should not go off on semantic flights, nor should he go to the other extreme and keep his statements and questions on the level of a fourth-grade reading assignment. He should aim for a middle balance.

The juror will have heard, somewhere along the line, that lawyers are a tricky body of skilled professionals who use legal terminology to cloud facts. The lawyer may counteract much of this propaganda by avoiding the usage of such words as "prior" and "subsequent," using instead, "before" and "after."

The jury a lawyer first questions—and later addresses—has great responsibilities that weigh heavily upon their collective mind. It is all they can do to sift through the mass of fact that confronts them. It is the lawyer's task to make them understand that fear, prejudice, malice, and the love of approbation bribe a thousand men where gold bribes only one.

The collected powers of the juror's mind must continually be fixed upon the issue of fact which he is sworn to try. But—unless the juror has a clear understanding of the law applicable to the issue—his efforts are in vain.

The law is always changing, expanding, contracting. I have recently heard of experiments being conducted that could, theoretically, allow counsel to make short psychological tests upon the poor juror's psyche as he sits in the jury box. Frankly, such a method does not greatly appeal to me. But, who knows? Perhaps the courts of the twenty-first century will consider such a device commonplace.

To me, the law is not only today but it is also rather beautifully colored and tinged with traces of yesterday. For example, when I think of making an opening statement for the plaintiff before a jury in a damage suit I hasten to become reacquainted with Charles Dickens's classic *Pickwick Papers*. You will recall Sergeant Buzfus, who represented the Widow Bardell and who read his dramatic and devastating peroration against the gentle and innocent—but greatly alarmed—Pickwick.

"But Pickwick, gentlemen, Pickwick, the ruthless destroyer of this domestic oasis in the desert of Goswell Street—Pickwick, who has choked up the well, and thrown ashes on the sward—Pickwick still rears his head with unblushing effrontery, and gazes without a sigh on the ruin he has made. Damages, gentlemen—heavy damages is the only punishment with which you can visit him; the only recompense you can award to my client. And for those damages she now appeals to an enlightened, a high-minded, a right-feeling, a conscientious, a dispassionate, a sympathizing, a contemplative jury of her civilized countrymen."

VENGEANCE IS MINE

FOR MANY YEARS I have made almost daily ventures into the incongruous structure that is San Francisco's Hall of Justice. When I depart it is always with a feeling of despair over the legal destruction of man occurring within its cold confines. These are harsh words. But murder is harsh, particularly when committed in the name of the People of the State.

Law is based upon the theory that justice owes something to each individual; that each gets what is owed him; neither more nor less. No man can quarrel with the theory of justice, but there is room aplenty for criticizing the methods and reasoning through which it is actually administered.

Charity and understanding and forgiveness should be unwritten mandates in every law. If not, our halls of justice would stand today as testimony of an uncivilized people who built them as defense against their own hatreds.

Today the guaranteed rights in our Constitution are idealistic in content, beautiful in print, circumvented in our mass thinking, and abridged by our fifty-five million laws. Legal revenge is the mood of the day, and each safeguard of liberty has been battered by revengeful reformers. The principle of law that every man is entitled to a fair trial is gone and almost forgotten. Most assume that arrest is synonymous with guilt.

For every crime there must be punishment. But what is crime? The misconduct in others we repress in ourselves? Or are we so pure that we delegate punishment to a judge who may or may not be just and understanding?

Before punishing, it is the judge's duty to weigh carefully not only his responsibility to the people who elected him or appointed him, but also his responsibility to the citizen who stands before the bar of justice convicted of a crime.

Those who clamor for more stringent penalties usually know nothing of the background or mental capacity of the defendant, nor do they care. When an eye for an eye was the only penalty theory, the offense determined the punishment without regard to responsibility, culpability, or mental capacity. There was no thought of rehabilitation and no desire to save a human wreck cast upon the rocks of despair.

A criminal is as much a part of the community and a product of society as you or I. Have any of us thought of the reasons for the crime, the contributing causes, the mental capacity of the defendant, the economics of his living, or whether the community, and not the defendant, is the guilty party?

Crime and punishment have been problems from the day the first law was set down. It is no solution to demand creation of new offenses or an increase in the penalties for those already in existence.

Almost half a century ago the State of Missouri published a survey of crime which eloquently reported that severity of punishment had no effect on man and does not deter crime. The report, in part, reads:

. . . Ever since creation's peaceful dawn was startled by the death cry of the murdered Abel and Jehovah placed his mark upon Cain and sent him forth a fugitive and a vagabond, cursed from the earth that had opened its mouth to receive his brother's blood from his hand, there has been a neverending conflict between those who make the laws and those who break them. Nothing has afforded such harrowing and conclusive evidence of man's inhumanity to man as has this age long struggle. It has meant the rack and the stake, banishment and bondage, the Bastile and the Tower, the mines of Siberia and the dungeons of Doges. With refinement of torture that has taxed the cruel ingenuity of man, it has claimed as its unhappy victims in every age and every race, the prince and the peasant, the noble and the nobody, the king and the subject, the savage and the saint. Still crime persisted. Indeed, never was it so flourishing as when torture was most barbarous, the punishment most severe. . . .

Conditions today are no different.

Mankind has progressed noticeably in his civilization. He has progressed from the torture chamber to the gas chamber, but he has insisted on and now has more sanitary surroundings at the place of execution. The defendant is still murdered by the State with the judge's soothing: "May God have mercy on your soul."

Crime is a disease. Evil must be treated with charity instead of anger. Love of man, no matter what kind he may be, must displace the gas chamber, the scaffold, the electric chair. Reason and experience must overcome hatred and revenge.

Psychiatry has proven that punishment is a need of both the prosecutor and the defendant. Analyze a cold-blooded prosecutor and there appears a man who reveals the intensity of his inner struggle to defend against his unacceptable moral and social urges; to defend against drives which he does not consciously admit. Human motivations are of an unconscious nature.

If we accept punishment as the only medicine for crime, shall man be punished for punishment's sake or is there another way? Humane treatment outside prison has a place in our criminal procedure rather than an emotional get-even attitude; rehabilitation not retribution.

Certain crimes are committed impulsively by men of previous good character who are not likely to threaten society again. In the commission he suffers more punishment than can be given by the law; the stigma of the crime is punishment enough.

If we desire to be just, let us first persuade ourselves that there is not one among us without fault; no man can acquit himself, and he who calls himself innocent does so with reference to a witness, and not to his conscience.

Bigger prisons will not end criminality. Rehabilitation will lessen the number who each day add to our national deterioration.

Vengeance is mine, sayeth the Lord.

GENTLEMEN OF THE JURY

TWENTIETH-CENTURY MAN has a multitude of obligations and responsibilities he must answer to, one of the greatest being his duty to serve on a jury.

Too many times such service is considered a burden, when in reality it is an honor to be sought instead of shunned.

True, it requires time and patience and thought to probe the evidence and determine guilt or innocence, right or wrong.

But it has to be such, for the jury is man's only defense against arbitrary laws, his only defense against arbitrary judges, his only defense against persecution, his only defense against the government.

When he dons the title of juror, man assumes a moral responsibility second to none, for his decision in a court case, especially one of a criminal nature, may mean the difference between life or death, imprisonment or freedom, ruination or exoneration.

Law has been subjected to the scrutiny of philosophers since the beginning of recorded history. St. Paul preached that the law is good, if man uses it lawfully. Cicero went much further and contended that if the fortunes of all cannot be equal, if the mental capacities of all cannot be the same, at least the legal rights of all ought to be equal.

To insure equality before the law, man adopted the jury system. This manner of trying issues by the people grew from the ancient trial before the elders sitting in judgment at the gates of every encampment and city in ancient Israel, and was the forerunner of trial by jury as established in England some time after the year 1066 A.D.

If the responsibility of the juror is great, the responsibility of the lawyers participating in the defense, or prosecution, of an individual is of no less importance. The lawyers must present their respective cases honestly and lucidly, and both must inform the jury of its duty to judge only on fact, and to presume innocence only until guilt should become apparent beyond a shadow of a doubt.

In the forty years I have been trying jury cases, it has been my most important effort to explain to each juror the importance of his position as a judge of his fellow man, and what is meant by trial of an individual by a jury of his peers.

In every instance, as the jury has filed out of the courtroom to begin deliberation, I have questioned my final address—was it sufficiently illustrative to make the jurors appreciate their responsibilities?

You can, therefore, understand my delight when I discovered, while perusing a law journal, the charge given to a jury by the Honorable Gordon W. Chambers, Judge of the City Court of Richmond County, Georgia.

I have never met Judge Chambers, but he is known to me from the wording of his charge. Here is a man who fully understands the juror's position in relation to the administration of justice and to the timeless phrase "a jury of your peers." This is what Judge Chambers said:

Gentlemen of the Jury, by being selected for jury service you have been elevated to the peerage of democracy. As such you have a noble opportunity for service, obligated by patriotic duty to God and Country. This duty is deserving of the consecrated dedication of a conscientious concentration of your abilities and the just impulses of your honor.

You are a shield of protection against false accusers, transitory passions and prejudice. You are determiners of truth revealing the character of our country as a land of the free and home of the brave.

You are the preservers of liberty that walks with progress and restrains only libertine license to insure its own freedom. You are the protectors of all legal rights of society, citizenship and the state. You are guarantors of justice, constitutional and statutory, exactly, evenly and universally applied.

You are the custodians of American civilization, for without law there can be no civilization, without courts there can be no law, and without truth and independence there can be no courts.

The only title of nobility recognized by America's loyal house is in the peerage of the jury box where trial by peers determines the truth of issues between the state and its citizens. This title carries no feudal privilege of materialistic value. However, it merits the accolade of achievement—the accomplishment of the aristocracy of service.

This high honor carries only the title as a word of address or as an adjective or description: Gentlemen of the Jury.

Every man should thank God that we have among us one such as Judge Gordon W. Chambers, and every judge and citizen should read his words.

WHAT'S WRONG WITH THE JURY SYSTEM

It has been said that we live in a world of illusion. If this be true, join me while I take a brief excursion into the impressionistic world of fantasy, for a moment, using one of the trial lawyer's most basic tools: the analogy . . .

You are a learned physician, a neurosurgeon (not a resident named Casey, I might add), and you have just opened up the skull of a living human being. On a table beside you are your complex, gleaming instruments; nurses and assistants wait for your very word to carry out your orders. You have examined the patient whose brain now stands revealed before your eyes; you and you alone know what must be done to save this man's life. You give a complex set of instructions to your assistant and . . .

Nothing. Absolutely nothing happens. You look up from your labors, desperate, for there is not a moment to lose, and instead of skilled associates, trained for years in the fine art of neurosurgery, you see before you twelve bank tellers, their fingers still green from counting money and their eyes wide with incomprehension of what you are doing. To make the analogy more biting, perhaps I ought to add that three of these bank tellers are dozing soundly on an unoccupied bench located near the door.

We are now back to reality, having left our literary Disneyland far behind. Of course we know that twelve bank tellers, no matter how fine or noble they might be, would never be allowed in an operating theater under any circumstances. Their background, their training—nothing they have experienced would qualify them to assist a surgeon in his occupational specialty. By the same token, few of us would presume to tell a skilled craftsman how to repair a two-thousand-dollar Patek Phillipe wrist watch. Finally, we all know what would happen if we attempted to lecture a plumber on how he should repair the leaky pipes in our house; we would have to hasten down to the dentist and have our bridgework repaired.

And yet in the most serious business of all—the sitting in judgment on a fellow human being—any adult citizen in our land is somehow automatically considered expert!

As previously pointed out, Cicero contended that if the fortunes of all cannot be equal, if the mental capacities of all cannot be the same, at least the legal rights of all ought to be equal. To guarantee at least partially this equality before the law, man adopted the jury system. The jury system, as I have said, stems from the ancient trial before the elders of Israel, which was the forerunner of the trial by jury, later established in England some time after 1066.

Today, the jury—representative human beings who are, ideally, from all walks of life—is our only defense against arbitrary laws, arbitrary judges; it is our only defense against persecution and, most important, our only defense against the cold and impersonal entity we know as Government. To make another analogy, our jury system can be compared to the Dutch boy with his finger in the dike; without this collective "finger" we would soon be inundated.

For some years, now, an organized attack from many quarters has been leveled against the jury system. While it is true that many arguments included in this attack may be valid, it is my belief that if anything is wrong with such a system, blame ought to be placed on the truly responsible party: the trial judge.

Few people outside the Law (and few within it, to be candid) really understand the function of the trial judge. Pulp literature, the public's awe of this black-robed figure, and human frailties that cannot, and should not, be discarded by him who wears these black robes have done much to cloud and disguise the duties of the modern-day trial judge. In keeping with my premise that we are in every sense a by-product of history, perhaps we should examine just how the role of trial judge came about.

In primitive times—long before man was judged by an aggregate of his peers—the primitive judge was expected to administer justice directly, determine the guilt or innocence of a defendant, and mete out punishment according to the gravity of the offense. For a parallel, I cite the action of God in the cases of Divinity versus Adam and Eve and Almighty versus Cain. This was the function of the earliest judge; he was the right hand of God, on earth. Authority for this may be found by the Doubting Thomas in St. Luke, where he may read: "He is an unjust judge if he fears not God nor regards Man, but gives justice lest he become weary of being troubled by those who seek it."

Well, we have come a long way in our legal, political, and moral travels since that time. Today, the role of the trial judge can often be compared to that of a referee in a boxing match. We expect the judge not to yield to the influence of partiality, prejudice, or sentiment; nor do we expect him to seek out strained analogies or blind himself to reality by a slavish adherence to technicalities. We want to fill the seat of Justice with good men, but not so absolute in goodness as to forget the frailty of the human being.

What a series of contradictions! We seem to be saying that we want a kind of Composite Man—a mixture of Nietzsche's "Superman," Albert Schweitzer, and a Mark VI computer with self-regulating feedback. If such a contradiction of values were put into effect we should all have to wait at least a thousand years before our cases came to trial. Unhappily, man is a cynical fellow, capable of paying lip service to an ideal while being capable, at the same time, of dealing in stark totalities. The result? Average man, with all his faults and foibles, cloaked in a black gown.

I once served with a fine noncommissioned officer during the days of Black Jack Pershing and Pancho Villa. This man had had many years of honorable service in the Army and he had advanced to the rank of sergeant. As a sergeant he was unquestionably brilliant. Then, some functionary in the War Department made a monumental blunder; on the assumption that a man who was a fine N.C.O. would make a brilliant second lieutenant, our sergeant was commissioned an officer. The result? Disaster!

As it is difficult to explain why a fine sergeant could be a poor officer, so it is equally difficult to explain the many elements that can make a pleasant, amiable, capable lawyer into a harsh and unrelenting judge. I suspect that a good test of the so-called reformer would be to make him a judge for six months. In the end, perhaps, he would discover that he should first practice upon his own heart that which he had proposed to try on others. Only mercy has a human heart; when man is in a position that has suddenly changed from the abstract to a swift, concrete reality, he often discovers what it is that truly dwells within his own heart.

I should not like this to be entirely construed to be a quarrel with the judiciary, but years of experience in trial courts have never completely restrained me from addressing some of these courts in rather caustic terms. And if I did so, it was because the judge had flatly indicated to me that he, and secondly God, was right. While there is no higher position of trust in all of our land than that of a judge, even the court must bear in mind that God never proposed to judge man until the end of his days.

Now, let us walk into court. We are about to try a man for his life and we shall first observe the judge and the jury. Let us try to search their hearts and minds to learn whether the so-called murderer will receive a fair trial; let us try and learn why man is charitable toward physical deformity and vengeful toward moral and mental deformity. Let us see if Justice will remove the bandage from her eyes long enough to distinguish between the vicious and the unfortunate.

In order for a jury to understand properly just what the charges, and their significance, against the defendant are, the jury ought to know that murder is the unlawful killing of a human being with malice aforethought. The judge may think that the term—malice aforethought—is easy for the jury to comprehend. But is it? And who, at the beginning of the trial, ought to determine just how much of this concept the jury comprehends? Well, inasmuch as the defendant's lawyer is fighting for his client's life it would follow that he, the attorney, should know something of what is going on inside the few cubic centimeters of the average juror's head. And yet there are those judges who will insist that the trial lawyer not take up his time—and the time of the jury—with what he considers to be useless questions while impaneling, or choosing, the jury. The judge says he will instruct the jury as to what malice is. Well, that is all fine and dandy—assuming (1) that such instructions are truly given, and (2) that the court's instructions so closely parallel defense counsel's that the defendant's interests have been scrupulously protected.

But if judges did these things, then we wouldn't even need a defense counsel, would we?

Well, we know that the judge will instruct the jury on the law, but is the average juror mentally equipped to understand what the judge is talking about? Is the average bank teller equipped to understand the instructions of a neurosurgeon in an operating theater? Instructing the jury has been described somewhat humorously as: "The process in which the judge detracts from and discounts counsel's multiple arguments, makes his own deductions, adds his own wisdom, divides the blame, and roundly charges the jury to deliver a square result."

Does that sound like a recipe for justice? To me, it smacks more of the formula for making dynamite!

As you may quickly gather, this system of instructing juries, so uniformly followed, is rank injustice to the litigants and a travesty of justice in the bargain! How few lawyers and judges there are who can define the various phases of the law of homicide without a book in one hand and a set of pince-nez glasses in the other, the better to perceive the fine print!

As I have mentioned before, murder is the unlawful killing of a human being with malice aforethought. This malice is an essential element of the crime and it is extremely important that its semantic and legal meaning be thoroughly explained to the jury. Therefore, the judge will instruct the jury:

> Malice may be express or implied. It is express when there is manifested a deliberate intention to take away the life of a fellow-creature. It is implied when no considerable provocation appears, or when the circumstances attending the killing show an abandoned and malignant heart.

Well, to begin with, such concepts of criminal law as learned

judge has just imparted belong to the fifteenth century and are
as alien to our modern world, today, as the witch's broom. In
each thousand-year cycle, it often appears, there is one brilliant
mind capable of laying down sound concepts of conduct; for the
next nine hundred and ninety-nine years, none dare touch them,
so in awe are they. Sir William Blackstone, the learned English
jurist, was the first to educate the world as to the features and
disadvantages of our basic law. Blackstone wrote his commentaries between 1765 and 1769 and our law has made little advance since his day. If our skilled neurosurgeon were to practice
some of this fifteenth-century medicine on an ailing skull, you
may be sure that the good doctor would be sent to the penitentiary with all due haste! And yet we continue, in the field of the
law—a field surely as important as the doctoring of ailing bodies
—to talk of concepts that were alien to our finest minds *before
the 1800s!*

Now, let us return to the courtroom and let us ponder just
how the jury has received the court's instructions. The answer to
all this pondering is quite simple: The jury doesn't know what
the court is talking about! Neither the jury—nor the judge—know
what the term "an abandoned and malignant heart" means. And
to further addle the juror, the judge will read for all to hear that
"the bare existence of hatred, ill-will, and the like does not
amount to legal malice."

At this point it is small wonder that the poor juror falls asleep
or seriously begins to wonder which way "up" is.

The court will not be halted and, like a deacon who is in
haste to get through a sermon and sit himself down to a fine
chicken dinner, rumbles on to read: "Malice aforethought is not
synonymous with the elements of deliberation and premeditation which must first accompany a homicide to characterize it as
murder of the first degree . . ."

Well, now he's done it! The legally uneducated juror will at
this point experience a revelation of the greatest magnitude! He
will now know exactly what the judge is talking about! And of

course his honor will gladly permit the trial lawyer—the man fighting for the life of his client—to explain minor and unimportant things such as deliberation and premeditation. Every juror must know how to apply the law in this connection—when the *other fellow* is on trial for his life!

The litany from the bench drones on and on: "The state must prove to a moral certainty and beyond a reasonable doubt that the accused person had the mental intent to take the life of the person killed, and that such mental intent was arrived at as the result of deliberation and premeditation . . ."

Simple? Yes, possibly, if you are able to read it, and read it again, and read it perhaps for a third time. But what does the juror, sitting in his chair in an oppressive and over-warm courtroom get from it? Do you believe for even a moment that the juror understands this instruction and, if he does, is capable of applying it to the evidence? Of course he can't, no more than I could listen to a lecture on nuclear physics and then go out and build an atomic reactor!

The judge will conclude his reactions, his voice rising sharply from time to time as one head after the other—all in the jury box —nods downward, snaps backward, then down again:

> "The state must establish to a moral certainty and beyond a reasonable doubt: (1) that the defendant did kill the deceased, (2) that such killing was accompanied by a mental intent to take the life of the person killed, and (3) that such mental intent was arrived at by the accused upon the result of the thought and weighing of considerations on his part. By his weighing the act in his mind and considering the reasons for and against such act, and by his having previously contrived and designed to do such act. Such contrivance and design having been arrived at as the result of deliberation."

The oration finished, a hush fills the courtroom. This sudden quiet awakens the jurors just in time to see the counsel for defense, and the district attorney, weeping and silently pulling out their hair!

My purpose is not to attack judges or to belittle juries. Instead, it is my purpose to put more understanding and humanity into our trials. It is not enough to search with our minds; we must reach with our hearts.

During long years of law practice it has been my duty to try many civil and criminal cases, and often the public has condemned the criminal trial lawyer as one who is full of tricks, who will do anything to win. It is sad to realize that such an attitude frequently finds willing believers, for no injustice should be done the criminal trial lawyer by attributing to him any want of loyalty to truth, or any deference to wrong, simply because he employs all his powers and attainments toward exhibiting and enforcing the merits of his case. And if sometimes the criminal trial lawyer works too hard, gestures too much, and raises his voice on occasion, it is often because he is working desperately to educate a jury that has been hopelessly muddled, or worse, by a combination of incomprehensible instructions and a malevolent prosecution. Would you not work as hard were you charged with protecting a man's life?

The profession to which we belong is, of all others, fearless of public opinion. It has ever stood up against the tyranny of power, on one hand, and the tyranny of public opinion, on the other. Coupled with these adversaries, always, is the most formidable enemy of all: the poorly instructed, legally uninformed jury. Perhaps the following little anecdote will go a long way toward explaining what I have been trying to say.

A juror was once asked, "Do you have any objection to capital punishment?"

The juror rolled his eyes, wrinkled his brow, licked his lips, and solemnly replied, "No, not unless it is too severe."

INSTRUCTIONS ON A KILLING

THE CONDUCT OF MAN has always been guided by certain rules. Even the Jívaro Indians, South African head-hunters, have a form of protocol they must follow as they go about the task of shrinking the head of the victim who was unfortunate enough to come their way.

In our so-called civilized society we too are guided by rules, whether we are operating an automobile, laying bricks, or trying lawsuits. These "rules of the road" are as necessary for existence as the very food and drink that sustain us, although I am inclined to believe that sometimes we have too many, rather than too few, rules to guide us.

When a trial by jury is about to end, the judge is required to instruct the jury on those phases of the law that are applicable to the facts, through evidence, that have been brought out by the witnesses during the course of the trial. The judge's interpretation of the rules of evidence are known as instructions, and while the judge must say nothing to the jury that will *directly* influence their verdict, he will nevertheless lay down certain "rules of the road" that will tend to guide them when they retire to ponder the case.

This function of the judge—the giving of instructions—requires that the instructions be legally correct. Beyond this, the judge should do his best to deliver the instructions in such a way that the jury will comprehend them. The judge must, in whatever wisdom he may possess, attempt to reduce legal complexities to the comprehension of the average man in the street. This task, by the way, can sometimes be compared to the job an American would have if he tried to explain the significance of a parking meter to a Siberian.

Most judges, alas, tend to read the instructions with the same monotony that one might expect to hear from an Indian fakir as he recites a plea for alms. And like the tourist who is in a hurry to get to one place or the other, the jurors will, at best, be bored by such a litany. At worst, they will fall asleep.

While it is acknowledged that Justice is blind, there is nothing in the law that says the judge must feed her tranquilizers.

To offset the effect of those judges who deliver instructions designed to stupefy and befuddle the jury, there occasionally comes a jurist who is not only a learned lawyer but also a just human being, a man greatly concerned with the equality of all men before the law. In the following instructions which such a judge delivered to a jury, you will decipher the story of a killing. You will learn something of the parties involved in the killing, their motives, and, perhaps, their degree of guilt.

It is unlikely, by the way, that you will be put to sleep.

"Ladies and gentlemen of the jury. I shall, in discharging the duty incumbent on me, consume as little more of your time as may be consistent with a clear exposition of the principles necessary to be understood in order to form a just and legal decision.

"You have heard the facts in the case stated by the witnesses, ably and ingeniously commented upon by counsel, and the principles of law discussed in forcible and eloquent arguments.

"It is now left to you upon the whole view of the case, both of the law as it shall be declared to you by the Court, and the facts as proved by the testimony, to pronounce your verdict.

"The crime charged is manslaughter. This crime consists of the unlawful killing of a human being, without malice. However, the killing of a human being, under some circumstances, is not only excusable but justifiable under the law.

"Some persons entertain the visionary notion that it is in no instance lawful to destroy the life of another, grounding their opinion upon the general proposition in the Mosaic code that 'whosoever sheddeth man's blood, by man shall his blood be shed.' There is always danger in taking general propositions as the rules of faith or action without attending to those exceptions which, if not expressly declared, necessarily grow out of the subject matter of the proposition.

"Were the position above alluded to true, then the judge who sits in the trial of a capital offense, the jury who may convict, the magistrate who shall order execution, and the person who shall execute, will all fall within this general denunciation, as by their instrumentality the blood of man has been shed.

"The same observations may be applied to one of the precepts in that the decalogue, 'Thou shalt not kill,' is the mandate of God himself. Should this be construed literally and strictly, then if a man attacked by a robber, or in the defense of the chastity of his wife, or of his habitation from the midnight invader, should kill the assailant, he would defend himself against the divine command. But the common understanding of mankind will readily perceive that the very nature of man, and principles of self-preservation, will supply exceptions to these general denunciations.

"Our laws abundantly negate such unqualified definitions of crime, and have adopted certain principles by which the same act may be ascertained to be more or less criminal or entirely innocent, according to the motive and intent of the party committing it.

"Thus, when the killing is the effect of particular malice or general depravity, it is murder and punished with death.

"When without malice, but caused by sudden passion and heat of blood, it is manslaughter.

"When in defense of life, it is excusable.

"When in advancement of public justice, in obedience to the laws of the government, it is justifiable.

"These principles are all sanctioned by law and morality, and yet they all contradict the dogma that 'whosoever sheddeth man's blood, by man shall his blood be shed.'

"A man who, in the lawful pursuit of his business, is attacked by another under circumstances which denote an intention to take away his life, or do him some enormous bodily harm, may lawfully kill the assailant.

"When, from the nature of the attack, there is reasonable ground to believe that there is a design to destroy his life, or commit any felony upon his person, the killing of the assailant will be excusable homicide, although it should afterwards appear that no felony was intended.

"To illustrate, take the following case: A, in the peaceful pursuit of his affairs, sees B rushing rapidly towards him, with an outstretched arm and a pistol in his hand and using violent menaces against his life as he advances. Having approached near enough, in the same attitude, A, who has a club in his hand, strikes B over the head before or at the instant the pistol is discharged, and of the wound B dies. It turns out that the pistol was loaded with powder only, and that the real design of B was only to terrify A. Will any reasonable man say that A is more criminal than he would have been if there had been a bullet in the pistol? Those who hold such doctrines must require that a man so attacked must, before he strikes the assailant, stop and ascertain how the pistol is loaded, a doctrine which would entirely take away the essential right of self-defense. And when it is considered that the jury who try the case, and not the party killing, are to judge of the reasonable grounds of his apprehension, no danger can be supposed to flow from this principle.

"As to the evidence, I have no intention to guide or interfere with its just and natural operation upon your minds. I hold the privilege of the jury to ascertain the facts, and that of the Court to declare the law, to be distinct and independent. Should I interfere with my opinion on the testimony in order to influence your minds to incline either way. I should certainly step out of the province of a judge, into that of an advocate.

"All which I conceive necessary or proper for me to do is to call your attention to the points of fact on which the cause may turn, state the testimony in the case which may tend to establish those points, give you some rules by which you are to weigh testimony if a contrariety should have occurred, and leave you to form a decision according to your best judgment, without giving you to understand, if it can be avoided, what my opinion of the subject is.

"Where the inquiry is merely into matters of fact, or where the facts and the law can be clearly discriminated, I should always wish the jury to leave the jury-box without being able to ascertain what the opinion of the Court as to those facts may be; that their minds may be left entirely unprejudiced to weigh the testimony and settle the merits of the case.

"An important rule in the present trial is that on a charge for murder or manslaughter, the killing being confessed or proved, the law presumes that the crime as charged in the indictment has been committed, unless it should appear by the evidence for the prosecution, or be shown by the defendant on trial that the killing was under such circumstances as entitle him to justification or excuse.

"On the point of killing, there is no doubt in this case. The young man named in the indictment unquestionably came to his death by means of the discharge of a pistol by the defendant.

"The great question in the case is: Whether, according to the facts shown to you on the part of the prosecution, or by the defendant, any reasonable, legal justification or excuse has been proved.

"From the testimony of several prosecution witnesses, it appears on the day set forth in the indictment, the defendant was in his office a little before one o'clock; that in a conversation about his quarrel with the father of the deceased, he intimated that he had been informed an attack upon him was intended, and that he was prepared. That a short time afterward, he went from his office towards the United States Bank. That as he walked his hands were behind him, outside of his coat, without anything in them. There is testimony that when the deceased approached, the defendant put his right hand in his pocket and took out his pistol, while his left arm was raised to protect his head from an impending blow.

"The manner of his going, the weapon which he had with him, the previous intimation of an attack which he seems to have received, and the errand upon which he was going, are all circumstances worthy of your deliberate attention.

"Passing down the street as before described, several witnesses testify that the deceased—who was standing with a cane in his hand, near the corner of the Norwalk Building—having cast his his eye upon the defendant, shifted his cane into his right hand, stepped quick from the sidewalk onto the street, advanced upon the defendant with his arm uplifted; that the defendant turned, stepped one foot back; that a blow fell upon the head of the defendant and the pistol was discharged at the deceased at one and the same instant. Several blows were afterwards given and were attempted to be parried by the defendant who threw his pistol at the deceased, seized upon his cane, which was wrested from him by the deceased, who, becoming exhausted, fell down and in a few minutes expired.

"One witness testified that having expected to see a quarrel on State Street, in consequence of the publication against the deceased's father in the morning, he went there for the express purpose of seeing what should pass; that he saw the defendant coming down the street, saw deceased advance upon him; that he had a full view of both parties, was within fifteen feet of them; that he saw a blow fall upon the head of the defendant with violence; that the arm of the deceased was raised to give a second blow which fell the instant the pistol was discharged. This is the only witness who swears to a blow before the discharge of the pistol; but he swears positively, and says he has a clear, distinct recollection of the fact. His character is left without impeachment. If you consider it important to ascertain whether a blow was or was not actually given before the pistol was fired, you will inquire whether there are any circumstances, proved by other witnesses, which may corroborate or weaken this testimony.

"You will consider the testimony of the witness who testified that the left arm of the defendant was over his forehead, as though defending himself from blows, when he saw the blow fall. You will consider that all the witnesses state that the blow which they saw, and thought the first, was a long blow across the head.

"If you find a difficulty in settling the fact of the priority of the blow, take this for your rule: that a witness who swears positively to the existence of a fact, if of good character and sufficient intelligence, may be believed, although twenty witnesses of equally good character swear that they were present and did not see the same fact. The confusion and horror of the scene was such that it was easy for the best and most intelligent of men to be mistaken as to the order of blows which followed each other in such rapid succession that the eye could scarcely discern an interval.

"You will, therefore, compare the testimony of the witnesses where it appears to vary, attending to their different situation, power of seeing, and capacity of recollecting and relating, and settle this fact according to your best judgment, never believing a witness who swears positively to be perjured, unless you are irresistibly driven to such a conclusion.

"When the defense is that the assault was so violent and fierce that the defendant was obliged to kill the deceased to save himself, it surely is of importance to ascertain whether the violent blow he received on his forehead, which at the same time that it would put him off his guard, would satisfy him of the design of the assailant.

"When a weapon is used, it seems to me that the effect produced is the best evidence of the power and intention of the assailant to do that degree of bodily harm which would alone authorize the taking of his life on the principles of self-defense.

"But whether the firing of the pistol was before or after a blow struck by the deceased, there are other points of more importance for you to settle, and about which you must make up your minds, from all the circumstances proved in the case, such as: the rapidity and violence of the attack; the nature of the weapon with which it was made; the place where the catastrophe happened; the muscular debility or vigor of the defendant, and his power to resist or to fly.

"If you believe his only resort for safety was to take the life of his antagonist, he must be acquitted unless his conduct has been such, prior to the attack upon him, as will deprive him of the privilege of setting up a defense of this nature. It has been suggested during the argument by the defendant's counsel that even if his life had not been in danger or no great bodily harm, but only disgrace was intended by the deceased, there are certain principles of honor and natural right by which the killing may be justified.

"These are principles which you as jurors, and I as a judge cannot recognize. The laws which we are sworn to administer are not founded upon them.

"Let those who choose such principles for their guidance erect a court for the trial of points and principles of honor; but let the courts of law adhere to those principles which are laid down in the books, and whose wisdom ages of experience have sanctioned.

"I therefore declare it to you as the law of the land that homicide is justifiable when committed in defense of the person, against one who manifestly intends or endeavors to do some great bodily injury upon the person of the defendant. But the circumstances must be sufficient to excite the fears of a reasonable person, and the party killing must have acted under the influence of such fears alone.

"I ought not to rest here, for although I have stated to you that when a man's person is fiercely and violently assaulted, under circumstances which jeopardize his life or important members, he may protect himself by killing his adversary; yet he may, from the existence of other circumstances proved against him, forfeit his right to a defense which the laws of God and man would otherwise have given him.

"If a man, for the purpose of bringing another into a quarrel, provokes him so that an affray is commenced, and the person causing the quarrel is overmatched, and to save himself from apparent danger he kills his adversary, he would be guilty of manslaughter, if not of murder, because the necessity, being of his own creating, shall not operate in his excuse.

"You are therefore to inquire whether this assault upon the defendant by the deceased was or was not by the procurement of the defendant; if it were, he cannot avail himself of the defense now set up for him.

"You have heard the whole story of the misunderstanding between the defendant and the father of the deceased. To call a man a coward, liar, and scoundrel in the public newspapers, and to call upon other printers to publish the same, is not justifiable under any circumstances, whatever.

"Such a publication is libelous in its very nature, as it necessarily excites to revenge and ill blood. Indeed, I believe a court of honor, if such existed, to settle disputes of this nature, would not justify such a proclamation as the one alluded to.

"Neither can I refrain from censuring the manager of the paper who admitted such a publication for so readily receiving and publishing what, in its very nature, would tend to disturb the public peace. But, gentlemen, it is one thing for a man to have done wrong, and another thing for that wrong to be of a nature to justify an attack upon his person. If personal wrong, done by the father of the deceased to the defendant, would not justify him in publishing a libel, neither would the libel have justified the deceased or his father in attacking the person of the author of the libel.

"No man can take vengeance into his own hands; he can use violence only in defense of his person. No words, however aggravating, no libel however scandalous, will authorize the suffering party to avenge himself by blows.

"If, therefore, the deceased's father—the object of the newspaper publication—would not be justified had he attacked the defendant and beat him with a cane, still less would the circumstances have justified the unfortunate young man, who fell a victim to the most unhappy and ever to be lamented dispute.

"For, however a young and ardent son may find advocates in every generous breast for espousing his father's quarrel from motives of filial affection and just family pride, yet the same laws which govern the other parts of the case would have pronounced him guilty, had he lived to answer for the attack which was the cause of his death.

"The laws allow a son to aid his father, if beaten, and to protect him from a threatened felony or personal mischief, and in like cases a father may assist a son; and should a killing in either case take place it is excusable; but neither one nor the other can justify resorting to force to avenge an injury consisting in words, however opprobrious, or writing, however defamatory.

"Upon the whole, therefore, should you be of the opinion that the defendant, in order to avenge himself upon the father of the deceased, prepared himself with the deadly weapon which he afterwards used; went with a view to meet his adversary and expose himself to an attack in order that he might take advantage of and kill him; intending to resort to no other means of defense in case he should be overpowered, then there is no doubt the killing amounted to manslaughter. But, if from the evidence in the case you should believe that the defendant had no other view but to defend his life and person from an attack which he expected, without knowing from whom it was to come; that he did not purposely throw himself in the way of the attack, but was merely pursuing his lawful vocations, and that in fact he could not have saved himself otherwise than by the death of the assailant—then the killing was excusable, provided the circumstances of the attack would justify a reasonable apprehension of the harm which he would thus have a right to prevent. Of all this you are to judge and determine, having regard to the testimony of the witnesses who have given evidence to these several points.

"The last subject on which I shall trouble you is the address which has been so forcibly urged upon your minds by the counsel on one side, and as zealously and ably commented on by the other, touching the necessity of excluding all prejudices and prepossessions relative to this cause. I do not apprehend these observations were in any degree necessary, as I cannot bring my mind to feel that the verdict of twelve upright, intelligent jurors, selected by lot from the mass of their fellow citizens, will be founded on anything beside the law and evidence applicable to the case.

"Every person of this numerous assembly, let his own opinion of the merits of the case be as it may, must be satisfied of the fairness, regularity, and impartiality of the trial, up to the present period; and sure I am that nothing which is left to be done by you will impair the general character of the trial. If you discharge your duty conscientiously, as I have no doubt you will whether your verdict be popular or unpopular, you may defy the censure, as I know you would disregard the applause of the surrounding multitude.

"You, Gentlemen, will not be the first to violate the solemn oath you have taken and seek for a conviction or an acquittal of the defendant upon any other principle than those which the oath has sanctioned. And as I trust that in performing my duty I have conscientiously regarded that oath which obliges me 'faithfully and impartially to administer the laws according to my best skill and judgment,' so that in discharging yours, you will have due regard to that which imposes upon you the obligation, well and truly, to try the cause between the State and the defendant, according to law and the evidence which has been given you. . . ."

The jury returned a verdict of Not Guilty.

Censorship

THE UNKNOWN CLERK

MEET MR. JAMES HARLAN.

Who is James Harlan? Judging by his accomplishments he should be easily remembered. He was a man of purpose and purity. Raised by God-fearing parents and schooled by God-fearing teachers, he entered adulthood well prepared.

His studies led him into the field of education and in 1853 he became president of Iowa Wesleyan University. He was well suited for the position of spiritual leader, as well as titular head, of the seat of learning.

One of Harlan's great loves was his collection of the works of the literary masters. Knowing this, it is not difficult to picture him in a comfortable chair before a roaring fire in his library thumbing through the offerings of Marlowe, Shakespeare, Keats, Shelley, and Byron.

To be sure, certain passages presented by these authors must have puzzled him, for purity of thought and action was an essential element in his make-up. But he accepted these and did not take issue with them because the world of letters accepted them and therefore they must be good.

This reasoning enabled him to thumb through such classics as Shakespeare's *Rape of Lucrece*, Dante's *Inferno*, Bacon's *Advancement of Learning*, Milton's *Paradise Lost*, Erasmus's *In Praise of Folly*, Montaigne's *Essays*, and other thought-provoking volumes that nestled side by side on his bookshelves.

Harlan left the university post in 1854, studied law, and entered the realm of politics. He was elected a Senator to represent the people of Iowa in Congress in 1855, serving in this capacity for ten years.

In Washington he soon became a close friend of Abraham Lincoln. This tie was strengthened when his daughter married Lincoln's son.

Lincoln recognized Harlan's ability by appointing him Secretary of the Interior in 1865.

That is when Mr. James Harlan established his place in history.

For one of his first acts was to fire an obscure six-hundred-dollar-a-year Interior Department clerk because he had written an obscene book of poems entitled *Leaves of Grass*.

We all know Walt Whitman.

But who is James Harlan?

SON OF PROCRUSTES

OCCASIONAL SCHOLARS, today, tell us we are rapidly headed for anonymity. We hear talk of government operating as a bulldozer, doing its bureaucratic best to reduce all of our respective personalities to a common level. We hear talk of "mass man," "the organization man," "the common man," and "the silent generation." Mass production, television, and urban complexes, so say the scholars, are reducing millions to the same dull level of conformity. Houses grow to look alike, language loses its color, and computers can, in a matter of seconds, reduce a man's name to a fingerprint classification number or a plastic strip called a credit card, good for three months, revokable at owner's option.

Alas, we have always had "adjustment experts" in our midst. True, there were never so many of them, nor were their techniques so effective, but the ecology of the "people adjuster" is almost as old as that of the cockroach. Here is how it all might have begun . . .

In the time of the ancient Greek, so says legend, there lived in a mountain cave a certain type named Procrustes. It develops that Procrustes ran a kind of Homeric Hilton, taking in weary travelers who stopped along the way, for the night. As was the case with most things ancient, Procrustes' accommodations were few and simple; his bed was nonadjustable, nonexpandable, was not hooked up to a Princess phone, nor did it come in a choice of interior decorator's colors. It was not, as far as I know, of giant, economy size. It wasn't made of plastic, either.

Procrustes was a man who believed in order, one of the first proponents of that insidious form of brainwashing known as life adjustment. Now, while these particular personality traits may be beneficial in moderation, Procrustes was one of those people who go through life saying: "Please, Mother, I'd rather do it *myself!*" A rather simple-minded fellow, Procrustes was the sort of man who, once he got an idea into his head, just had to worry it and expand on it, being incapable of either moderation or original thinking.

You know his type; a lot of them are in government.

Being an expert in the field of "adjustment," it was Procrustes' notion that rather than go to the trouble of adjusting things to people, it would be better to adjust people to things. Thus, when it came time to retire for the night and it developed you were too long to properly fit in the bed, Procrustes solved this by lopping your feet off. If, on the other hand, you were too short, he would put you on the Greek equivalent of the rack and stretch you until your body better fitted his bed.

I am not sure what finally became of Procrustes; some say he was arrested for practicing medicine without a license. I personally prefer to believe he took a bride from the mattress maker's association and retired to the country to try his hand at olive growing.

While Procrustes is no longer with us, his memory persists, even in modern times. If you look about you today, you will see people who, save for a few thousand years' progress, could be his double. You know their kind; the bright ones write political speeches about "images" or spend their working day meddling in affairs that concern them not. These latter-day sons of Procrustes —the bright ones—are paid handsomely to "adjust" the man to fit the society.

But what, you ask, of the not-so-bright sons of Procrustes? Are they starving for want of work? No, indeed. The stupid ones are working in government.

THE FOUR-LETTER WORD ON TRIAL

This is part of a court argument in the case of The People of the State of California versus Lawrence Ferlinghetti, the publisher of *Howl and Other Poems* by the talented young poet Allen Ginsberg.

JUDGE CLAYTON W. HORN: Mr. Ehrlich, you may proceed.

MR. EHRLICH: Your Honor, much has been made by the Prosecution concerning the four-letter word—fuck—and there's been nervous hesitance on the part of the District Attorney to use it.

I am wondering whether my opponent knows the meaning of this word, or whether he attaches it lewdly to sex. During the time of Queen Elizabeth, it was in ordinary usage; an old Anglo-Saxon word meaning to plant, to occupy. It has been used in story, in poetry, and in song. Many scholars have and do contend that Christopher Marlowe was England's greatest dramatist and one of its great poets. Some researchers have and now insist that Shakespeare copied several of Marlowe's great dramas.

Certainly it cannot be said that Marlowe was a man who thought only of loose language or of lewd descriptions of sex, yet I must read three stanzas from a poem he wrote sometime during his life, which commenced in 1564 and ended in 1593:

> I love thee not for Sacred Chastity.
> Who loves for that? Nor for thy sprightly wit:
> I love thee not for thy sweet modesty,
> Which makes thee in perfection's throne to sit.
> I love thee not for thy enchanting eye,
> Thy beauty, ravishing perfection:
> I love thee not for that my soul doth dance,
> And leap with pleasure when those lips of thine,
> Give musical and graceful utterance,
> To some (by thee made happy) poet's line.
> I love thee not for voice or slender small,
> But wilt thee know wherefore? Fair sweet, for all.
>
> 'Faith, wench! I cannot court thy sprightly eyes,
> With the base viol placed between my thighs;
> I cannot lisp, nor to some fiddle sing,
> Nor run upon a high stretching minikin.
> I cannot whine in puling elegies.
> Entombing Cupid with sad obsequies:
> I am not fashioned for these amorous times,
> To court thy beauty with lascivious rhymes:
> I cannot dally, caper, dance and sing,
> Oiling my saint with supple sonneting:
> I cannot cross my arms, or sigh "Ah me,"
> "Ah me forlorn!" Egregious foppery!
> I cannot buss thy fill, play with thy hair,
> Swearing by Jove, "Thou art most debonnaire!"
> Not I, by cock! But I shall tell thee roundly,
> Hark in thine ear, zounds I can fuck thee soundly.

That was written by one of the great men of literature, who, if he lived today, would be prosecuted by our District Attorney for obscenity.

There are those who attribute wrong and improper thoughts to what they read because mentally they want it that way. You do not think lewd or lascivious thoughts just because you have read something in a book, unless it is your mental desire to think so. Impure sexual thoughts or prurient interest is self-generated by a desiring mind disposed to lewdness. The four-letter word "fuck" is not used in the book on trial to cater to prurient interest, but to express ideas necessary to the situation and the theme.

THE COURT: May I interrupt you there for a minute? I don't think you contend that the word is used in so-called polite society, do you?

MR. EHRLICH: Well, I don't know what your Honor means by polite society. Polite society? Are there degrees?

THE COURT: In other words, if you were invited to a party, would you use that word while discussing something with someone there, some ladies, for example?

MR. EHRLICH: I do not think that the mere use of one word is going to destroy anyone's morals or cause them to embrace that which is base and unworthy of an intellect of decency.

THE COURT: No, I am not approaching it from that standpoint. I am approaching it from the standpoint that . . . let me ask you this question: Are you willing to concede that there are certain words in the book that generally at this time, in this place—I don't mean this courtroom: I mean in the community—may be considered coarse and vulgar?

MR. EHRLICH: Yes, I will concede that there are words that may be so considered. I can't visualize the use of the four-letter word, whether acceptable or unacceptable, unless it is relevant to the theme. Our problem is whether the word is relevant to the theme of the book and it is not the question of where and when we should or should not use this word.

As has been aptly said, a word is not a crystal, transparent and unchanged. It is the skin of a living thought and may vary greatly in color and content according to the circumstances and the time in which it is used.

Is the word relevant to what the author is saying, or did he use it just to be dirty and filthy? In the book, is the word relevant to what the author is saying when he cries out:

America I've given you all and now I'm nothing.
America two dollars and twenty seven cents January 17, 1956
I can't stand on my own mind.
America when will we end the human war?

He answers his question:

Go fuck yourself with your atom bomb.
I don't feel good don't bother me.

What prurient interest is the author seeking to generate with that cry of pain? He is at the end of the road; crying out in the wilderness. Nobody is listening. Your Honor can't feel that anguished cry nor can I. We do not understand it. We have never lived his life. A man doesn't know the pain of a toothache unless he has a toothache. In love with your wife and devoted to her, you cannot share or feel her toothache.

We do not know what the author's mind was saying at the moment he wrote these lines. We haven't experienced hunger; we haven't reached the bottom of the pit. And who knows what man would say or do in any given set of circumstances unless these circumstances surrounded him.

The Prosecution refers to that part where the author is telling us, and the figurative Carl Solomon is saying:

I saw the best minds of my generation destroyed by madness,
    starving hysterical naked,
Dragging themselves through the negro streets at dawn
    looking for an angry fix.

He talks about what he sees. The endless subways from the Battery to the Bronx, benzedrine, noise of wheels . . . battered bleak of brain all drained of brilliance . . . a lost battalion . . . screaming vomiting whispering facts and memories and anecdotes . . . whole intellects disgorged in total recall . . . describes the man who studied philosophy . . . studied St. John of the Cross . . . the Kabala . . . who jumped in limousines with the Chinaman of Oklahoma . . . who lounged hungry and lonesome through Houston seeking jazz or sex or soup . . . seeking, seeking, always, broken, crying, everything is wrong.

The people about whom the author writes are doing everything Solomon is doing and everything he ought not be doing.
He associates with many girls . . . red-eyed in the morning but
prepared to sweeten the snatch of the sunrise, flashing buttocks
under barns and naked in the lake. He continues through
Colorado, sees what he terms the Adonis of Denver, who is
proud of his innumerable conquests. Instead of saying innumerable conquests, the author says . . . Lays of girls in empty
lots and diner backyards, moviehouses, rickety roads on mountaintops. . . .

After reciting all this turmoil and all he had seen, he could
have said that the secret hero of these poems, this cocksman,
this Adonis of Denver luxuriated in the memory of his innumerable conquests in the Waldorf-Astoria, or after dinner at Chasen's
or after a drink or two in the 21 Club. I presume he could have
said that, but that isn't the situation he is writing about; he is
writing about this man Solomon, this figurative man who marches
through all this turmoil and degradation.

If the Prosecution contends that because Adonis laid girls in
empty lots and moviehouses and on mountaintops and in caves,
and not in hotels or apartments, this book is an obscene book,
then the law is silly. It isn't for us to choose the words. When the
author tells his story, he tells it as he sees it, uses the words as he
knows them, and portrays in his language that which he sees,
hears, and feels.

And another place referred to by the Prosecution . . . the kitchen
has no door, the hole there will admit me should I wish to enter
the kitchen . . . I remember when I first got laid, H. P. graciously
took my cherry, I sat on the docks of Provincetown, age 23, joy-
ful, elevated in the hope with the Father . . . the door to the
womb was open to admit me if I wished to enter. . . .

There are passages in the Holy Bible describing the same
situations, but they do so in much clearer descriptive content.
Does the fact that the author has come to a realization of one
of the natural urges of life, which is the opening of an entire new
world to him, and he says so, and says it reverently—elevated in

hope with the Father—is it this description which the Prosecutor claims creates and encourages lewd and lascivious thoughts in the reader? I find nothing that is salacious, filthy, dirty, lewd, lascivious, or licentious in these references.

There is no evidence of obscenity. I can find no evidence here of any salacious appeal, nor is there any evidence of anything which urges that the book be bought and read because the author uses the word "fuck."

There is no evidence of the lewd intent required by law, or that the defendant sold this book lewdly. The Prosecution seeks to make the point that the book was published by the bookshop. But, that isn't enough, your Honor. The law requires more. The fact that someone published the book and the fact that the publisher sold it is not enough to establish guilt. There must be some specific act on his part. Let us remember that a man is on trial. What was his conduct in relation to the sale of the book? Did he sell it with the intent and purpose of creating lewd interests? Did he sell it with the intent to awaken the prurient interest of others? The only evidence before this court is that a police officer bought the book.

THE COURT: Stopping you there for a moment, it has been proved that the book was published by the bookshop, and the testimony is also in the record that the defendant is the owner of the bookshop. So, therefore, he published it. And that there was no one else on the premises at the time he sold it, so the only charge against the defendant would be confined to publishing and keeping for sale.

MR. EHRLICH: The law is that the sale or the keeping of a prohibited book will support an inference that the defendant acted lewdly only if there is some evidence that he knew or believed the book to be obscene in content. Your Honor will recall that we introduced reviews from magazines and newspapers, each of which praised the book and not one called it obscene. The defendant could and did rely on the opinion of those who are qualified to weigh the literary merit of a book.

The Prosecutor inquired whether the Court would like to

have the book read over the radio or on television. While it is not in the record, I inform the Court that it has been televised and broadcast. It is a book that has been so highly publicized by this trial that it is being discussed in literary circles and groups throughout the country, groups interested in literature and not in lewd publications.

Your Honor, great works of literature and classics of literature are at first condemned by those who see destruction in everything they cannot or will not understand and who find pornographic skeletons in every book closet.

Voltaire's *Candide* was originally condemned as obscene because it dealt with sex. The Prosecution and its witnesses admit this work is a classic. Words dealing with and describing sex do not destroy literary merit.

Shall we cull the lines from Balzac's stories? Shall we ban his works, take the volumes off the library shelves and hide behind the barn to read? Seek filth and you will find it. Seek beauty of narration and you will find that too. But to find filth you must search for it with a wanton mind and a willing application.

Any book can be declared obscene since a moron could pervert the listings in a seed catalogue to some sexual fantasy to which his mind is open. Not even the Bible is exempt. Annie Besant once compiled a list of 150 passages in Scripture that might fairly be considered obscene—it is enough to cite the story of Lot and his daughters.

Portions of Shakespeare and Chaucer could also be offensive, to say nothing of Aristophanes, Juvenal, Ovid, Swift, Defoe, Fielding, Smollett, Rousseau, Maupassant, Voltaire, Balzac, Baudelaire, Rabelais, Swinburne, Shelley, Byron, Boccaccio, Marguerite de Navarre, Hardy, Shaw, Whitman, and a host more.

One Prosecution witness testified that copying does not produce literature. He must have overlooked *The Jew of Malta,* a tragic drama by Christopher Marlowe written about 1590 and anticipating Shakespeare's *The Merchant of Venice* in plot.

Much of the plot of *The Merchant of Venice* first appeared in the *Gesta Romanorum* in the fourteenth century. Who copied whom, and who created literature?

There are books that have the power to change men's minds, and call attention to situations which are visible but unseen. Whether the book on trial is or is not obscene is of little importance in our world faced, as it is, with the problem of physical survival, but the problem of what is legally permissible in the description of sex, of art, and of literature is of the greatest importance in a free society.

It is generally established that the intention of a book as a whole, rather than the language of any particular passage, is the criterion in judging obscenity. There is not now, nor has there ever been, a workable definition of obscenity. Every person will react to sex writings according to his own sexual tastes.

The so-called legal yardstick of prurient or obscene when applied to books is much like judging the color of a horse by how fast he can run. What is prurient? And to whom? Prurient, it is said, means lewd, lascivious, or some other synonym that defies precise definition. And that the material so described is dangerous to some unspecified susceptible reader. It is interesting that the person applying such standards in censorship never feels that his own physical or moral health is in jeopardy.

The desire to censor, however, is not limited to crackpots and bigots. There is in most of us a strong desire to make the world conform to our own ideas, and it takes all the force of our reason and our legal institutions to defy so human an urge. The courts have long wandered in a maze in their efforts to apply the concept of contemporary community standards, and have often appeared to be deciding matters of law by the watery drippings of public opinion.

No one wishes to give free license for the publication of obscene works. Yet the difficulties in deciding what is or is not obscene have forced many into extreme positions. The liberal sees the threat of censorship and would let everything pass to give freedom to what is good. Another man would risk the suppression of an occasional book to guard the community from what he considers the danger of obscene literature.

The battle of censorship will not be finally settled by your Honor's decision, but you will either add to liberal, educated thinking or by your decision add fuel to the fires of ignorance.

I have seen the efforts of the Prosecution to build its case by counting four-letter words. I have seen the honest confusion of honest men trying to determine what is obscene with no real background of information to help them. I have seen the struggle with the semantic nonsense that is written into the lawbooks as definitions of obscenity.

Let there be light. Let there be honesty. Let there be no running from nonexistent destroyers of morals. Let there be honest understanding. In the end the four-letter words will not appear draped in glaring headlights, but will be submerged in the thinking of small minds.

Your Honor, Dr. Samuel Johnson could have been speaking of our self-appointed censor, when he described Iago, the villain of Shakespeare's tragedy *Othello*, who deliberately strings together such a mass of circumstantial evidence in proof of Desdemona's love of Cassio, that the Moor kills her out of jealousy.

> The cool malignity of Iago, silent in his
> Resentment, subtle in his designs, and studious
> At once of his interest and his vengeance . . .

To which I add:

His ignorance.

Let the matter stand submitted.

Is Poverty or Disease a Crime?

WARD OF THE STATE

I THINK it may be safely said that law is nothing more nor less than a kind of written memorandum outlining our obligations and responsibilities toward others. The best laws are those that coincide with the times we live in, and to do this they have been modified, over the centuries, by wise men. The worst laws are fool's laws and they have been created by frightened men who have glimpsed into themselves and have been frightened by the things they saw. They then sat down, assuming their wickedness was universal, and wrote laws punishing people for being what they are.

I am about to write some elemental history, here, showing how laws come about. While I have earlier written about obviously bad laws, the legal codes I shall presently discuss are not, on the face of it, bad. To the contrary, they came into being only recently and they owe their existence to the reformers, the kind of heart, and the compassionate. And yet, as they stand, they are bad laws. These laws may be compared to the decent impulse the unknowing have when they come upon the scene of an automobile accident and try and move the broken-bodied victims. We are a curious breed of cat, we of the human race. Like a pendulum, we swing back and forth in our attitudes toward our fellows, never constant, never quite sure of why it is we do the things we do. To get a better picture of what we were, what we are, and what we may be in the future, let us pause for a few moments and review some ancient and modern history.

Man is a tribal animal, a social animal. Since man first drew breath and began dragging his family from place to place, we have always lived as a unit. The family has always been the rule, the outlander or "loner," the exception. Accordingly, earliest man had a definite role to play out; he was the hunter, the maker-of-things, the farmer. The provider. It was earliest man's job to take care of his family the best way he knew how, and the fact that many of our ancestors hardly lived long enough to take a mate and make the barest start toward a family is mute proof that many of our earliest breed were not as successful in the role of the provider as others. We do know, however, that even in those earliest days—thousands of years before recorded history—the race for survival often went to those who were fleetest of foot, most cunning of all, or else a small minority who were merely lucky.

What happened to the rest of these earliest men? Some were slaughtered by their fellows, or by wild beasts. Some died in infancy, others by such accidents as forest fires, or being caught in their own animal traps. A very tiny few probably died of old age or whatever its prehistory equivalent was in those times.

The role of man has been, traditionally, that of the provider. Even the most barbaric and uncivilized of our ancestors had a moral obligation to provide food and shelter for his family. That tools were invented somewhere along the way surely attests to the fact that early men—at least some of them—decided that the business of getting enough to eat was practically a full-time job and that even a savage should have a little leisure time to devote to improving his cave or helping his wife. In any event, progress from man the savage toward man the tool-maker was prompted, largely, by the necessity of getting enough food to keep his wife and family quiet. And so it is to this day, I might hasten to add, recalling the words of a friend who once said: "Behind every successful man there is at least one empty belly."

There was no welfare as we know it today, no Social Security payments and unemployment pay, in those prehistoric times.

Perhaps some tribes had certain arrangements for taking care of the old and infirm, such as they were. If so, there is no record of these activities. Indeed, prehistoric man was so busy taking care of his own basic needs that he had no time to do much of anything for any person not a member of his family. Possibly when man became a member of a larger family, a tribe, the weaker members existed on a kind of sufferance, doing menial chores in exchange for sharing the meat provided by the hardy hunters; but it is unlikedly. Meat was exceeding hard to come by and, not unlike today, the slayer of the mastodon was exceedingly reluctant to share his good fortune with another.

The role of man went, as we know, from a creature little better than an ape to the more sophisticated person we know today. Always, man lived on at least a tribal level, each member of the tribe having a definite place in the scheme of things. We know that some early peoples tended first toward agricultural work, with each family working a small plot of ground, usually located near a river. Some members of the tribe—probably those unable to do the backbreaking work that is often the farmer's lot—became craftsmen. Arrangements were no doubt made to the effect that the tribe's potter could share the bounty of the farmer's fields in exchange for a few vases or dishes. Thus, the barter system began.

The more civilized peoples began to recognize a certain responsibility toward their elders, now that man was starting to live long enough to be able to know his father and mother as they reached middle age. Much of the threat of wild animals and marauding, unfriendly tribes was being eliminated and, as man developed his tool-making abilities, he had a certain amount of time left in which to educate himself. It was now becoming possible for a farmer to learn something of the trade of pottery-making or metal-making, skills he could pass on to his children as they began to grow up. From the simple role of farmer, man became a more diversified creature, sometimes mastering several crafts within his lifetime.

Cities, as we know them today, began to spring up along

the rivers that early man had instinctively gravitated toward. Again, the role of man became more diversified. Some men became merchants, bankers, specialized artisans, while many of their elders became counselors and advisors to the tribe, a role somewhat like today's lawyer's. Ideally, at this time, every member of what had once been a tribe and was now fast becoming a race had a purpose, a goal, a role to play out, a reason, perhaps, for justifying his own existence. Still, we must also take note of the fact that the crippled, the lame, the halt, the feeble-minded—unless they were of a family wealthy enough to support them—probably died at an early age, unwanted and uncared for. Some of these very early civilizations might have had some kind of a retirement plan for those reaching old age who were not capable of sitting on the high tribal councils or the like, but it is doubtful. It was not until the Roman Empire was in full sway—perhaps several hundred years before Christ— that man began to be concerned enough about the mysteries of the future to purchase group insurance for the afterlife in the form of burial plans that allowed each participating member, at the time of his death, to be buried in a manner considered fitting in those times.

And what of the unemployed at this time? Well, they were there, though not in the proportionately great numbers we have today. Many of them starved, cut off from family ties and work abilities that might have supported them. Also, during the many phases of the Roman Empire there was a plain-and-simple surplus of warm bodies from time to time. The army could not hold all of them, an agricultural surplus hit the market every so often, and slaves, who worked for less and ate correspondingly less, generally served to keep a portion of free Roman citizens "at liberty." Several plans, all of them cynical and designed to buy votes, were inaugurated whereby the unemployed were bought off by the use of special gold coins or a small amount of food. These plans were generally unsuccessful and it may be noted that about the time the Roman Empire commenced to hit the skids a substantial unemployment problem was in the making.

Subsequent history shows us much the same thing. At the point where a tribe of men settle permanently, build a city, develop skills and trades peculiar to their society, a certain percentage near the bottom are unable to get work, or, once obtaining work, soon lose it. The Industrial Revolution in Europe shows the plight of small farmers, relatively self-sufficient on their land, being dragooned into the cities to toil impossibly long hours on looms, in mills, on lathes. Industry cared not for the welfare of these people and as their jobs were made obsolete by a kind of crude form of automation they were declassed, let out to pasture with less consideration than one would show for an old mule who had spent its best years in harness for Old Master.

At this point I think it is well to "take a breather" and consider several important things about work, civilization, and the nature of man. First of all, history shows us that those societies that were relatively content and stable were so because of several factors: (1) All members of the society were, first and last, attached strongly as a familial unit. Each had his place, his position, his own sense of worth relative to the whole. (2) Each member of the family—or tribe—had a sense of worth because he felt *needed*. The youngest child had certain tasks or chores he was required to fulfill. The father, as we have seen, was the breadwinner, in the most literal sense of the word. From the early hunter down through the ages to the craftsman of the eighteenth and nineteenth centuries, the man supplied the food, the shelter for his family. Perhaps more important, his method of supplying these things was his own and if he was dependent upon the tribe it was a dependency based upon the tribe's greater interests as shown in mutual aid against hostile tribes and the like. The main thing of importance, it seems to me, was that man— until the last few centuries—was involved in the *whole* of his work; he labored not to make a part of a thing, but the whole of a thing. A cobbler made shoes, not just heels. A hunter made traps, skinned wild animals, did not serve merely as a trap-spring repairman, GS-5, junior-executive trainee.

Thus, each person had a true sense of value, of belonging to the larger group. This state of being, I should like to add, is allegedly with us today in its bastardized concept known as "status." It is a weak substitute for what our elders had in mind, and our sick and troubled society, I believe, knows this on all levels.

America beckoned all the world, in the beginning, for it promised a bounty of land, of crops. It promised that here there would be no rigid caste system such as had developed in Europe when the huge cities ceased to be in a state of flux and gradually became fixed in attitude. I suspect that much of contemporary America's concern with the television Western and the concept of "Cowboy Free Will" might spring from the faintest dreams that were inculcated in all of us, in school, of the freedom that the West might have promised our grandfathers. Here, so said our schoolbooks—and so says the television, today—each man could again be a part of the familial unit. Goals were there for the man who would work. All men were needed for tasks and the rewards for the completion of these tasks were bread, a place to live, a chance to participate in a larger share of the wealth, and, most important, *a sense of belonging!*

But to dismiss the West—or even the whole of early America —as a paradise lost, would be too easy and we would not be telling the entire truth. For in early America we were plagued with problems of unemployment, though not in anywhere near the proportions that confront us today. The specter of men going hungry, many through no fault of their own, began to stalk the civilized portion of our land even before the Civil War; by the time this great conflict had subsided, our larger cities had become pestholes, in many quarters, because they were jammed with people whose skills—if they had such—were not wanted. It was during this same era, and as far in the future as the 1930s, that it was publicly acknowledged by many business leaders that it was a good thing if a large pool of the unemployed were continually on hand to serve as a kind of ballast necessary to keep wages depressed.

We read our history books and we learn what the price for keeping a "large pool of unemployed" has cost us. We read of the Homestead Strike, of mines and tipples being dynamited, of goons and scabs retained by management, serving as private armies to make continual war on the unemployed. What these tragedies cost us in money, in production, and, most important, in the lost lives of men, women, and children, no one can imagine. We do know that these management practices were, to a large degree, eventually curtailed, for to continue them placed our country in great peril; a free society cannot exist when a large portion of its citizens, through no fault of their own, are poorly housed, worked like dogs, and receive the tiniest fraction of the profits from their labors. This is simply sound economy, the bettering of conditions, and when it was finally realized, concessions were gradually made, until we have, roughly, society as we know it today.

And what is today's society? Well, there is no doubt that there are depressed areas, large pockets of them, all over America. Specifically, we have those portions where our mining industry is located: Kentucky, Virginia, and other states hard hit by changing times and obsolete work skills. We have the tragic spectacle of men who wish to work but who cannot; their trades and crafts are outmoded and their willing hands and backs are unwanted. Patiently, they sit on the stoops of their cabins and wait for word to return to work. This word will never be given them; machines have taken their place.

There are other areas where men have been declassed, and not all of them are in the South, by any stretch of the imagination! Every northern city has its slum area, its depressed area, and living conditions here are surely as mean and as wretched as they were in industrial England, the England Dickens immortalized in *Oliver Twist*. In these areas of our country there is no hope existing in the hearts of these slum dwellers that work will ever be forthcoming; there is only the father-to-son continual knowledge that living in this manner is a way of life that may be questioned but rarely challenged.

And this brings me to subsidized poverty and our entire relief, unemployment, and welfare program.

To appreciate better the contradictions that dwell within us and are often reflected in the inane and mystifying laws we make, I shall ask the following question: What is it that a movie star, a retired colonel of the Army, an out-of-work shipping clerk, and an industrial magnate drawing a company pension all have in common? It is this: They all may be found at the Unemployment Compensation Benefit window of any local state office of employment, drawing unemployment compensation. Now, while it is quite understandable that the shipping clerk, out of work, strapped, and looking for work would immediately qualify for unemployment compensation, it is hard to fathom why a colonel, an actor, and an industrial executive would need this pittance. But it is the law; anyone out of work who alleges he or she is looking for work is qualified to draw unemployment benefits. Now, we know that the industrialist needs not one penny of state aid, nor does the actor who will be out of work this week and working two weeks hence; especially when his gross income has been about $50,000 a year over the past ten or so years. We also know that the "professional" compensation-drawer, the man who takes a six-month vacation from time to time, surely has not lost his job through no fault of his own; he has "arranged" to be let go. Well, this is fine and dandy; a six-month state-subsidized vacation.

And all of this, fellow taxpayer, at your expense!

Like most of our laws, the codes covering unemployment insurance were inaugurated with good intent. Also, we were fast reaching the point where the unemployed, the poor, were beginning to raise a clamor that shocked and no doubt made a number of politicians think twice about the coming elections. Therefore, unemployment insurance as a concept was introduced in our states. It was introduced *specifically* to cover those who had lost their jobs through no fault of their own, *who were actively looking for work!* Does this appear to cover the status of retired industrialists and army colonels? Does it sound as if actors and others who yearly earn half as much again as the President should qualify for benefits? Not to me, it doesn't!

I hold that the unemployment insurance laws, far from covering those who need it most—the genuinely unemployed who are walking their feet off, daily, in search of honest toil—have become perverted . . . and dearly expensive, too! Consider such a state as Michigan, bankrupt a few years ago because while many of the unemployed were genuinely out of work and doing their best to seek labor, a large number of the lazy, the indolent, the fat of head and lean of character were flocking to this state to get on "that old unemployment."

I believe that he who knowingly draws unemployment insurance, who has contrived to lose his job, who searches not for toil while he is supping at the table of the state, is as guilty of fraud as was Ponzi, one of the most gigantic swindlers of our lifetime. Such persons, by deliberately lying in order to take funds from those who truly need them—the unemployed—are as guilty of larceny as the bank robber! Indeed, there is a similarity in the *modus operandi* of these two cheats, for both slip a sheet of paper across to the teller. Of the two, the bank robber is the more honorable, for he boldly states: "Your money or your life," while the unemployment fake cozens his way into the state coffers, shuffling, rubbing his belly, moaning—all part of his calculated act to bilk you and me out of money that rightfully should go to the genuinely unemployed.

What's to be done? In all truth, there are laws on our books that cite penalties for such swindlers. These laws are not being enforced, for the unemployment cheat, it seems, must be legion in number. I say this because our politicians appear to be so

fearful of what would happen if such a mountebank were prosecuted and sent off to jail, where he rightfully belongs. And I
want to make it very clear, here, that I *am not* referring to a
particular class or ethnic group in this condemnation of the
unemployment swindler either! I am talking about all of them!
Ideally, they should be made to pay back every dime they have
taken from the state and, in the bargain, it would be a good
thing if the state had special camps for them. Inasmuch as
they are all purportedly "out of work," let's give them a new
skill that has been with us since earliest recorded history: hard
labor. I am convinced that as the blisters began to form on the
soft hands of these labor fakers they would most quickly "git
religion," as they used to say in my boyhood home in Maryland,
and "see the light."

As to another facet of this problem, I should now like to call
your attention to a hard core of persons in our land who might
as well be from another country. Technically, these people are
citizens of America, though none of them will ever exercise an
important right of citizenship by obtaining a passport. Most
of these persons have a literacy rate that is about equal to that
of a high-grade seven-year-old child. Naturally, few—if any—
of these persons vote in the national elections, though they have
traditionally been used as a moving force in municipal and state
politics by those astute enough to go out and round up their
votes. Most of these persons are members of what is euphemis-
tically called a "minority group," though the Caucasians are by
no means absent among them. This group of people I am speaking about is noted for its high crime rate, especially when compared to the crime rate of the nation as a whole. This group
almost never owns real property, as we know it; such possessions
as they may have are leased, never owned, being continually
repossessed by one loan-shark outfit or another. The amount of
rent this group is compelled to pay, in relation to the quality of
the dwellings they must occupy, is astronomical. But then this
group is often referred to as a "captive population" and naturally

they are in no position to protest, unless you consider pulling a stick-up, getting drunk, or taking to narcotics a valid form of protest.

This "captive population" I am speaking of is our captive poor, our legally subsidized wards of the state. While our various county and state relief laws have made meager provisions for their upkeep, they have done nothing constructive in the way of eliminating the existence of these wards of ours. In the land of "opportunity and freedom" they are our lowest strata. And they are our continual responsibility, for a chunk of our taxes goes toward their upkeep and, in a roundabout way, toward the upkeep of unscrupulous landlords, political ward heelers, fly-by-night moneylenders, and others who are cheap and mean enough to make a profit on misery.

On the other side of the coin, we are also the ones who finally lose patience with them, send them to the penitentiary, the gas chamber, or the mental wards. They are our children, these wards of the state, and it behooves us to examine them.

What one single thing characterizes these children of ours? They are not working. They cannot work. They are unable to work. They are absolutely unprepared, in the main, to work if work were offered them! They cannot provide bread for the mouths of their children, they cannot earn their keep. They are the losers, the rock-bottom, 10 per cent hard core of our lowest level. They have been referred to, collectively, as a "disaster area." Individually, the state calls them the "unfortunates."

As I have stated earlier, these persons are unprepared for work. Why? Because they are ignorant, as all of us would be ignorant had we not received an education. Few of these persons have ever had any kind of education; like their parents before them, most are barely literate. They cannot read, they cannot possibly hope to compete in a twentieth-century job market. Finally—and most tragically—because their parents, and sometimes their grandparents, have also been on relief, they have come to accept their plight as a way of life! They have come to accept the continual visits made by some social workers and others interested in keeping these people ignorant, barefoot, and indigent—the invasions of privacy you and I would rebel at—as something quite natural.

What, you ask, is the law on this? It is difficult to cite chapter and verse, as each state has its own specific laws governing the treatment of the poor. In California our treatment of the indigent is governed by the Welfare and Institutions Code. This is a thick volume, some 678 pages long, covering every conceivable aspect of the administrative details of public relief, welfare, call it what you will. This volume deals with such esoteric subjects as delinquents and wards of the juvenile courts, orphans and other needy children, indigent persons, and even the oft-neglected American Indian.

And not one word will be found in this volume about what legal provisions are most sorely needed: how to get these people off the rolls of the state and, as could be the case with so many of them, give them the dignity that should at least be a way of life for all human beings.

What is the impact on a person who is on relief? What are one's obligations to the state? As we surely must know, there is no such thing as "something for nothing." When one takes something from the state, one loses certain rights. For example, if you are an ex-serviceman and you become ill, you may turn in at a Veteran's Administration hospital. You will be given the finest medical attention that is available. You will also lose certain rights, perhaps only token rights, but lose them you will! You will be subject to a semblance of military discipline, even though technically a civilian. And if you do not like it, the authorities will be quick to tell you that you are at liberty to go elsewhere and *pay*, naming your own terms and conditions.

On the ultimate level, service in the military is an example of what happens to a person when he receives "something for nothing." You will be fed and clothed while serving your enlistment; your medical attention will be the finest. Every necessity of life will be provided you. And in such circumstances, you will be surrendering all of your civil rights to the man who has one more stripe than you have! There is no other way it can be done.

Of those drawing relief, how many are restored to society? Few, if any. On the other hand, does their population remain stable? It does not! Their numbers continue to grow and grow, for the state, in most jurisdictions, pays a premium for every new child. Inasmuch as most women on relief are also without a husband to support them, we have the curious spectacle of the state supporting bastardy! The tragedy of this whole farce, really, is that there is a growing mutter of protest in our land from those who are frequently without pity or compassion for their fellows, those who contend that we are paying too much to support idlers. There are some who would have the poor cut off without another state dime; they would have the indigent sterilized, the better to prevent their multiplication. And what if such a totalitarian attitude crept into our laws? Frankly, there would probably not be too much protest. Surely those on relief—the ignorant and the uneducated—would be in little position to do much, save turn to crime.

It is my opinion that relief, per se, is wasteful. More important, it is criminal, for we pay these people a pittance, a small amount of money that allows them to survive at a marginal level and, as mentioned earlier, acts as an inducement to have unwanted and uncared-for children at a rate that staggers the imagination. We are subsidizing poverty where we ought to be eliminating it. We have thoroughly perverted the concept of "my brother's keeper," and have twisted it to read: "my brother's warder, subject to certain behavior."

What do I offer as a solution? Modesty forbids that I call it Ehrlich's Law; better to simply term it Common Sense Statute Relative to the Welfare Code:

(1) All persons on the relief rolls *will* attend school each working day of each week. All such persons will obtain profi-

ciency in reading and writing on at least a tenth-grade level. Further, such subjects as Conduct, Personal Hygiene, and Civics shall be taught such persons in addition to courses designed to enable them to read, write, and work arithmetic.

(2) Failure to attend such a school would *immediately disqualify* the recipient of welfare from further benefits.

(3) All such persons as designated in (1) who have obtained a certificate of graduation from school will be taught a trade or other, appropriate work skill. Trades shall be all-inclusive and the trade to be taught shall be determined by tests of the individual's proficiency. Persons with a higher intelligence quotient will be encouraged to enroll in university-level classes.

(4) Failure to learn a trade as a result of willful negligence shall be grounds for immediate termination of further benefits.

(5) Monies advanced the indigent welfare recipient during the course of his trade-education period shall be reimbursed the state by the recipient following his employment. Payment of sums owed may be in modest amounts, spread out over a period deemed reasonable, considering the individual worker's circumstances, wages, etc.

What I have proposed is nothing radical, nothing new, nothing untried. Several of the Scandinavian countries have experimented with trade-education programs and have even stood the expense of moving the worker and his family to another part of the country when he was unable to find work in his original place of residence. Needless to say, the worker is obliged to pay the state back.

We would have little or no problem obtaining qualified instructors on the trade level. Our society is cruel and heartless in its treatment of the aged; we have many useful oldsters who are slowly dying of ennui, whose lives could be prolonged if they felt they were of value. Many of these older people have retained job skills that should be passed on to the next generation. Of especial concern ought to be all the artisan skills, handmade products the like of which we rarely see in this country any more. The sale of these products could partially help defray the cost of such a program.

Most important, the trade unions and organized capital are

going to have to recognize their responsibility in these matters, and I want to make it crystal-clear right now that I will not give credence to the union leader or the industrialist who says: "This is no responsibility of mine!" It *is* their responsibility, for they too pay taxes, and these taxes go to the subsidization of the welfare recipients. Trade unions, inactive as far as work-trade programs go, must be made to realize that they would do well to have a larger membership rather than continually yammering for a few pennies more an hour, a few pennies, I might add, that are quickly gobbled up by the state for bigger taxes. The same applies to management. Industry failed to read the entrails of history during the late 1800s and 1900s and paid a high and unnecessary price for its poor augury. A pool of skilled and well-trained workers would be a great saving to industry, make no mistake about it!

True, there will be a certain plateau in every society representative of those who cannot be trained, cannot be employed. Well, get them out of the slums, too! There is manual labor in our forests, on our farms, in our cities. The important thing is that all of these people be given the feeling that they *belong*, that their existence serves some kind of purpose. Can you imagine anything more self-defeating than the knowledge that you are not wanted, that you serve neither the state nor yourself by even existing? Well, this is the feeling that runs rampant among our wards of the state and it is a sickness that must be eliminated! And the only way to eliminate it is by giving these people knowledge, trades, skills. We have failed to do this and, if you need proof, visit your local slum and talk to some of these not-so-legitimate children. Then, imagine that you were an employer and this person were presenting himself for a job. Would you hire him? Not likely!

We do not spend money to subsidize cancer; we spend millions to eliminate it. When we take an ailing automobile to the garage for repairs we tell the mechanic to fix it, not simply keep it in its faulty state. Yet with our relief program, our monies spent on subsidized poverty, we do nothing more than perpetuate the ignorance, the squalor, the heartlessness of these shameful conditions. We offer those on the bottom levels nothing more than charity—money charity—and I assure you that those on our lower levels are not grateful. Neither would you be grateful if you were given a dole once a week, knowing that the giver despised you or, at best, pitied you as one pities a mangy dog.

The pendulum, as we have seen, has swung from one extreme to the other. From lawless prehistoric man who abandoned the weak to the wild animals, we have now gone to lawful new man who subsidizes weakness and ignorance. The pendulum, in time, may begin to swing back to the old ways, the jungle ways, and if it does, it is important that we have as few of the weak and the unfortunate as is possible. If we do not, the brutalities that will be done to these future wards of the state will be done in our names.

The laws that perpetuate subsidized poverty are your laws. If you agree with me that they are bad laws, incomplete laws, change them. This is your prerogative, as an American.

THE NARCOTICS ADDICT

IT IS THE YEAR 2064. For many years now, the use of tobacco in any form whatsoever has been banned. Historians now write of the effects of tar upon the lungs of our ancestors, and to completely destroy the smoking habit, lurid movies and books have been written about "nicotine fiends." Because the state considers a person who has cancer of the lungs to be a confirmed smoker of cigarettes, all such persons are now tried before special tribunals where, when automatically found guilty, they are quickly put to death.

A special investigative body has been created to stamp out the last remnants of the once flourishing society of cigarette smokers, the Special Hearings Investigative Tribunal, abbreviated . . . well, no matter. This apparatus, without the necessity of procuring search warrants, may enter any place at any time of day or night. To be seen with brown stains on one's forefinger is enough to be remanded to the Tribunal's office, where certain fluids will be injected into the suspect's body. A positive reaction immediately indicates that the suspect is a confirmed smoker of cigarettes.

Naturally, although the state has done its best to stamp out the smoking vice, there are those, even on pain of death, who will continue this unnatural practice. When apprehended they will readily admit that they know they face the death penalty. They have seen the state's propaganda films against smoking, they will tell you, but so great and so powerful is the urge to place a contraband cigarette in their lips, light up, and draw the tarry smoke deep into their lungs, that they are unable to control themselves. Yes, they say, they know that smoking is a filthy vice; that the state is correct when it preaches abstinence, if for no other reason than the prohibitive economics involved, for that which is banned is expensive, and cigarettes on the black market now sell for about $3 apiece. The better-grade tobacco, the so-called Mexican Brown, sells for $5, and daily one reads of the FeToPo (Federal Tobacco Police) engaging smugglers out of Mexico in running gun battles.

A new national hero, the Smoke Cop, has emerged. Television series regale the citizen of 2064 with lurid stories of his exploits. In the first three reels of any such series, we see nicotine fiends as they go about the business of debauching themselves with tobacco—smoke orgies, they are called—and in the final reel the Smoke Cop arrives, to take them all off to jail. Children, emulating his example, are encouraged to turn in smokers, especially their parents. Indeed, the state now offers a bonus of $1,000 to him who will report to the proper authorities the act of possession for sale of tobacco.

For a brief time the state sets up institutions to treat smokers, but to no avail. In spite of the withdrawal cures the state provides, in spite of the lectures that the members of the FeToPo and the S.H.I.T. make in schoolrooms all across the land, there is still a hard core of about 60,000 smokers in the land. Penalties are stiffened: five to ten years for possession for use, first conviction; life in prison for sale to a minor; death for two previous convictions and/or lung cancer. It is all for nothing; daily, young men and old ladies are hauled off to jail by the authorities.

Occasionally, medical authorities attempt to make themselves heard above the hue and cry of the mob. These authorities would like the citizens to believe that smoking is not a police problem but a medical problem. Nonsense, retort the police; smokers are lawbreakers and you know what happens to lawbreakers. Hospital is for sick people, not lawbreakers.

The doctors reply that smokers *are* sick people; to this the authorities reply that any person who wants to stop smoking *can* stop. Why, before smoking became a crime, they reply, look at how many people were able to quit.

Yes, say the doctors, but look at how many, even when their physicians told them to quit, were unable to do so, knowing that cigarettes were absolute poison to their systems.

We wouldn't know about that, say the police. All we know is that in the old days our fathers had the same problem with narcotics addicts and you know how we solved *that* one!

Yes, say the doctors, sadly; you shot them all!

Having indulged in my analogy, I now offer you the above as a parody on our narcotics problem. True, 2064's solution to our contemporary problem may seem rather drastic to those of us alive in 1964, but you must remember that the hydrogen bomb, in the eyes of George Washington, would have seemed rather drastic by comparison too!

Narcotics have always been with us. It is thought that the Chinese, or possibly the Persians, discovered *Papaver somniferum*, the opium poppy; the date of discovery is unknown. In any event, it was probably Marco Polo who brought this black, gummy substance back to Europe, along with the poppy and some of its seeds. Physicians immediately put opium and laudanum, one of its derivatives, in their medicine chests as a good medicine for pain and sleeplessness. While we do not know how many addicts this drug produced while it was taken orally, it may be assumed that if addicts existed, they were not a great threat to the state. Indeed, history tells us that such men as Coleridge and Poe used opium or laudanum. Recent reports indicate that Sir Walter Scott was not above an occasional bout with Morpheus, and we all know of De Quincey's work, based upon personal experience, *Confessions of an English Opium Eater*.

If we may say that a narcotics problem was created, it would be correct to say that the American Civil War ushered it in, in the United States, with the invention of the hypodermic needle. By this time opium had been further treated to give us morphine, an extremely powerful narcotic. Many soldiers had been given morphine injections during the War between the States, and the doctors, at that time not knowing morphine's addictive nature, had no way of gradually withdrawing the dosages as the soldiers recovered from their wounds. By the end of the war, it was estimated that about 60,000 persons in the United States were addicted to the use of morphine by means of self-administered hypodermic injections.

In the following years—up to 1916—any person who so desired could walk into a drugstore and lay down a small amount of cash for drugs that today may be sold only to physicians. There were literally hundreds of commercial preparations on the open market that contained opium, laudanum, morphine, etc. Cough syrups containing enough laudanum to lay a grown man cold were recommended for "crying children" and older women. So-called soothing syrups and various tonics for women undergoing the menopause were nothing more than narcotic preparations that, if taken too rapidly, would produce coma or death.

Heroin, the most widely know addictive drug today, was extracted from opium in 1898. Curiously enough, the chemist who performed this history-making event announced that now there was a new, nonaddictive drug on the market, safe for use by all.

Even in 1898, it develops, people were being besieged by the "new, all-new" charlatans.

The Harrison Act of 1916 was enacted by our federal government in an attempt to control the spread of narcotic drug abuses. By then, incidentally, it was estimated that about 500,000 men, women, and children throughout the land were addicted to narcotic drugs. Without going into the technicalities of the Harrison Act, suffice it to say that it was a tax act, enforceable by the Internal Revenue Department, and it provided that certain narcotic drugs could be bought after a tax was paid to the government. There were various licensing requirements attached to this act, making it virtually impossible for anyone other than a doctor or a pharmacist to buy narcotic drugs in this country.

Well, the Harrison Act shut off the supply of legal drugs in this country. Now, what was to be done with some 500,000 addicts? Clinics were tried in a few states and by the middle 1920s the doctors were crowded out of the field of treating addicts. The various local, state, and federal agencies gradually pre-empted the field of medical treatment of addicts until finally the addict became a police problem, not a medical problem.

What is addiction? Is it a state of mind or a state of being? Medical authorities, when allowed to speak on this problem, tend to agree that it is *both* a state of being and a state of mind. It is impossible, so say responsible physicians, to treat one without treating the other. While the federal authorities in their clinic-hospital at Lexington, Kentucky, seem to partially recognize this fact, if no one else does, the fact remains that most states do not and, beyond this, even the federal people have not had any great degree of success in getting an addict off narcotics and then *keeping* him off.

What is an addict? Briefly, he is a person who has voluntarily or involuntarily so changed his body metabolism that drugs have become as essential to him as the air he breathes. Science still has a long way to go in understanding the mechanical process of addiction and we may lay the blame for this largely at the feet of our lawmakers and our police. In all our states it is a crime for a physician to treat an addict, save in what the legislators consider a "proper facility." Usually, a "proper facility" is a stinking cell in a county jail or a city prison. Therefore, by making it a crime for a physician to treat addicts, it is quite understandable that the physician, on the average, knows little or nothing about addiction. Of course I will not go so far as to say that the police, by keeping things this way, also keep the supply of addicts at such a point as to justify their own existence. I cannot believe that the police and the legislators would *intentionally* do such a thing; I can only assume that they are acting in "our own best interests."

Back to the business of addiction. Morphine, opium, heroin, and the like are poisons. They depress the entire bodily function. Now, in the beginning, the would-be addict can use only a small portion of a narcotic drug and, as he gradually uses more, it follows that his body develops a tolerance for larger doses. In much the same manner as tolerance to a narcotic drug is developed, I might add, a would-be poisoner can develop a tolerance to, say, arsenic, over a period of time. At such a time as a tolerance has been reached, this poisoner could give a friend some arsenic-spiked candy, eat some from the same batch, and be completely unaffected while the friend died of arsenic poisoning.

The addict becomes "hooked," or addicted, at the point at which his system absolutely has to have the drug, and it presents no great problem to determine when this time has arrived. The addict will awaken one morning and discover that he has a condition something like intestinal flu, only much more pronounced. Further, the addict will discover that he will feel "normal" only when he has injected another batch of narcotics into his arm, or other preferred site of injection. From this point on the addict's life becomes the most vicious kind of circle; from month to month the amount of drug needed just to make the addict feel "normal" increases.

Now, the addict may have started taking drugs for a number of reasons. We know that some addicts started using drugs because of their environment; their friends were doing it and they did it "just to be one of the gang." A small percentage of addicts—how small or large we do not know—were accidentally addicted by their physicians. Barney Ross, the fighter, had such a tragic experience as a result of wounds suffered in World War II.

But there are other facts about addiction that few people know. For one thing, one injection of a drug will not, in itself, produce an addict. Nor, for that matter, will two or three or four. Being an addict, along with building up a tolerance for the drug, which will take no small amount of time to develop, is also a psychological problem. Science has been able to demonstrate that so-called normal people experience no great amount of elation when given morphine or similar drugs. As a matter of fact, if you are not in pain and take a quarter-grain of morphine, the reaction will decidedly not be pleasant . . . unless you have a certain built-in tendency toward addiction. Chances are if you were taking a drug on a "dare" you would become ill, frightened, and probably repelled by the whole affair.

If we have learned much during our thousands of years on earth, we have learned that not all people are built alike, think alike, or should be treated alike. Until we know what makes every single person on the face of the earth do the things he does, we have no right to single out a group of people and attempt to label them as a botanist labels a bush of roses. And yet this is what we do with the addict; we label him as to cause, motivation, and degree of criminality.

The state of being an addict is a pitiful thing. For one thing, drugs—illicit drugs—are expensive and a day's supply is about equal to a day's wages. So, right off, if the addict were able to work—and few are—he would have to work all day for his drugs and exclude such necessities as food, lodging, clothing, and the like. But perhaps this is a minor consideration alongside the other difficulties he will encounter.

The addict *must* have his drugs, else he will become quite ill. Now, remember, that while you or I can make no sense out of why a person should want to poison himself, we must remember that the addict's make-up is quite different from ours; if we do not condemn the lunatic, how can we condemn the addict? So the addict, in the plight I have mentioned, will have to concentrate most of his waking hours upon obtaining enough drugs to make him feel "normal." And in the process of obtaining these drugs it will be a weekly occurrence that his source of supply will attempt to cheat him by means of giving him a "turkey," or harmless pinch of face powder or a similar substance.

Now, let us assume that the addict has bought his day's ration of drugs and is now in his room. I say "room," by the way, because it is extremely unlikely he has a house or even a flat of rooms. What does the addict do now? Well, he will, by rule of thumb, calculate what his dosage is. He cannot do this with scientific equipment, by the way; he has none. If he had such equipment, he probably would have pawned it long ago. But it is very important that the addict not overestimate his dosage, for if he does, he may die. While he has a far greater tolerance for this poison than do you or I, he cannot estimate the purity of his drug until he has injected it into his body. I hasten to add, by the way, that the illicit manufacturer of this drug cannot guarantee its purity either.

The addict has now cooked or heated his portion of the drug. He will draw it up into a syringe of homemade manufacture and will probably inject it into a vein somewhere on his arm. If he has been addicted for any length of time he will have to take the dull needle on the end of his syringe and probe for a little bit, trying to locate a vein that is still open and un-clogged by the residue left from previous injections.

The addict finds the proper vein—whether it be on his arm, on his hands, between his toes, or beneath his penis—and in-jects the drug. And what are the results? Sleep! The drug puts the addict to sleep. Failing to do this, it will make him feel woozy. To the addict's tragic and warped way of thinking, this sensation is to be sought after at any price! And this person, by law, we consider to be "normal."

And so the addict's problems continue. After four or five hours have gone by—and unless his dosage was too great and he killed himself—he will awaken, stupefied, to ponder anew where his next supply of drug can be bought. In the interim he will have such minor problems as continual constipation, blood poisoning, air embolism, venereal disease (from the needle, not as the result of intercourse; the drug deprives the addict of normal sexual desire), and the ever-present police to contend with. Incidentally, the addict's life "on the street," or out of jail, is a relatively short one. Although the police would like you to believe otherwise, the average addict will remain at large less than two years from the time he becomes addicted or is released from prison, until he is again apprehended.

I certainly do not advocate that we commence peddling drugs to all who desire them, but I do maintain that federal, state, and city police should bow out of the practice of medicine and leave the whole business of treating addicts to physicians. What is perhaps so ironic is that all of our law enforcement agencies follow the lead of the Federal Bureau of Narcotics, which has been doubly wrong by dictating the practice of medicine and by further insisting on unsound treatment. This bureau has main-tained a rigid, stereotyped, one-track policy in a situation that demands flexibility plus a great deal of medical and scientific background. A cop cannot, under any set of circumstances, scientifically treat a sick man. The result is a sorry mess, of course, which is what happens when revenue agents take it upon themselves to become dictators of medicine.

Worse yet, our courts are gradually permitting narcotics police to make violations of our Bill of Rights that have been heretofore proscribed. In narcotics cases, so say some courts, the police are granted extraordinary powers of search and seizure. Further, a whole network of informers, telephone spying, and secret police devices completely foreign to our way of life have been created, largely by narcotics agents. Look at our courtrooms; they are jammed with narcotics offenders, many of them coming back for the second or third time! Unhappily, under most state laws a third conviction for violation of the many and varied narcotics laws can now send such a sick and wretched person to the penitentiary for the rest of his natural life!

It should be patently obvious, to anyone who cares to inform himself, that our whole program—from arrest to treatment—for dealing with narcotics addicts is absolutely hopeless! True, by fantastic prison sentences and extraordinary methods of search and seizure, we have been able to keep the entire addict population down to about 60,000. But if this is such a remarkable figure, one the police would care to brag about, I answer: Hitler was able to do much better when he dealt with his "undesirables." There is no such thing as "bending the law a little bit for special offenses." Today's persecution of the addict may well become tomorrow's persecution of you or me or someone else.

Until each and every narcotic agent in our land has become a licensed physician, and an attorney to boot, I say: Give the practice of medicine back to the physicians. Addiction is a medical problem and no policeman is qualified to either treat it or understand it.

LEGAL INSANITY

BECAUSE OUR LEGAL CONCEPT of insanity, like most of our law, is so closely influenced by Great Britain, I am going to begin this essay with a quotation from Winston S. Churchill. Speaking before the House of Commons during the now dimly remembered early days of World War II, Mr. Churchill said, "Never in the field of human conflict was so much owed to so few by so many."

Someday, when man has evolved into a higher state than any of us can now comprehend, perhaps as much will be said when it is remembered how we of the twentieth century went about the task of determining, in court, who was mentally fit to stand trial and who, according to archaic tradition, was mentally unsound.

We should like to think, today, that our treatment of the mentally ill has never been better. We should like to think, today, that by law we differentiate between those possessed of reason and those who, through no fault of their own, are unable to account for their behavior. We may continue to think this way; if we do, we are wrong.

A careful examination of history, an examination stretching back before the time of Christ, tells us that our ancestors, poor unenlightened souls that they were, were far more charitable toward the mentally afflicted, in spite of science, than we are. In the Scriptures we may read of the lunatics who dwelled amongst the tombs, who were allowed to wander, unmolested, through the cypress groves on quiet, moonlit evenings. In Egypt, as we now know, the insane were acknowledged to be afflicted in such a way as to prevent them from comprehending what their duties and obligations to Pharaoh were.

Classic Greece and pagan Rome had special laws for the insane, and if they failed to understand the causes of insanity —as we, today, often fail to understand them—these ancient societies nevertheless made provisions for them. In many cases, these now three-thousand-year-old societies considered the insane to be under the special protection of a deity we, today, call God.

So much for the "unenlightened pagans."

By the dawn of Christianity, shortly after the political assassination of Christ, we find the insane being cared for by monks, in churches especially prepared for them. By this time, however, the attitudes held toward the insane were somewhat less charitable than had been the attitude of the pagans. By now there was dogma to the effect that the insane were possessed with demons; treatment consisted of exorcising or purging these devils from the body of the person afflicted. Special tribunals of religious exorcists were created and we read: "Water and salt are exorcised by the priest, and so withdrawn from the power of Satan, who, since the Fall, has corrupted and abused even inanimate things."

As history moved along, the West's practices toward the psychotic became more rigid, less understanding, less sympathetic. For a while it was common practice to tie these poor people to crosses, cutting them down at the close of each day. Other forms of "psychotherapy" consisted of chaining them to special stones in the church or dipping them in holy wells. In some monasteries it became accepted for the monks to give each afflicted psychotic ten lashes per day as a kind of "therapeutic" for driving the devil from the creature's body. For a time this treatment was codified to read, in part: "In case a man be a lunatic, take skin of a mereswine or porpoise, work it into a whip, swinge the man well therewith, soon he will be well. Amen."

It is likely that the practice of "swingeing" became corrupted from exorcism to the granting of license to any sadist who might be inclined to thrash one who, by law, was insane. One Andrew

Boorde, writing in London, England, in 1542, cautions us: "I do advertyse every man the which is mad or lunaticke or demoniacke, to be kept in save garde in some close house or chambre where there is lytell lyght. And there he have a keper the which the mad man do feare."

Inasmuch as Boorde differentiates between "lunaticke" and "demoniacke," it must be safe to assume that he was the sixteenth century's answer to today's "expert witness." That Boorde's technique of custody was probably standard practice in the community can be established if we read Shakespeare, who says, in *Twelfth Night:* "We'll have him in a dark room and bound."

The British had founded the Priory of St. Mary of Bethlem in 1247 and by 1403 it was being used, exclusively, as a place of detention for the insane. Four centuries later this cattle pen for humans was still being used, its name now corrupted to "Bedlam." As St. Mary's began to fill up, a second institution, St. Katherine's by The Tower, was created "for the better sort of mad folks." In both of these places, it should be noted, a complete absence of treatment existed. Like much of today's penal system, custody, and not therapy, was the guiding force.

Conditions in these places have been recounted many, many times. We know of beatings, chainings, solitary confinement, and the like. And, as sometimes happens even today, we know that many persons were railroaded into madhouses, often so that their relatives could expropriate their property.

The *Gentleman's Magazine* of London for the year 1765, dealing with the subject of private asylums for the insane, tells us that "persons were taken forcibly to these houses without any authority, instantly seized by a set of inhuman ruffians trained up to this barbarous profession, stripped naked, and conveyed to a dark room."

What progress! From God's protection, to prayer, to dark rooms!

Even royalty was subjected to the sort of treatment our Bill of Rights proscribes. A Mr. W. Massie, writing in 1865 of King George's mental affliction, states:

Mental disease was at that time a branch of art little understood, and the specific treatment of lunatics was worthy of the barbarous age of medicine. The unhappy patient upon whom this most terrible visitation of Heaven had fallen, was no longer dealt with as a human being. His body was immediately enclosed in a machine, which left it no liberty of motion. He was sometimes chained to a staple. He was frequently beaten and starved, and at least he was kept in subjection by menacing and violent language.

Could it be that George's physician had his best interests at heart as he subjected his patient to this treatment? It is more likely than not that the good doctor, overcome by the importance of his patient, went beyond his wildest dreams when the corpulent George fell into his hands. Then, again, it could be that the doctor simply didn't like kings.

The earliest English test for sanity appears to be the Arnold case, also known as the "wild beast test." This ruling dates from 1724 and it generally held that a person could be exempted from punishment if he "be totally deprived of his understanding and memory and not know what he is doing, no more than an infant, than a brute, or a wild beast."

A little later on this test was implemented by the "delusion test," arising out of an action brought against one James Hadfield who fired a pistol at the same George III we earlier encountered "enclosed in a machine." The trial court in the Hadfield case ruled that the accused was suffering from delusions even though he knew, at that time, that he was shooting at his king.

Up to this point—and for some time afterward, actually—if a defendant could qualify under one or the other of these two conditions, he was not executed. He was only shut up in Bedlam or some other similar place for the rest of his natural life.

Since that time—the eighteenth century—we have progressed no end in the field of criminal responsibility, insanity, and other such meaningless areas. We owe all this progress to one Daniel McNaghten, a British citizen who was, in all likelihood, a paranoid personality, a man who believed people were conspiring to do him wrong.

In 1843—and mark this date carefully, for these standards are still applicable in most states in America—McNaghten gunned down Sir Robert Peel's secretary, killing him. It appears that the shooting of this unfortunate gentleman was an accident; McNaghten was actually intending to kill Sir Robert. But no matter. There was no disputing that McNaghten was the killer.

The case was submitted to trial and, after considerable deliberation, fourteen out of fifteen trial justices made the following ruling:

> To establish a defense on the grounds of insanity, it must be clearly proved that, at the time of the committing of the act, the party accused was laboring under such a defect of reason, from disease of the mind, as not to know the nature and quality of the act he was doing; or if he did know it, that he did not know he was doing what was wrong.

Now, for those times the McNaghten Rule was probably a great step forward, especially if we consider that, prior to this time, many persons were being killed for such offenses as pocket picking, handkerchief stealing, and poaching. Now, at least, it might be held that such nonviolent crimes, while still capital offenses, could nevertheless be excused on the grounds that their perpetrators were insane. Especially if they had the wherewithal to retain skilled counsel.

No, it must be concluded that the McNaghten Rule of 1843 was extremely farsighted, especially if we note that in 1843 Sigmund Freud was still not born, Cesare Lombroso, founder of the school of criminal biology, was only seven years old, and a work entitled *Elements of Phrenology*, which stated the brain "was divided in three compartments, one the seat of active propensities, a second of moral sentiments, and the third of intellectual facilities, of which three were definitely associated with criminal behaviour," had been published eighteen years earlier.

For 1843, the McNaghten Rule was certainly a modern and long-overdue innovation. For 1964, the McNaghten Rule is a disgrace! It is a bad, old law and in most cases, in America, it is the law of the land.

I say the McNaghten Rule is a foolish and archaic concept, for does not even the idiot eat? Does not the idiot drink? Does not the idiot know his mother and father? He does all this because he is a man. Does he not smile and weep? He smiles and weeps because he is moved by human joys and sorrows. Has not the idiot anger, rage, revenge? Take from him his food and he will stamp his feet and scream. Think you he does this for nothing? He does it all because he is a man, and because, however imperfectly, he exercises reason.

By McNaghten's standards, the idiot, being a reasonable man, may be thought, in the eyes of Justice, to be fit to stand trial. In the eyes of today's nineteenth-century Justice, the idiot may be found sane. And by the standards set over one hundred years ago the idiot may be led to a place of execution and there be put to death.

There are a few exceptions to McNaghten in this country. A very few. In 1954 the judges of the federal court in the District of Columbia decided that our tests of criminal responsibility had decidedly failed to keep pace with modern psychiatric progress. These judges were deeply disturbed with the McNaghten English import, based on the conception that he who can distinguish between those two ephemeral concepts—"right" and "wrong"— is not insane. Accordingly, the District of Columbia court adopted a new test, holding that if the unlawful act was the product of a mental disease or *defect*, the accused could not be convicted.

The word "defect" modifies "mental disease," and it is an important modification. We know, today, that a psychotic, or one afflicted with psychosis, rarely resembles the "wild beast" of old English law. We also know that there are subtle forms of mental affliction that could not possibly have been recognized as such one hundred and twenty years ago. "Defect," as interpreted by the District of Columbia court, helps take this into consideration.

A generation ago Justice Benjamin Cardozo, our paragon of moral ideals on the bench, said: "I have faith that a century or less from now, our descendants will look back upon the penal system of today with the same surprise and horror that fills our own minds when we are told that only about a century ago one hundred and sixty crimes were visited under English law with the punishment of death, and that in 1801 a child of thirteen was hanged for the larceny of a spoon."

Today, we are using the McNaghten Rule of 1843 to send men to their death. In an era that has produced such wonders as nuclear power, television, the most subtle forms of brain surgery, we continue, in almost all states, to decide who may die and who may be absolved of his crime, on the basis of a law enacted *not by physicians, but by judges,* in an age where medicine, by today's standards, was in its infancy.

I can only fervently pray that generations of the future, who look back on our society today, will not judge us too harshly. For if even retention of the death penalty now seems, to many today, an anachronism too discordant to be suffered—mocking with grim reproach all our clamorous protestations of the sanctity of life—how will the future think of us, today, with our practice of nineteenth-century medicine and law?

Persecution and Religion

PAPIST, PROTESTANT, JEW, AND TURK

NOTHING, IT WOULD SEEM, is more sacred in this country than the practice of religion. Daily we have the spectacle of certain "radio pastors" blasting various Christian sects, condemning all manner of free speech—in the name of "religious liberty." While one's rights to worship when and where one chooses are guaranteed by a myriad of state and federal laws, I suspect that many truly unreligious souls use the cloak of religion in much the same way that the school bully of old used his glasses; when confronted by a bigger boy he would clap them over his nose and cry "foul."

A most recent U.S. Supreme Court case—School District of Abington Township, Pennsylvania, *et al.* v. Schempp *et al.*—raised a high-pitched, feverish howl I can best compare with the sound of a mashed cat, from certain quarters all across the land. On close examination of this case we see that the Supreme Court has done nothing more nor less than many courts in our country have been doing for a long, long time: the Court has said that religion is independent of the state and all of the state's appendages, namely the schools. This is surely not a radical decision and it is of considerable interest to me that those who cried "foul" the loudest are those selfsame persons who daily moan that the federal government—the state, if you will—controls *too much* of our activities.

Well, as a sage once told me, Nothing in this world is consistent, not even stupidity.

In the beginning, our founding fathers were anything but tolerant. Contrary to the "Jim and Judy" history books that our children are obliged to read, the early Puritans were bigots of the worst sort; they came here not seeking freedom for *all* but merely freedom for *some*. Indeed, New England, in the early days of the 1600s, was governed by its clergymen, and so strong was their hold over the populace that they were able to decree that church affiliations—in their particular church, of course— were necessary *before a man could even vote!* These stern ministers, who themselves had sought religious sanctuary in the New World, made certain no one else could have any freedom, except as prescribed by them. Church attendance was mandatory and anyone who did not attend these particular services was indicted and prosecuted, an accomplishment not at all difficult, since jurors and magistrates sat at the pleasure of the church leaders.

Religious freedom? Here, then, are the records of the County Court of Middlesex, sitting at Cambridge, Massachusetts, on April 17, 1666:

> . . . Thomas Goold, Thomas Osburne and John George being presented by the Grand Jury of this County for absenting themselves from the public worship of God on the Lord's Day for one whole year now past, alleged respectively as followeth, viz., Thomas Osburne answered that the reason of his non-attendance was, that the Lord hath discovered unto him from his word and spirit of truth that the society, wherewith he is now in communion, is more agreeable to the will of God, asserted that they were a church and attended the worship of God together, and do judge themselves bound to do so, the ground whereof he said he gave in the general court.
>
> Thomas Goold answered, that as for coming to public worship, they did meet in public worship according to the rule of Christ, the grounds whereof they had given to the Court of Assistants, asserted that they were a public meeting, according to the order of Christ Jesus, gathered together.
>
> . . . John George answered, that he did attend the public meeting on the Lord's Day where he was a member; asserted that they were a church according to the order of Christ in the Gospel, and with them he walked and held communion in the public worship of God on the Lord's Day. . . .

Well, let us pause for a moment and examine this situation. Messrs. Osburne, Goold, and George are surely not atheists, communists, or heathens by any stretch of the imagination. Indeed, they have just admitted faith in Christ Jesus and the other tenets of the Christian faith. Surely, the local magistrates, church officials, and other, assorted functionaries can have no quarrel with them? Can they? Read on . . .

> . . . Whereas at the General Court in October last, and at the Court of Assistants in September last, endeavors were used for their conviction, the order of the General Court declaring that said Goold and company to be no orderly church assembly and that they stand convicted of high presumption against the Lord and his holy appointments was openly read to them and is on file with the records of this court.
>
> The Court sentenced the said Thomas Goold, Thomas Osburne and John George, for their absenting themselves from the public worship of God on the Lord's Day, to pay four pounds fine, each of them, to the county order. And whereas by their own confessions they stand convicted of persisting in their schismatical assembling themselves together, to the great dishonor of God and our professions of his holy name, contrary to the act of the General Court of October last prohibiting them therein on penalty of imprisonment, this Court doth order their giving bond respectively in 20 pounds, each of them, for their appearance to answer their contempt at the next Court of Assistants.
>
> The above named Thomas Goold, John George and Thomas Osburne made their appeal to the next Court of Assistants, and refusing to put in security according to law, were committed to prison. . . .

An end to this bigotry came in 1691, at the hands of King William III, during a reorganization of the Colonies. King William ordered freedom of religion and abolished religious qualifications for voting.

Thus tolerance and religious liberty first came to our nation. In time, this liberty and the equality of man was reduced to writing in our Constitution.

Thanks to the efforts of an English king, I am compelled to add.

These, then, were the roots from which our country first drew life. A lesson was learned from these early religious misadventures: that no belief, no dogma, no absolute doctrine can be comfortably incorporated into our form of government; to do so would bring us a state religion, and with it all of the miseries of a Torquemada or a Savonarola. While no one denied each and every man the sacred right to practice his belief as he saw fit, our country finally got off to a start in the right direction by making absolutely certain that church and state were separated by a comfortable, legal margin.

Let us turn the clock forward, now, on the problem of law, religion, and state. The year is 1821 and the place is a neighborhood grocery store in New York City. Two usually meek and mild men have been engaged in a political discussion and as the evening has progressed, angry and violent words have been uttered by the disputants. When the boiling point of this "political discussion" had finally been reached, history tells us, one or the other of these gentlemen went before a magistrate and swore out a criminal complaint against the other, charging him with committing blasphemy during the "political discussion."

Subsequently, an indictment was returned, alleging that the defendant:

> . . . Not having the fear of God before his eyes, but being moved and seduced by the instigation of the Devil, contriving and intending to scandalize and vilify the Christian religion, as received and publicly professed in this State, and to blaspheme God and our Lord Jesus Christ, on the first day of April, 1821, at the City and within the County of New York, unlawfully, wickedly and blasphemously, in the presence and hearing of divers citizens of this State, spoke and pronounced and with a loud voice published these profane and blasphemous words following, that is to say: God Almighty was a fool, and, Jesus Christ was a fool; to the great dishonor of Almighty God, in contempt and disgrace of the Christian religion, to the evil example of all others in the like case offending, and against the peace, etc., etc. . . .

What had begun with two men exercising their rights to argue

political differences ended in a courtroom trial before a jury.
The charge was a most serious one, with imprisonment the
penalty for conviction.

The trial was the usual affair. The prosecution thrust and the
defense parried. At the end, the presiding judge, a man of
understanding, charged the jury:

> . . . Although by the Constitution every man in this country has
> a right to entertain any religious opinion, and all sects have free
> toleration in their respective modes of worship, though the
> Unitarian, New Mahometan, and even Pagan, remain here free
> from persecution, yet it is contrary to the principles of the Com-
> mon Law for any man to revile the religion generally prevailing
> here, or its author; or to impeach or call in question the attributes
> of the Deity.
>
> While, on the one hand, we say to the Unitarians, Jews, Ma-
> hometans, and even Pagans, enjoy your own religious notions
> free from restraint, so on the other, we say, and such is the lan-
> guage of the Law, revile not the religion we profess, or its
> author. It is from religion that oaths in Courts of Justice derive
> their efficacy; and to undermine the religious opinions of men
> would deprive us of the security we place upon oaths in judicial
> proceedings and others, and would finally operate to the sub-
> mersion of civil society.
>
> If you believe the words laid in the indictment to have been
> uttered by the defendant, it is your duty to convict him. But
> considering the testimony adduced on his behalf, in contradiction
> of the testimony of the prosecutors, and considering the testi-
> mony of his good character, and his peculiar religious opinion, it
> is hardly possible that he could have uttered the words laid in
> the indictment.
>
> If the jury should believe that he did not, and that the prosecu-
> tion originated from mistake or malice, it is your duty to acquit
> him. . . .

This Solomon-like speech by the judge resulted in the jury's
swiftly finding the defendant not guilty. Possibly the fact that
the jurors themselves had often engaged in heated political discussions had something to do with the defense verdict too.

Belief, as we know it and as we must forever know it, is a

personal and private affair. All have the right to believe in a deity of their own choice and no man, no state, no apparatus of any kind, has the right to challenge, modify, or in any other way tamper with another's belief. This is the American way and it is important that all of us, believers and nonbelievers, ever fight to keep it such.

Perhaps one of the most eloquent and poetic expressions of belief and each man's right to believe as he sees fit was expressed several hundred years ago by Roger Williams, who said:

> There goes many a ship to sea, with many hundred souls in one ship, whose weal and woe is common, and is a true picture of a commonwealth, or society. It hath fallen out sometimes, that both Papists and Protestants, Jews and Turks, may be embarked in one ship; upon which supposal, I affirm that all the liberty of conscience I ever pleaded for, turns upon these two hinges, that none of the Papists, Protestants, Jews or Turks be forced to come to the ship's prayers or worship, if they practice any. . . .

Don't rock the boat; let the other man worship as he sees fit, for, in another time and another place, he may be the captain of the vessel upon which you are quartered.

WITCHCRAFT

COTTON MATHER (1663–1728) could not be criticized as to his right to don the garments of a Puritan clergyman. After all, hadn't his father, Increase Mather, and his father's father, Richard Mather, been men of the same cloth?

Endowed with such heritage, it is little wonder that the colonial populace of seventeenth-century Massachusetts readily accepted as divine truth Mather's revelations of the dangers of witchcraft being practiced in the community. In 1685, the twenty-two-year-old religious leader published his *Memorable Providences Relating to Witchcraft and Possessions.* The tome cited actual cases of men and women, boys and girls who had signed pacts with the Devil and received supernatural powers in return. Cotton Mather's memorable providences played no small role in inciting the people to perpetrate the tragedy we know as the Salem Trials. Not content with causing the violence, Mather compounded his participation by acting as an investigator and testifying against many of the accused.

There are those who today regard Cotton Mather as having been a righteous, albeit confused, man of God. It is fortunate that a true profile of this demented creature exists, in the form of a book on the Salem Trials written by a Bostonian, Robert Calef, who was witness to much of the happenings. Calef's Mather emerges as vain, pedantic, narrow, prejudiced, bigoted; an individual who hated without reason and condemned without cause.

Witchcraft hysteria was nothing new. It erupted in ancient Rome where offenders were stoned to death in streets. The Middle Ages produced different methods of executing those possessed by the Devil: Thousands were burned at the stake in France and other countries of Europe. The English kept laws relating to witchcraft through the seventeenth century. These were among the customs brought over to the colonies of America.

Take a look at America in 1692 through the eyes of Robert Calef, who writes:

"Mr. Parris had been some years a minister in Salem village, when this sad calamity, as a deluge, overflowed them, spreading itself far and near. He was a gentleman of liberal education; and not meeting with any great advantage in merchandising, to which for some time he applied himself, betook himself to the work of the ministry.

"After he had been there about two years, he obtained a grant from a part of the town, that the house and land he occupied, and which had been allotted by the whole people to the ministry, would be and remain to him as his own estate. This occasioned great divisions both between the inhabitants themselves, and between a considerable part of them and their said minister; which divisions were but as a beginning, or proeludium, to what immediately followed.

"It was the latter end of February, 1691, when divers young persons belonging to Mr. Parris' family, and one or more of the neighborhood, began to act after a strange and unusual manner, by getting into holes, and creeping under chairs and stools, and to use sundry odd postures and antic gestures, uttering fooling, ridiculous speeches, which neither they themselves nor any others could make sense of.

"The physicians that were called could assign no reason for this; but it seems one of them, having recourse to the old shift, told them he was afraid they were bewitched. Upon such suggestings, they that were concerned applied themselves to fasting and prayer, which was attended not only in their own private families, but with calling in the help of others.

"March the 11th, Mr. Parris invited several neighboring ministers to join with him in keeping a solemn day of prayer at his own house. The time of the exercise, those persons were for the most part silent; but after any one prayer was ended, they would act and speak strangely and ridiculously; yet were such as had been well educated, and of good behavior; the one, a girl of 11 or 12 years old, would sometimes seem to be in a convulsion fit, her limbs being twisted several ways, and very stiff, but presently her fit would be over. Those ill affected or afflicted persons named several that they said they saw, when in their fits, afflicting them.

"The first complained of was an Indian woman, named Tituba: she confessed that the Devil urged her to sign a book, which he presented to her, and also to work mischief to the children. She was afterwards committed to prison, and lay there till sold for her fees. The account she since gives of it is that her master did beat her, and otherways abuse her, to make her confess and accuse (such as he called) her sister-witches; and that whatsoever she said by way of confessing, or accusing others, was the effect of such usage: her master refused to pay her fees, unless she would stand to what she had said.

"The children complained likewise of two other women, to be the authors of their hurt, viz., Sarah Good, who had long been counted as a melancholy or distracted woman; and one Osborn, an old bed-ridden woman; which two were persons so ill thought of, that the accusation was the more readily believed; and, after examination before two Salem magistrates, were committed.

"March the 19th, Mr. Lawson (who had been formerly a preacher at the village came thither, and hath since set forth, in print, an account of what then passed; about which time, as he saith, they complained of Goodwife Cory, and Goodwife Nurse, members of churches at the village and at Salem, many others being by that time accused.

"August 5th, the court again sitting, six more were tried on the same account; George Burroughs, some time minister of Wells; John Proctor, and Elizabeth Proctor, his wife, with John Willard, of Salem Village, George Jacobs, Sr., of Salem, and Martha Carrier, of Andover; these were all brought in guilty, and condemned; and were all executed, August 19, except Proctor's wife, who pleaded pregnancy.

"Mr. Burroughs was carried in a cart with the others, through the streets of Salem to Execution. When he was upon the ladder, he made a speech for the clearing of his innocency, with such solemn and serious expressions, as were to the admiration of all present: his prayer (which he concluded by repeating the Lord's Prayer) was so well worded, and uttered with such composedness, and such (at least seeming) fervency of spirit, as was very affecting and drew tears from many, so that it seemed to some that the spectators would hinder the execution. The accusers said the Black Man stood and dictated to him.

"As soon as he was turned off, Mr. Cotton Mather, being mounted upon a horse, addressed himself to the people, partly to declare that he (Burroughs) was no ordained minister, and partly to possess the people of his guilt, saying that the Devil has often been transformed into an Angel of Light; and this did somewhat appease the people and the executions went on.

"When he (Burroughs) was cut down, he was dragged by the halter to a hole, or grave, between the rocks, about two feet deep, his shirt and breeches being pulled off, and an old pair of trousers of one executed put on his lower parts; he was so put in, together with Willard and Carrier, that one of his hands and his chin, and a foot of one of them were left uncovered. . . .

". . . And now 19 persons having been hanged, and one pressed to death, and eight more condemned, in all 28, of which above a third part were members of some of the churches in New England, and more than half of them of a good conversation in general, and not one cleared; about 50 having confessed themselves to be witches, of which not one was executed; above 150 in prison, and above 200 more accused; the special commission comes to a period, which has no other foundation than the governor's commission; and had proceeded in the manner of swearing witnesses and by receiving evidences in writing, according to the ancient usage of this country.

"In the trials, when any were indicted for afflicting, pining and wasting the bodies of particular persons by witchcraft, it was usual to hear evidence of matter foreign, and of perhaps 20 or 30 years standing, about oversetting carts, the death of cattle, unkindness to relations, or unexpected accidents befalling after some quarrel.

"Whether this was admitted by the Law of England, or by some other law, wants to be determined; the executions seemed mixed, in pressing to death for not pleading, and sentencing women to be hanged for witchcraft, according to the former practice of this country, and not by burning, as is said to have been the Law of England. . . ."

During many years of law practice it has been my duty on occasions to argue before judge or jury, or both, in civil as well as criminal cases. It is always an important concern to present a point clearly and briefly. This becomes an art developed through years of experience and hours of trial and error.

A Mary Easty, before her execution in Salem in 1692, made the greatest closing argument I have read or heard when she addressed her convictors in her quiet and hopeless request for the lives of others:

> I petition your honors not for my own life, for I know I must die and my appointed time is set; but the Lord he knows that it is that if it be possible, no more innocent blood may be shed, which undoubtably cannot be avoided in the way and course you go in. I question not but your Honors do the utmost of your powers in the discovery and detecting of witchcraft and witches, and would not be guilty of innocent blood for the world. But by my own innocency, I know you are in the wrong way.

The insane wanderings of Cotton Mather led men to believe in supernatural power obtainable by entering into compact with the Devil. Mather believed that the witch abjured God, and dedicated herself to the Devil, and that she rode to her meetings with the Evil One on broomsticks.

Following Mather's line of thought, it does not seem too insane to presume that witchcraft could have been stamped out by burning all broomsticks and forbidding new ones to be made.

Origins

FOURTEEN LITTLE WORDS

In RECENT YEARS the words *"nor shall be compelled in any criminal case to be a witness against himself"* have been the subject of interminable debate. They are a part of the Fifth Amendment to the Constitution of the United States.

While they may have protected some criminal, they have also protected the innocent from those who are dedicated to hate and revenge.

Moral cowards and intellectual liars have proclaimed themselves heroes for the moment by demanding the impeachment of the members of our Supreme Court because of its insistence that the Fifth Amendment is part of the law and must be enforced.

Our United States Senate and House investigating committees are a disgrace to the ethical profession of enforcing the law. Here is where it ends: Answer truly and you have given evidence leading to your conviction for a violation of federal law; answer falsely and you will be convicted of perjury; refuse to answer and you will be found guilty of criminal contempt and punished by fine and imprisonment.

Is this what our forefathers had in mind when they insisted on the Fifth Amendment to our Constitution?

The Fifth Amendment in part provides that no man shall be compelled in any criminal case to be a witness against himself. This clause has a long history. In the sixteenth century it was brought forward in England in protest against the inquisitorial method of the ecclesiastical courts. During this time the common law permitted accused defendants to be questioned. After 1660 it became a fixed rule that no one was compelled in any criminal case to be a witness against himself.

Our United States Supreme Court has ruled that a witness in a civil proceeding may refuse to answer any question his answer to which might be used against him in any criminal proceeding.

Many facets of this rule are not covered here since the purpose is to trace the origin of the maxim that no man is bound to accuse himself—*nemo tenetur se ipsum accusare*.

This rule was first enunciated by the great Hebrew scholar and Talmudist Rava, who lived in exile in Babylon in the fourth century A.D. His rule was that a man is nearest himself, and no man calls himself a wrongdoer. It is interesting to note that while Rabbi Rava was announcing this rule, the Roman law provided for judicial examination of accused persons under torture.

Under Biblical law near relatives and wrongdoers are incompetent witnesses. The incompetence of near relatives was based on an interpretation of Deuteronomy to the effect that a man may not be put to death either on the testimony of his parents or children; or more clearly for the sins of his parents or of his children.

In compliance with the rule laid down in Deuteronomy, punishment for false testimony was severe, being the same punishment to which the accused was liable, had he been convicted. If, however, the accused was convicted of a capital offense: "the hands of the witnesses shall be first upon him to put him to death."

The incompetency of wrongdoers was derived from the book of Exodus: "put not thine hand with the wicked to be an unrighteous witness," which has been interpreted to mean that the wicked are bound to be unrighteous witnesses and therefore are incompetent to testify.

At one time a person could not testify in his own favor. This dates from a period earlier by at least two centuries than Rava's time. The Mishnah is the earliest part of the Talmud and was finally completed about 200 A.D. In the Mishnaic text there is a rule to the effect that the presumption that a woman is violated by the enemy while held prisoner cannot be rebutted by the solemn oath of her husband that "her hand did not move out of my hand from the day the enemy entered Jerusalem until he left" because nobody is a witness in his own cause.

The law did provide, however, that a man must be heard in his defense, not as a witness, but to argue his own case.

The evolution of Rava's rule into a general prohibition of self-incrimination took time. In several Mishnaic texts the rule commenced to grow and to be definitely used.

In the Scriptures there is the instance of questioning a person accused of crime and obtaining his confession: "And Joshua said unto Achan . . . make confession unto him; and tell me now what thou hast done; hide it not from me. And Achan answered Joshua, and said, Indeed I have sinned . . . and thus and thus have I done."

This was interpreted in the Mishnah as if the confession had been asked for and made only after trial and conviction, and then only for the purpose of expiating the sin before God so as not to be revisited again after death.

Later Hebrew jurists dismissed this and similar Biblical stories simply as exceptions to the general rule. However, there is not a single instance of the application of the rule in the Bible.

The confession of sin in repentance before God is, of course, always encouraged and, at certain times (the Jewish Day of Atonement), even prescribed. But these confessions have no legal significance and are not admissible in evidence against the confessor or at all; it is a sin even to remind a man who has confessed before God of the misdeeds he has confessed to.

It is worthy of note that Lilburne, the English political reform leader and pamphleteer (1614–1657), was whipped, pilloried, and imprisoned after defending himself against the claim by the judges that he was, although an accused, under obligation to be examined. He relied on the law of God for his refusal to answer; but gave no particular text in the Scriptures as authority for his proposition, except Christ's trial by Pilate. The judges ruled against him.

There finally emerged an additional rule, that the neutral part of a confession is admissible only for the purpose of corroborating other independent evidence. Thus, where the issue requiring proof is the death of a man, the evidence of a witness to the death may be corroborated by that part of the confession of the killer which testifies to the death having occurred; but the killing can never be proved by the confession of the killer even where corroborated by the evidence of one independent witness, because under Biblical law at least two witnesses are required and the confessor is not a witness against himself.

Since, under this Biblical law, the accused was never compelled to testify against himself, a confession of guilt was only accepted in evidence and considered in connection with other facts of the case, but standing alone it could not be the basis of a conviction.

Maimonides, the great Hebrew lawyer and philosopher, in his commentaries on the Mishnah, discusses this rule: "We have it as a fundamental principle of our jurisprudence that no one can bring an accusation against himself. Should a man make a confession of guilt before a legally constituted tribunal, such confession is not to be used against him, unless properly attested by two other witnesses, for our law never condemns on the single confession of an accused. . . ."

The question arises whether the injunction of the Scripture: "ye shall have one manner of law," as is directed in Leviticus, should not read to prohibit any distinction between civil and criminal law with regard to admissions and confessions; the question must be answered in the negative because the Scripture itself says in civil cases: "he shall pay," but in criminal cases: "he shall die."

This question arises because, in later history, the rule that the confession to a criminal act would serve as a civil cause of action, but would not be admitted as evidence in criminal proceedings, was applied to confessions of arson, embezzlement, the taking of usurious interest, and, by analogy, adultery—the confessing wife losing her claim to maintenance and other monetary benefits, but not her status as a married woman, and incurring no liability to be divorced or punished on the strength of her confession only.

The earliest version of the rule against self-incrimination appears in Deuteronomy to be that "at the mouth of two witnesses, or three witnesses, shall he that is worthy of death be put to death, *but* at the mouth of one witness he shall not be put to death," and ". . . no one may be condemned otherwise than on the evidence of witnesses, as distinguished from the evidence of himself."

Maimonides adds a reason of his own:

> It is a scriptural decree that the court shall not put a man to death on his own admission of guilt. This is done only on the evidence of two witnesses. It is true that Joshua condemned Achan to death on the latter's admission, and that David ordered the execution of the Amalekite stranger on the latter's admission. But those were emergency cases, or the death sentences pronounced in those instances were prescribed by State law. The Sanhedrin [the highest tribunal in Biblical Israel], however, is not empowered to inflict the penalty of death on the admission of the accused. For it is possible that he was confused in mind when he made the confession. Perhaps he was one of those who are in misery, bitter in soul, who long for death, thrust the sword into their bellies or cast themselves down from the roofs. Perhaps this was the reason that prompted him to confess to a crime he had not committed, in order that he might be put to death. To sum up the matter, the principle that no man is to be declared guilty on his own admission is a divine decree. . . .

Another reason is based on the words of the prophet Ezekiel, who said that all souls are the Lord God's—hence no admission by which a man may forfeit his life can be of any effect, his life being not his own but God's to dispose of.

Another theory was that if confessions were accorded any probative value in criminal proceedings, the courts might be inclined to overvalue them, as did King David: "And David said unto him, thy blood be upon thy head; for thy mouth hath testified against thee, saying I have slain the Lord's anointed. . . ."

Today, even in the State of Israel, self-incrimination as prohibited in the Scripture is no longer regarded as unlawful per se, but is now controlled by the English common law privilege which leaves to individuals the choice either to testify or not.

The guaranteed right in the U.S. Constitution that no man shall be compelled in any criminal case to be a witness against himself is so rooted in our traditions, heritage, and conscience that to question its value to mankind is incompatible with democracy and the equal protection of the law.

We must condemn the practice of imputing a sinister meaning to the exercise of a person's constitutional right under the Fifth Amendment, nor should we permit any inference of wrongdoing to flow from the invocation of any constitutional right.

DANIEL AND THE LIE DETECTOR
(WITH NO MOVING PARTS)

ONE OF THE LESSER-KNOWN ASPECTS of modern courtroom technique is that of the exclusion of witnesses not actually under examination. This procedure is sometimes used by trial lawyers to prevent one witness from hearing what may be said on the stand by another witness. This is a good play, somewhat like that a wise father uses on two sons as he goes about questioning each of them, in privacy, as to which of the two was the one that used (and ruined) his razor strop.

The rule of exclusion of witnesses, strictly construed, applies only to a witness of the party adverse to the party making the request. Thus, I can request that the opposition's witnesses be excluded from the courtroom at the time the opposition puts on their first witness. The opposition, of course, can make the same request. It is a court-made law that the matter of exclusion of witnesses is a request addressed to the sound discretion of the trial court.

What real benefit is gained from this technique? Well, to be quite candid, trial and error have taught us one sound lesson: Man will not always tell the truth. He will manufacture stories out of cloth too thin to hold the ravelings of his absence of intellect, or—in the case of an intelligent man—the absence of imagination. If only people told the truth, perhaps such a rule would not be necessary. But, then, if man told the truth both I and many of my dear friends would have to occupy ourselves elsewhere than in our courts of law, for there would be no great need for lawyers, judges, bailiffs, and the like.

For those of you who are, like myself, amateur historians, it is interesting to explore just how the concept of exclusion of witnesses came about. Unlike such relatively modern concepts as trial by a jury of one's peers, the history of exclusion of witnesses is very old, surely as old as recorded history. I mention this last to show some of my altruistic friends that man is really just about the same person—no better and no worse—that he was thousands of years ago.

The first case ever reported on exclusion of witnesses is not to be found in any volume we, today, know as a lawbook. Unless, of course, you and I are in agreement that our law is really history, experienced and recorded for posterity, dating back far before the time of Christ. In any event, if we examine the Apocrypha of the Holy Scriptures we will come upon the History of Susanna, which is really a part of the Book of Daniel but has been set apart in the Apocrypha because it is not in the Hebrew. It is an interesting story and good trial technique. Should the reader be a trial judge who has, on occasion, refused to exclude witnesses from a courtroom, I advise the learned jurist—and anyone else so inclined—to read the following as it appears in the English translation. Aside from being a good lesson in the law, it is beautiful prose, and no amount of rewriting or updating in modern phraseology would do it justice:

> There dwelt a man in Babylon, called Joachim:
>
> And he took a wife, whose name was Susanna, the daughter of Chelcias, a very fair woman, and one that feared the Lord.
>
> Her parents also were righteous, and taught their daughter according to the law of Moses.
>
> Now Joachim was a great rich man, and had a fair garden joining unto his house: and to him resorted the Jews; because he was more honourable than all others.
>
> The same year were appointed two of the ancients of the people to be judges, such as the Lord spake of, that wickedness came from Babylon from ancient judges, who seemed to govern the people.
>
> These kept much at Joachim's house: and all that had any suits in law came unto them.
>
> Now when the people departed away at noon, Susanna went into her husband's garden to walk.
>
> And the two elders saw her going in every day, and walking; so that their lust was inflamed toward her.
>
> And they perverted their own mind, and turned away their eyes, that they might not look unto heaven, nor remember just judgments.
>
> And albeit they both were wounded with her love, yet durst not one shew another his grief.
>
> For they were ashamed to declare their lust, that they desired to have to do with her.
>
> Yet they watched diligently from day to day to see her.
>
> And the one said to the other, Let us now go home: for it is dinner time.
>
> So when they were gone out, they parted the one from the other, and turning back again they came to the same place; and after that they had asked one another the cause, they acknowledged their lust: then appointed they a time both together, when they might find her alone.
>
> And it fell out, as they watched a fit time, she went in as

before with two maids only, and she was desirous to wash herself in the garden: for it was hot.

And there was nobody there save the two elders, that had hid themselves, and watched her.

Then she said to her maids, Bring me oil and washing balls, and shut the garden doors, that I may wash me.

And they did as she bade them, and shut the garden doors, and went out themselves at privy doors to fetch the things that she had commanded them: but they saw not the elders, because they were hid.

Now when the maids were gone forth, the two elders rose up, and ran unto her, saying,

Behold, the garden doors are shut, that no man can see us, and we are in love with thee; therefore consent unto us, and lie with us.

If thou wilt not, we will bear witness against thee, that a young man was with thee: and therefore thou didst send away thy maids from thee.

Then Susanna sighed, and said, I am straitened on every side: for if I do this thing, it is death unto me: and if I do it not, I cannot escape your hands.

It is better for me to fall into your hands, and not do it, than to sin in the sight of the Lord.

With that Susanna cried with a loud voice: and the two elders cried out against her.

Then ran the one, and opened the garden door.

So when the servants of the house heard the cry in the garden, they rushed in at a privy door, to see what was done unto her.

But when the elders had declared their matter, the servants were greatly ashamed: for there was never such a report made of Susanna.

And it came to pass the next day, when the people were assembled to her husband Joachim, the two elders came also full of mischievous imagination against Susanna to put her to death;

And said before the people, Send for Susanna, the daughter of Chelcias, Joachim's wife. And so they sent.

So she came with her father and mother, her children, and all her kindred.

Now Susanna was a very delicate woman, and beauteous to behold.

And these wicked men commanded to uncover her face (for she was covered), that they might be filled with her beauty.

Therefore her friends and all that saw her wept.

Then the two elders stood up in the midst of the people, and laid their hands upon her head.

And she weeping looked up toward heaven; for her heart trusted in the Lord.

And the elders said, As we walked in the garden alone, this woman came in with two maids, and shut the garden doors, and sent the maids away.

Then a young man, who there was hid, came unto her, and lay with her.

Then we that stood in a corner of the garden, seeing this wickedness, ran unto them.

And when we saw them together, the man we could not hold: for he was stronger than we, and opened the door, and leaped out.

But having taken this woman, we asked who the young man was, but she would not tell us: these things do we testify.

Then the assembly believed them, as those that were the elders and judges of the people: so they condemned her to death.

Then Susanna cried out with a loud voice, and said, O everlasting God, that knowest the secrets, and knowest all things before they be:

Thou knowest that they have borne false witness against me, and, behold, I must die; whereas I never did such things as these men have maliciously invented against me.

And the Lord heard her voice.

Therefore when she was led to be put to death, the Lord raised up the holy spirit of a young youth, whose name was Daniel:

Who cried with a loud voice, I am clear from the blood of this woman.

Then all the people turned them toward him, and said, What mean these words that thou hast spoken?

So he standing in the midst of them said, Are ye such fools, ye sons of Israel, that without examination or knowledge of the truth ye have condemned a daughter of Israel?

Return again to the place of judgment: for they have borne false witness against her.

Wherefore all the people turned again in haste, and the elders said unto him, Come, sit down among us, and shew it us, seeing God hath given thee the honour of an elder.

Then said Daniel unto them, Put these two aside one far from another, and I will examine them.

So when they were put asunder one from another, he called one of them, and said unto him, O thou that art waxen old in wickedness, now thy sins which thou hast committed aforetime are come to light:

For thou hast pronounced false judgment, and hast condemned the innocent, and hast let the guilty go free; albeit the Lord saith, The innocent and righteous shalt thou not slay.

Now then, if thou hast seen her, tell me, Under what tree sawest thou them companying together? Who answered, Under a mastick tree.

And Daniel said, Very well; thou hast lied against thine own head; for even now the angel of God hath received the sentence of God to cut thee in two.

So he put him aside, and commanded to bring the other and said unto him, O thou seed of Chanaan, and not of Juda, beauty hath deceived thee, and lust hath perverted thine heart.

Thus have ye dealt with the daughters of Israel, and they for fear companied with you; but the daughter of Juda would not abide your wickedness.

Now therefore tell me, Under what tree didst thou take them companying together? Who answered, Under an holm tree.

Then said Daniel unto him, Well; thou hast also lied against thine own head: for the angel of God waiteth with the sword to cut thee in two, that he may destroy you.

With that all the assembly cried out with a loud voice and praised God, who saveth them that trust in him.

And they arose against the two elders, for Daniel had convicted them of false witness by their own mouth;

And according to the law of Moses they did unto them in such sort as they maliciously intended to do to their neighbour: and they put them to death. Thus the innocent blood was saved the same day.

Therefore Chelcias and his wife praised God for their daughter Susanna, with Joachim her husband, and all the kindred, because there was no dishonesty found in her.

There is a place in every law office for a good trial lawyer—especially if his name is Daniel.

WHAT A DIFFERENCE
A YEAR MAKES

JOHN BROWN died on the gallows in 1859 because he believed the concept that all men are equal.

The belief resulted in a series of acts that the government termed murder, treason, and insurrection when it placed John Brown on trial.

Brown was a rabid abolitionist who believed he had been given a divine command to enforce the law of God that forbade the keeping of slaves. In the beginning, Brown was content to limit his actions to ferrying freed Negroes to sanctuary across the border of Canada by way of an underground network of sympathizers.

In the fall of 1859, however, John Brown decided his previous efforts had produced little effect and he came to the conclusion that he must lead an army of freedom into the South. He banded together an assortment of followers, that included several of his sons, and went to war.

On October 16, Brown's motley militia, needing weapons to wage their fight for freedom, attacked and seized the government arsenal at Harper's Ferry.

It was a short-lived victory. The government dispatched troops to Harper's Ferry, under the command of Union Army officers Colonel Robert Edward Lee and Lieutenant James Ewell Brown Stuart, and the abolitionist army fell after a bloody battle. Brown was ordered to stand trial for his crimes, found guilty, and executed. The hanging was carried out under the direction of Union Army officer Colonel Thomas Jonathan Jackson.

John Brown presented a pathetic picture during his trial. He seemed unable to comprehend what he had done. When asked by the court whether he had anything to say before sentence was passed, John Brown stood tall and proud and said:

I deny everything but what I have all along admitted; of a design on my part to free slaves. I intended certainly to have made a clean thing of that matter, as I did last winter, when I went into Missouri and there took slaves without the snapping of a gun on either side, moving them through the country, and finally leaving them in Canada. I designed to have done the same thing again on a larger scale. That was all I intended. I never did intend murder, or treason, or the destruction of property, or to excite slaves to rebellion, or to make insurrection.

I have another objection, and that is that it is unjust that I should suffer such a penalty. Had I interfered in behalf of the rich, the powerful, the intelligent, the so-called great, or in behalf of any of their friends, either father, mother, brother, sister, wife or children, or any of that class, and suffered and sacrificed what I have in this interference, it would have been all right.

Every man in this court would have deemed it an act worthy of reward rather than punishment.

This court acknowledges too, as I suppose, the validity of the Law of God. I see a book kissed, which I suppose to be the Bible, or at least the New Testament, which teaches me that all things whatsoever I would that men should do to me, I should do even so to them. It teaches me, further, to remember them that are in bonds as bound with them. I endeavored to act up to the instruction. I say I am yet too young to understand that God is any respecter of persons. I believe that to have interfered as I have done, as I have always freely admitted I have done, in behalf of His despised poor, I did not wrong, but right. Now, if it is deemed necessary that I should forfeit my life for the furtherance of the ends of justice, and mingle my blood further with the blood of my children and with the blood of millions in this slave country whose rights are disregarded by wicked, cruel and unjust enactments, I say, let it be done. I feel no consciousness of guilt. . . .

Thus it was that John Brown paid the supreme penalty.

What a prologue to our greatest trial as a nation: Robert E. Lee, Stonewall Jackson, and Jeb Stuart righteously keeping the law of the day, and Brown dying in his attempt to change it.

THE EMANCIPATION
PROCLAMATION

IT IS SOMEHOW part of the human mystique to take a man—a man good or a man bad—and then embellish his character according to the original colors he has been painted in. It is not enough, sad to say, that a man lives, does certain things, and is remembered as the man he was; we must go further and give him "an image." And there are always image-makers on the scene, just as there are always those who will accept an image if it is repeated often enough. When man learns to love his own kind without the necessity of having to sugar-coat him and endow him with qualities definitely not found in man, as we truly know him to be, perhaps we shall all be the better for it. Until that time arrives, I fear, we shall be destined to play a dual role; the role of a child who has grown too old to believe in Santa Claus but who will not admit this fact to his parents.

Lincoln's Emancipation Proclamation is an example of what I have been talking about; it is nothing more than a human face, hidden by a Halloween mask. The fact is, my friends, that the Emancipation Proclamation has always been surrounded by an aura of misconception and exaggeration. Abe Lincoln did not free the slaves.

Lincoln, in the words of certain minority leaders on the scene today, would have been guilty, in his time, of "tokenism." The fact is that Abraham Lincoln opposed emancipation, save on condition that there be organized a gradual emancipation based upon the voluntary action of the states, but with federal compensation to the slaveholders. Needless to say, Congress would not enact Lincoln's concepts into law. Were our incumbent President to hold to a comparable attitude, you may rest assured the very roof of the White House would tremble and rock with the cries of the outraged!

Such law as we have regarding the abolition of slavery first came about in 1862, when Congress passed a bill emancipating the slaves and prohibiting slavery in the Territories, along with the District of Columbia. No doubt Congress, during the heat and passion of the Civil War, was aware that already the ring of "all men are created equal" was fast becoming a peculiar American legend and, as such, was astute enough to keep its own back yard clean, even though many of the individual states were untouched by this particular bill. Sometimes a gaudy billboard, strategically placed alongside a busy highway, may hide the county dump.

On September 22, 1862, Abraham Lincoln declared that the slaves in areas of rebellion against the United States—the South —would be free on and after January 1, 1863. This proclamation did not, however, apply to Tennessee, nor did it apply to portions of Louisiana and Virginia. Further, it did not apply to the border slave states, areas of the Midwest that, today, many would like us to think were far above the venal practice of holding human beings in chattel. This proclamation, in essence, can be compared to an act of Franklin Roosevelt, during his tenure in the White House in the days of World War II, ordering that the Germans free all prisoners of concentration camps located in one particular portion of Germany. Such an order, had it been issued, would have been totally unenforceable and thoroughly lacking in any kind of all-encompassing effect. But a similar proclamation would have been very good "press" and perhaps that was what was in the minds of certain politicians at the time it was issued, during the Civil War. In any event, it was not, and cannot be, considered a blow against slavery.

In a second proclamation, on July 8, 1864, Lincoln said he would not admit the right of Congress to abolish slavery in the states. I leave it to you to make of this what you will. As far as

I am concerned, Lincoln was always apologetic for an act many historians would have us believe was the most important thing he ever did during his entire life!

In 1868 the Constitution of the United States of America—*during the administration of Andrew Johnson*—truly emancipated the slaves when the Thirteenth Amendment became part of our basic law! It reads:

> Neither slavery nor involuntary servitude, except as punishment for crime whereof the party shall have been duly convicted, shall exist within the United States, or any place subject to their jurisdiction.

Lincoln's proclamation, history books and Hollywood to the contrary, freed no slaves; it simply duplicated what Congress had already done, and it applied *only* to areas over which the federal government had no control. If this comes as something of a shock to those among us whom author Eric Hoffer calls the "true believers," it is a pity. As far as I am concerned, there are enough half-truths, hokum, and politically inspired legends floating around in the minds of the uninformed, as it is. We need not perpetuate the Lincoln legend; we have enough to contend with in the twentieth century, without having to fall back on stories that are already almost a hundred years out of date.

On a brighter note, and as a postscript, I offer the following bit of intelligence. The Emancipation Proclamation was written by William Henry Seward, Lincoln's Secretary of State. Seward is known, among the informed, as one of the great lawyers in America's history. Distinguishing himself in the defense of William Freeman, a psychotic Negro who massacred an innocent family in 1864, Seward, who had nothing to gain and everything to lose—such was the climate of the times—willingly involved himself in a case which was certain to cost him his friends, his law practice, and his political support.

And this, really, is the cloth of which great lawyers—and great men—are made.

Marriage, Divorce, and Juvenile Delinquency

FOR BETTER OR FOR WORSE

ALFRED, LORD TENNYSON created one of literature's most pathetic characters in Enoch Arden.

Enoch Arden was an English sailor who survived a shipwreck only to be washed ashore onto a mid-ocean island, where he lived for years in solitary confinement. Finally, he is rescued and returns home, only to learn that his wife, assuming him dead, has married in his absence. Staggered by the news, Enoch Arden approaches his dwelling with heavy heart, peers through a window into a candlelit room and beholds:

> His wife his wife no more and saw the babe,
> Hers yet not his upon his father's knee,
> And all his own children tall and beautiful
> And him that other reigning in his place
> Lord of his rights and of his children's love,
> Then he tho' Miriam Lane had told him all
> Because things seen are mightier than things heard,
> Staggered and shook holding the branch and feared
> To send abroad a shrill and terrible cry
> Which is one moment like the blast of doom
> Would shatter all the happiness of the hearth. . . .
> There speech and thought and nature failed a little
> And he lay tranced; but when he rose and paced
> Back toward his solitary home again,
> All down the long and narrow street he went,
> Beating it in upon his weary brain,
> As tho' it were the burden of a song
> Never to tell her; never to let her know. . . .

Tennyson created in Enoch Arden a hero whose image has not been shattered to this day. But, if Enoch Arden is a hero, how does one account for the classification allocated Teunis Van Pelt, who in 1816 was prosecuted and convicted of bigamy under similar circumstances by the State of New York? Returning from service in the War of 1812, Van Pelt discovered his wife had deserted him and married another. Van Pelt consoled himself by acquiring a new wife.

The State of New York brought Van Pelt to trial and a jury returned a verdict of guilty. It was fortunate, however, that the presiding judge was a man of the world, for he suspended the sentence, by reason of the circumstances, and set Van Pelt free.

Though Van Pelt's judge took into consideration the provocation which led to violation of the bigamy law, he did not see fit to criticize the divorce laws as applied to the common people, as did the celebrated Mr. Justice Maule when he had a case before him in the London courts a few years later.

A man who had been deserted by a worthless wife and had married again had been convicted of bigamy and was called up for sentence before Justice Maule, who said:

> . . . prisoner at the bar, you have been convicted before me of what the law regards as a very serious and grave offense, that of going through the marriage ceremony a second time while your wife was still alive. You may plead in mitigation of your conduct that she was given to dissipation and drunkenness, that she proved herself a curse to her household while she remained mistress of it, and that she had latterly deserted you; but I am not permitted to recognize such plea.
>
> You entered into a solemn engagement to take her for better or for worse, and if you got infinitely more of the latter, as you appear to have done, it was your duty to patiently submit. You say you took another person to be your wife because you were left with several young children, who required the care and protection of some one who might act as a substitute for the parent who had deserted them; but the law makes no allowances for bigamists with large families. Had you taken the other female to live with you as your concubine, you would never

have been interfered with by law. But your crime consists in having, to use your own language, preferred to make an honest woman of her.

Another of your irrational excuses is that your wife had committed adultery, and so you thought you were relieved from treating her with any further consideration; but you were mistaken. The law, in its wisdom, points out a means by which you might rid yourself from further association with a woman who had dishonoured you; but you did not think proper to adopt it. You ought first to have brought an action against your wife's seducer, if you could discover him. That might have cost you money and you say you are a poor working man, but that is not the fault of the law. You would then be obliged to prove by evidence your wife's criminality in a court of justice, and thus obtain a verdict with damages against the defendant, who was not unlikely to turn out to be a pauper. But so jealous is the law (which you ought to be aware is the perfection of reason) of the sanctity of the marriage tie, that in accomplishing this you would only have fulfilled the lighter portion of your duty. You must then have gone, with your verdict in your hand, and petitioned the House of Lords for a divorce. It would cost you, perhaps, five or six hundred pounds, and you do not seem to be worth as many pence. But it is the boast of the law that it is impartial, and it makes no difference between the rich and the poor. The wealthiest man in the kingdom would have to pay no less than that sum for the same luxury, so that you could have no reason to complain. You would of course have to prove your case over again, and at the end of a year or possibly two, you might obtain a divorce which would enable you legally to do what you have thought proper to do without it.

You have thus wilfully rejected the boon which the legislature offered you and it is my duty to pass such a sentence as I think your offense deserves, and that sentence is, that you be imprisoned for one day; and inasmuch as the present assize is three days old, the result is that you will be immediately discharged. . . .

JUVENILE DELINQUENCY

THE SCIENCE known as sociology, a Johnny-come-lately among the "ologies," has given mankind a good-sized glossary of many-syllabled, definite words and expressions. Among the latter is the term "juvenile delinquency," which purports to encompass a myriad of youthful sins ranging from failing to honor one's parents to the supreme crime of murder.

Judging from the texts, one might easily draw the conclusion that juvenile delinquency emerged to plague society at about the same time the social worker came into being and began combating the menace. The daily journals, civic leaders, and a multitude of sociologists and psychiatrists continually remind us that juvenile delinquency is a major problem of the moment.

The problem of youthful offenders is of particular interest to those who enforce the law. San Francisco Police Chief Patrick Crowley felt it serious enough to rate mention in his annual report to the Mayor and Board of Supervisors, which reads as follows:

> I am glad to be able to report that the City enjoys peace and tranquillity, and the laws are respected and obeyed to a degree not surpassed in any period in her history. The number of arrests was eleven percent greater two years ago, and twenty-three percent three years ago, than they have been the year just closed. This is remarkable because the population has steadily increased within the three years spoken of, and the diminution of arrests against the increase of population notably exhibits the peace and order enjoyed by our citizens.
>
> There exists, however, one evil which I mention with regret—it is the disposition on the part of many young men and lads to commit acts of violence and mischief. And as brutality and cow-

230

ardice frequently go together, the victims of their violence have usually been those whose voice was silenced in our Courts, and whose ignorance of our language and peaceable disposition were accepted as an invitation to the attack.

The possession and use of deadly weapons by those whose passions and prejudices are strong, and whose judgments are immature and unripe, has produced much mischief and threatens much more. The police are doing what they can to check and resist this wrong; but unless supported by public opinion and assisted by the citizens at large, they may labor long and hard before the evil is suppressed.

If every person who should be a witness to the commission of an outrage would promptly arrest the perpetrator, or, if not inclined to such active effort, would note the offender, the circumstances of the offense, and the witnesses present, and give the prosecuting officers the benefit of such knowledge, these wrongs could not continue. The sooner the efforts of our community rise to the height of this emergency, the better it will be for our reputation abroad, and the greater will be our security and happiness at home.

Not only was Chief Crowley concerned with the problem but others were worried, including James Denman, Superintendent of the San Francisco Public Schools, whose concern in his annual report to the Board of Education reads in part:

> In my last report I urged the necessity of adopting severe and effective measures to check the growing evils of truancy and vagrancy, which are rapidly corrupting the youth of our city. I am happy to report that while our schools have largely increased, the cases of truancy have decreased during the year. Three hundred and twenty-four truants, who have been reported as the most incorrigible, have been induced to return to school through the exertions of the officer and the influence of the teachers, who in some instances have shown a commendable zeal and interest in visiting parents to reclaim the wayward and abandoned youth under their charge, which should entitle them to our kindest consideration and gratitude.

> Forty incorrigible boys, who have defied all attempts at reformation by their teachers and parents, have been brought before the Police Judge and sentenced to the Industrial School, to rescue them from lives of infamy and crime.

Much remains to be done to free the city of a large class of youthful vagrants who are educating themselves in the streets and byways, and around the wharves, in all the crimes of a large metropolis. There are at least 2,000 children in San Francisco leading idle and vicious lives, who do not attend any school, and who are growing up in ignorance and vice.

I cannot therefore too strongly recommend the necessity of passing and enforcing the most stringent laws to repress youthful vagrancy. If parents will not control their children and educate them for useful members of society, it is the duty of the state, for self-protection, to assume the responsibility.

Society should also be educated and aroused to the importance of reclaiming the wayward youth infesting our city, for no laws can effect any great moral remedy unless sanctioned by an enlightened public sentiment.

It would not come as a surprise to read these reports in tomorrow's newspaper. But it might come as a surprise to learn that Superintendent Denman's report is dated for the year 1870, and that of Chief Crowley, 1872.

We have come a long way since then; we have given a name to a human failing that has been part of society since its birth.

DIVORCE

MUCH HAS BEEN WRITTEN about divorce and its evils, not only to the parties, but primarily to the children of the marriage. The man and woman who enter into an agreement to love, honor, and obey sometimes find, after the excitement of the acquisition of a mate, that little traits of character or personality appear which were not noticed during the lovey-dovey period. There is somewhat less love and respect, and practically no "obey."

Under Mosaic law, only the husband could have a divorce, by merely giving his wife a writing saying that he had divorced her. The teachings of the Christian faith have put certain restrictions on divorce, but the civil laws of our fifty states outline the rules that make divorce possible by either party.

There are so many elements leading to divorce that no two cases are exactly alike, nor do judges in the courts always agree in their judgments. Some judges require more proof than do others. Some attempt to reconcile the parties, knowing full well that they are wasting time. If two people decide that they are not getting along in mutual harmony and happiness, I don't see how any judge can implant in their minds high and lofty ideals against fixed facts and circumstances.

Denying a divorce to the husband or wife where it is indicated creates hatreds, miseries, adultery, and other moral aberrations.

A classical discussion of this subject is found in an early decision handed down by a judge in 1836 in which the learned man points out:

". . . The parties in this case were married in March, 1816. They have no children. The husband is proved to be a man in easy circumstances, and of a hasty and irritable temper. The wife is shown to be a very active and efficient manager of her household affairs, and of a high, bold, masculine spirit; somewhat impatient of control; in a high degree jealous of the liberty that belongs to her as a wife, and not always ready to submit, even to the legitimate authority of her husband. For aught that appears in this case, they lived in peace and harmony until some time since the year 1830, when the wife, having become a professor of religion, united herself to a church whose doctrines and opinions the husband did not approve. This diversity of sentiments in religious matters seems to have been the original fountain whence has flowed all the bitterness which has since existed between them, and which has driven them into quarrels, squabbles and encounters, that certainly do no credit to either party. The result of these broils was, that the wife left the house of the husband, and has since resided separate and apart from him; and she now seeks to have the bonds of matrimony dissolved, on the ground that in the contest which ended in their separation, he exercised a tyranny over her which amounted to extreme cruelty.

"In a contest about religion between two persons standing in the relation, and having the dispositions and tempers of these parties, it is hardly to be conceived that the blame could have been all on one side. Mere profession of religion weighs nothing in such a case. If the spirit of the gospel abide with one of the parties, not in word only but in its power, there can be no contest; whatever wrong or injury there may be on the one side—all will be patience and suffering on the other. Where strife is, there is every evil work. But that wisdom which is from above is first pure, then peaceable, gentle, and easy to be entreated, full of mercy and good fruits. This is the language of inspiration.

"The evidence in this case shows much strife between these parties; and an attentive examination of that evidence will enable us to see who has been to blame.

"One of the complaints of the wife in this case is that the husband has often addressed her in harsh, abusive, and profane language. This charge is sustained by the evidence, and his conduct in this respect can be viewed in no other light than as unmanly, indecorous, and in the highest degree reprehensible. And in the case of a woman of a meek and quiet spirit, incapable of rendering evil for evil, or railing for railing, but patient in all her tribulations, such language on the part of a husband often repeated, wantonly and unprovoked, would go a great way, and be a circumstance of much weight, in making out a case of extreme cruelty.

"But here much of the evidence on both sides, and even the tone and temper of the affidavit which she has drawn up herself and filed in the case, indicate in the wife anything rather than a meek and quiet spirit. And one of her own witnesses says that her conduct was often provoking and vexatious. She herself admits, in her affidavit, that she sometimes used passionate language, but says she used it only when he gave her occasion. It is very likely that she may think she had always an occasion for the passionate language she used; and it is equally likely that he may think he had an occasion for the harsh and abusive language he used towards her. It is not proved that he used such language wantonly and unprovoked on any occasion. And if a wife chooses so to act and to talk as to raise a storm in the temper of an irritable husband, it is doing her no injustice to say to her, when it has come attended only with harsh and abusive language, that she has had in its peltings her just and merited reward. However reprehensible his conduct may have been in this respect, she is not to be heard, when she would complain of it. She ought not to be heard to complain of abuse which she has wantonly provoked.

"Her next complaint grows out of a contest between them with respect to some wood, in August, 1833. Her story is that she sent a little girl out to procure some wood—that the husband met the girl at the door and told her 'she should not'—that she then went herself for the wood, and as she went out, he went into the house. When she returned she found the door fastened—upon which she threw her wood into the house through the window, and took a crowbar and knocked at the door; that he came out in a great passion, and using very profane language, which she repeats, but which we shall not, took the crowbar from her by force; that she screamed murder, and he stopped her mouth. But at length she escaped, and soon after deserted the house.

"Now in this account it is virtually admitted that she went out in open rebellion against the known will of her husband. And the throwing of the wood into the house by the window, the use she made of the crowbar, and her screams of murder when he took the crowbar from her, indicate a spirit and temper quite too belligerent, when indulged against a husband, to be becoming in a lady. But her witness adds other material circumstances, which she has omitted, and says that the husband told the girl not to take the wood that was on the other side of the road, but to take it from the mill-house, because he wanted to clear that—that upon this the wife came out and said that she sent the girl, and intended to have the wood. He further says, that she struck the door with the crowbar and made several dents in it, which are still visible; and that after the husband took the bar from her she threatened to go to a magistrate and compel him to give sureties of the peace, and that he told her that she had better go into the house.

"Such is the transaction, as it stands disclosed in the evidence. There seems to have been nothing unreasonable or improper in the direction which the husband gave to the little girl. And the temper in which the wife went forth from the house, and her declared intention of having her own will and her own way, in defiance of him, which was immediately carried into overt acts of rebellion against his authority, show her to have been entirely in the wrong on that occasion. She was to blame in the beginning: and she carried out the quarrel in a manner which all candid and impartial minds must pronounce to have been equally inconsistent with her connubial duties and her religious professions. In the skirmish which ended in his taking the crowbar from her, she seems to have been rather roughly handled. But considering the irritable temper of the husband, it seems to us that she escaped with quite as little injury as she could have had any right to expect, in such an attempt to take his castle by storm.

"Her next complaint is founded upon a quarrel between her and her husband which took place upon the Sabbath. The account which she gives of the matter in her affidavit is, that she asked him to let her have the horse and chaise to go to church. This he refused, because he did not like the minister. Then she ordered the boy to put the horse to the chaise, and went out herself to the chaise-house to assist the boy. Finding the chaise-house locked, she requested him to let her have the key, which he refused. She thereupon took hold of the door, 'and made as though she would open it.' Upon this, the husband came out and struck her upon the head, and made her head ache for several days. Such is her account of the affair. But her witness states other material circumstances, which she omits. He says that she went out to the chaise-house and attempted to force the lock with a wedge; that the husband came out, and took the wedge from her, and ordered her to go into the house. She, however, still persisted in her attempt to obtain the chaise, until he struck her.

"Now, in this instance, the quarrel had its origin in the misconduct of the husband. No good reason is shown why the use of the horse and chaise should not have been freely accorded to her. And his refusal of her reasonable request, not only has the appearance of great unkindness, but of a tyrannical attempt to embarrass her in the enjoyment of that religious liberty which belongs to every wife.

"But it was the Sabbath—and, under the circumstances, what course of conduct did duty prescribe to a Christian wife and to a member of the church? The very essence of the religion she professes is, that charity suffereth long and is kind, which vaunteth not itself, doth not behave unseemly, is not easily provoked, and not only believeth and hopeth, but beareth and endureth all things. What course of conduct, then, did duty prescribe to one who professed to have adopted that religion as the guide of her life? If when ye do well and suffer for it, yet take it patiently, this is acceptable with God, says the bible. What course of conduct did duty then prescribe to one who professes to believe the bible to be the word of God? In my judgment, there cannot be any diversity of opinion on these questions. It was due to the day, it was due to the religion she professes, it was due to the relation in which she stood to her oppressor, that, if she could not obtain his consent by kindness and condescension, she should have submitted in silence to the wrong he was doing her. But instead of this, regardless of the day and of the modesty and of all the sober virtues that belongs to the character of a pious matron, at the head of a respectable family, and setting her husband completely at defiance, she at once undertook to accomplish her purpose by force and violence;

and in this course she persisted, until, provoked by her perverse obstinacy, the husband was led so far to forget himself as to strike her.

"Whatever the old books may say upon the subject, there never was, in my opinion, in the relation between husband and wife, when rightly understood, anything that gave to a husband the right to reduce a refractory wife to obedience by blows. And at this day the moral sense of the community revolts at the idea that a husband may inflict personal chastisement upon his wife, even for the most outrageous conduct. The blow given by the husband in this case deserved the severest censure. All must condemn it. But I am much mistaken if the stubborn obstinacy with which the wife set him at defiance, and the violence she used in her rebellion against his authority, will not, under all the circumstances, be quite as revolting to the moral sense of an enlightened and a religious community as the unmanly conduct of the husband.

"She further complains of personal violence, inflicted by the husband in the quarrel about making matches. The account she gives of the transaction in her affidavit is, that while she was making the matches, according to his directions, and obeying him in all things, he, without any provocation, became violently enraged, and having beaten her cruelly with a horsewhip, imprisoned her in the cellar. The story is confirmed in some particulars by one witness who says he heard a dispute between the parties, and two blows of a whip, and saw her come up from the cellar, and by another witness who says he saw the husband strike her two or three times with a whip, but not very heavily. He also saw him carry her into the cellar. This witness further says that the parties talked very angrily. Still another witness says she heard blows of a whip and afterwards saw marks of violence upon the person of plaintiff.

"She has another complaint of personal chastisement, inflicted by the husband, in the dispute about certain papers belonging to the society for educating pious young men, of which society she was treasurer. Her account of this affair is, that the husband took the papers from her drawer and put them into his desk; that she demanded them, and he refused to restore them; that a few days afterwards she had an opportunity to obtain possession of them, in his absence, and took them away. When he came home and was informed of this, he flew into a violent passion, and using very profane and abusive language, finally horse-whipped her. Her account is, in some respects, confirmed by the testimony of a witness.

"Such is the case presented by the evidence laid before us on the part of the wife. And I shall, in the first place, consider whether, upon the case thus presented, she is entitled to the decree she asks. It then becomes necessary to consider the true nature of the relation between husband and wife, and what is to be deemed extreme cruelty, within the meaning and intent of the statute.

"In scripture the wife is represented as standing, in some re-spects, in the same relation to the husband as the husband stands to the Redeemer, and the Redeemer to God. The words are: The head of every man is Christ, and the head of the woman is the man, and the head of Christ is God. And in our law the wife is considered as being, in some respects, subordinate to the husband, who is the head of the house. The husband and wife are, in the contemplation of the law, one. Her legal existence and authority are suspended during the continuance of the matrimonial union. He is bound to support and maintain her in a manner suitable to her situation and his condition. He is made answerable for her debts contracted before the marriage. And during the continuance of the union he alone is responsible for crimes committed by her in his presence—the law not considering her, in such a case, as acting by her own will, but by his compulsion. He is answerable for all torts and frauds committed by her; and if committed in his company he alone is answerable. And she is wisely made subject in many things to his authority, as he is subject to the laws under which he lives. But a wife is neither the slave nor the servant of a husband. He is the head of the house, to whom as such she is subordinate. But she is at the same time his companion, the partner and sharer of his fortune, in many respects his equal; who in her appropriate sphere is entitled to share largely in his authority.

"He is bound, not only to honor and support her, but to accord to her freely and liberally all her rights, and to guarantee to her the full and free enjoyment of all her just privileges and prerogatives as the mistress of the family.

"He is bound to leave her free to enjoy her own religious opinions, and worship God according to the dictates of her own reason and conscience; and not to molest or restrain her in this respect, provided she does not in her zeal disturb the public peace, nor rebel against his lawful authority. Such is the equality and dignity which our laws confer upon the female character; and such the relation in which husband and wife stand to one another.

"What then is extreme cruelty? It is not mere austerity of temper, petulance of manners, rudeness of language, a want of civil attention, or even occasional sallies of temper, if there be no threat of bodily harm. It is not the denial of little indulgences or particular accommodations. Such denial may in many cases be extremely unkind and unhandsome, and disgraceful to the character of a husband, and yet not amount to the cruelty intended by the statute. To constitute extreme cruelty in a husband, his misconduct must be such as to show that the inward knot of marriage, which is peace and love, is untied, and that he exercises over his wife, not the mild and salutary authority of a husband, but a harsh and cruel tyranny. In the judgment of the law, any willful misconduct of the husband, which endangers the life or the health of the wife; which exposes her to bodily hazard and intolerable hardship, and renders cohabitation unsafe, is extreme cruelty.

"In order to amount to such cruelty it is not necessary that there should be many acts. Whatever force and violence, preceded by deliberate insult and abuse, have been once wantonly and without provocation used, the wife can hardly be considered as safe. But it is a well-settled rule, that a wife is not entitled

to be divorced on the ground of ill treatment received from
her husband, if that ill treatment has been drawn upon her
by her own misconduct. The cruety which lays a just and legal
foundation for a divorce, must be unmerited and unprovoked.
When she is ill treated on account of her own misconduct, her
remedy is in a reform of her manners, unless the return from
the husband is wholly unjustified by the provocation, and quite
out of proportion to the offense.

"Such are the rules of law that are to govern this decision;
and there is very little difficulty in the application of them to
the facts in this case. With respect to the quarrels and contests
between the parties about the wood, and about the horse and
chaise, there is no doubt. Whatever may have been the ill
treatment which the wife received on those occasions it is very
manifest she drew it down upon herself by her obstinacy and
ill conduct. Nor does the return made by the husband appear to
have been much out of proportion to the offense.

"With regard to the quarrel about the matches, it is very
clear that such was the conduct of the husband on that occasion,
that if it is to be considered as altogether wanton and unprovoked, it entitles the libelant to the decree she asks. To beat
a wife with a whip, and then put her into the cellar without
any provocation, is both unjust and tyrannical; and, even in a
case of great provocation, it could hardly be considered as manly
conduct. It is not denied that he struck her with a whip, or
that he put her into the cellar; and she states in her affidavit
that she gave him no provocation whatever. This, however, is
denied by him in his affidavit. The parties were alone when the
quarrel began, and no other person knows in what it originated.
It is proved that both very soon became very angry. It is not
at all probable that all the fault was on one side. Nor is it
likely that he would have proceeded to blows if there was no
provocation, but all was submission on her part. The proofs
which are in the case of her conduct and spirit on other occasions, render it quite improbable that she was at this time beaten
and abused for her meekness and condescension. Besides, we

have had an opportunity to compare her accounts of other transactions between herself and her husband, with the accounts which her witnesses give of the same transactions; and this comparison shows very clearly, that however fair her general character for truth and veracity may be, very little reliance can be placed upon her statements, when they relate to her disputes with her husband.

"Perhaps it would be too much to expect that she should, under the circumstances, give a full and fair account of those transactions. It is certain, if her witnesses are to be believed, her accounts are neither full nor fair; and we cannot presume that her account of the occurrence we are now considering, is perfectly correct. We entirely condemn the use of the whip by the husband, as unlawful and unmanly. But no very serious injury was done to her person; and her own affidavit, unsupported as it is by any other testimony, has failed to satisfy us that the conduct of the husband was wanton, unprovoked, and un-merited, which is essential, to make it a legal ground of a divorce.

"Indeed, taking all the testimony together, it seems to us to be rather more probable, on the whole, that she may have de-signedly used means to provoke him to acts of violence, in order that she might have a pretense for leaving him, than that, wantonly and unprovoked, he inflicted personal chastisement upon her. The same remarks, to a very great extent, are ap-plicable in all their force to the quarrel between the parties about the papers belonging to the society for educating pious young men. The parties were alone during the whole contest, and they alone know the spirit and temper in which it proceeded. There are, however, two circumstances to be considered in this instance, which did not exist in the contest about the matches. The wife was the treasurer of the society, and to take the papers from her without her consent and lock them up in his desk, certainly had the appearance, not only of unkindness, but of an unmanly meddling in a concern which was exclusively under the management of the ladies who belonged to the society, and must have been calculated to vex and irritate the wife. On the other hand, her taking advantage of his absence to open the desk and take away the papers, has in it too much of a disposition to have her own will, and her own way, by foul means if not by fair, to be commended in a wife, and was calculated to exasperate her husband.

"Now, considering the temper and disposition this lady is proved to have exhibited on other occasions, what is the probability as to her course of conduct when the husband came to reproach her for taking away the papers from his desk in his absence? Did she endeavor to avert the gathering storm by meek and submissive behavior, or did she retort upon him as unmanly interference in the concerns of a female society, with which he had nothing to do? It seems to us much more probable that he was driven to violence by her provoking taunts—taunts which may have been the more provoking, because he felt in them the sting of truth and justice—than that he should have resorted to blows without any new provocation on her part at that time. And this presumption is much strengthened by the consideration that the husband although quick and hasty in his temper, does not seem to be naturally vindictive; while the wife is shown to have been at other times quite as busy and active in a quarrel with her husband, as in the management of her ordinary household affairs. And we are of opinion, on the whole, that however obnoxious to censure the conduct of the husband may have been on any, or on all the occasions to which we have averted, the wife has no right to complain; because it is in the highest degree probable that in every instance she drew down upon herself the chastisement she received, by her own improper conduct. And it does not appear that on any occasion the injury she received was much out of proportion to her offense.

"Her remedy is to be sought, then, not in this court, but in a reformation of her own manners. Let her return to the path of duty; and if to a discreet and prudent exercise of her just rights and privileges as a wife, she will join that meekness, patience, and kindness which the religion she professes inculcates, and temper all her conduct towards her husband with that sweetness and goodness which belong to the true character of a wife, we think she will have no reasonable ground to apprehend any further injury to her person. Let her submit to the authority of her husband, and remember that the dignity of a wife cannot be violated by such submission. Let her return to the path of duty; and by displaying in all her conduct the mild and gentle spirit of the gospel, make that path a path of peace and safety.

"And let the husband recollect that the first duty of the head of a family is to be master of himself, and to have his temper and feelings in due subjection to his reason and understanding, so that no provocation shall drive him, on any occasion, to unjust and unmanly acts of violence, or even to the use of profane and abusive language. And remembering his own infirmities let him generously go forward, and not only invite but encourage his wife to return to her duty, by satisfactory assurances, not only that her person shall be safe, but that her feeling shall not be insulted again by profane or abusive language, and that her religious rights shall not be in any way abridged. And let all those who attempt to advise them, consider who it is that has said, 'Blessed are the peacemakers, for they shall be called the children of God.'

"Between these parties there is much to be forgotten and forgiven on both sides. But if they shall be disposed to retrace their steps; and if those who are around them shall aid and encourage them in all their attempts at reconciliation, it is to be hoped that they will encounter no serious obstacle in finding their way back to domestic peace and happiness. . . ."

All reasonable-minded people will agree with the Biblical Ecclesiasticus, which cautioned that an evil wife is a yoke shaken to and fro; he that hath hold of her is as though he held a scorpion, and adds: "I had rather dwell with a lion and a dragon, than to keep house with a wicked woman."

States' Rights

SECESSION

On april 12, 1861, a cannon manned by prideful men was fired against Fort Sumter. The echoes of that shot are still heard today.

When the Supreme Court in 1954 handed down its decision on integration, directing that public segregation between the black man and the white man shall no longer exist, it merely re-emphasized a social problem that cannot and will not be settled by court decision.

After this historic decision there was much talk in the southern states about secession, but more bitterly about our Supreme Court. Hatreds slowly dying out were rekindled and the North and the South are at it again. The United States Army and the National Guard are used to enforce the Supreme Court's decision. This is not new; history is replaying one of its greatest tragedies.

In 1857 the Supreme Court decided the famous Dred Scott case—which upheld property rights in slavery—and Abraham Lincoln, in his inaugural address on March 4, 1861, criticized the Court, saying:

> . . . I do not forget the position assumed by some that constitutional questions are to be decided by the Supreme Court, nor do I deny that such decisions must be binding in any case upon the parties to a suit as to the object of that suit, while they are also entitled to very high respect and consideration in all parallel cases by all other departments of the Government. And while it is obviously possible that such decision may be erroneous in any given case, still the evil effect following it, being limited to that particular case, with the chance that it may

247

be overruled and never become a precedent for other cases, can better be borne than could the evils of a different practice. . . .

At the same time, the candid citizen must confess that if the policy of the Government upon vital questions affecting the whole people is to be irrevocably fixed by decisions of the Supreme Court, the instant they are made in ordinary litigation between parties in personal actions the people will have ceased to be their own rulers, having to that extent practically resigned their Government into the hands of that eminent tribunal. Nor is there in this view any assault upon the court or the judges. It is a duty from which they may not shrink to decide cases properly brought before them, and it is no fault of theirs if others seek to turn their decisions to political purposes. . . .

This country, with its institutions, belongs to the people who inhabit it. Whenever they shall grow weary of the existing Government, they can exercise their constitutional right of amending it or their revolutionary right to dismember or overthrow it.

These words of Lincoln are, one hundred years later, becoming a fresh bloom of tragedy. The country is in a turmoil. The colored man is pressing his advantage and the white man is resisting—some actually and openly, others quietly and underground.

Since the formation of our national government, the people in the various states, as today, were fearful and dissatisfied. Many believed that they had surrendered their rights as state citizens to receive instead grandiose promises and guarantees from a "phantom" federal government. Some people today, as then, are sure that the right of each state to handle its own business is paramount to the right exercised by the federal government. As early as 1777 Vermont declared itself an independent republic under the name of New Connecticut and maintained it was not only free from England, but also from the Colonies.

In 1814 the Federalist Party in New England was extremely ill-disposed toward the government. The purchase of Louisiana, the admission of new states in the South and West, and the war of 1812, were extremely unpopular, and culminated in the Massachusetts legislature calling a convention to meet at Hartford in December of that year. Twenty-six delegates responded from Massachusetts, Connecticut, Rhode Island, and Vermont and sat for three weeks behind closed doors. This secrecy made the public think that treason was being hatched and many believed that the New England states were about to secede and that the convention was framing a new constitution. All it did was to pass resolutions and adjourn.

The constitutional issues concerning States' rights had been agitated for decades. When South Carolina claimed the right to nullify a federal law on tariffs, President Jackson, on December 10, 1832, issued his proclamation against nullification saying:

> . . . I consider, then, the power to annul a law of the United States, assumed by one State, incompatible with the existence of the Union, contradicted expressly by the letter of the Constitution, unauthorized by its spirit, inconsistent with every principle on which it was founded, and destructive of the great object for which it was formed. . . .
>
> This right to secede is deduced from the nature of the Constitution, which, they say, is a compact between soverign States who have preserved their whole sovereignty and therefore are subject to no superior; that because they made the compact they can break it when in their opinion it has been departed from by the other states. Fallacious as this course of reasoning is, it enlists State pride and finds advocates in the honest prejudices of those who have not studied the nature of our Government sufficiently to see the radical error on which it rests. . . .
>
> The Constitution of the United States, then, forms a Government, not a League; and whether it be formed by compact between the States or in any other manner, its character is the same. It is a Government in which all the people are represented, which operates directly on the people individually, not upon the States; they retained all the power they did not grant. But each State, having expressly parted with so many powers as to constitute, jointly with the other States, a single nation, cannot, from that period, possess any right to secede, because such

secession does not break a league, but destroys the unity of a nation; and any injury to that unity is not only a breach which would result from the contravention of a compact, but it is an offense against the whole Union. . . .

On January 21, 1861, when Jefferson Davis, Senator for Mississippi, said farewell to his colleagues in the United States Senate, secession was not a new subject for debate in Congress. South Carolina, Alabama, Florida, Georgia, and Louisiana had already seceded, and now Mississippi. States' rights was the issue, and time was marching toward the greatest military struggle of all time. Davis, a graduate of West Point, veteran of the Mexican War and a former Secretary of War, was fifty-two years of age when he took his state out of the Union.

Lincoln will be inaugurated on March 4, Virginia is about to secede, and the remaining southern states are waiting to follow. The Confederate States of America is slowly being organized. Fort Sumter is just ahead. The man who was to be the first and last President of the Confederacy is now addressing the Senate:

> . . . I rise, Mr. President, for the purpose of announcing to the Senate that I have satisfactory evidence that the State of Mississippi, by a solemn ordinance of her people in convention assembled, has declared her separation from the United States. Under these circumstances, of course, my functions are terminated here.
>
> It has seemed to me proper, however, that I should appear in the Senate to announce that fact to my associates, and I will say but very little more. The occasion does not invite me to go into argument, and my physical condition would not permit me to do so if it were otherwise; and yet it seems to become me to say something on the part of the state I here represent, on an occasion so solemn as this.
>
> It is known to Senators who have served with me here that I have for many years advocated, as an essential attribute of state sovereignty, the right of a state to secede from the Union. Therefore, if I had not believed there was justifiable cause; if I had thought that Mississippi was acting without sufficient provocation, or without an existing necessity, I should still, under my theory of the Government, because of my allegiance to the state

of which I am a citizen, have been bound by her action. I, however, may be permitted to say that I do think that she has justifiable cause, and I approve of her act. I conferred with her people before that act was taken, counseled them then that if the state of things which they apprehended should exist when the convention met, they should take the action which they have now adopted.

Secession . . . is to be justified upon the basis that the states are sovereign. There was a time when none denied it. I hope the time may come again when a better comprehension of the theory of our Government, and the inalienable rights of the people of the States, will prevent any one from denying that each state is a sovereign, and thus may reclaim the grants which it has made to any agent whomsoever. . . .

This is done not in hostility to others, not to injure any section of the country, not even for our own pecuniary benefit; but from the high and solemn motive of defending and protecting the rights we inherited, and which it is our sacred duty to transmit unshorn to our children.

I find in myself, perhaps, a type of the general feeling of my constituents toward yours. I am sure I feel no hostility to you Senators from the North. I am sure there is not one of you, whatever sharp discussion there may have been between us, to whom I cannot now say, in the presence of my God, I wish you well; and such, I am sure, is the feeling of the people whom I represent toward those whom you represent. I therefore feel that I but express their desire when I say I hope, and they hope, for peaceful relations with you, though we must part. They may be mutually beneficial to us in the future, as they have been in the past, if you so will it. The reverse may bring disaster on every portion of the country; and if you will have it thus, we will invoke the God of our fathers, who delivered them from the power of the lion, to protect us from the ravages of the bear; and thus, putting our trust in God, and in our own firm hearts and strong arms, we will vindicate the right as best we may.

In the course of my service here, associated at different times with a great variety of Senators, I see now around me some with whom I have served long; there have been points of collision; but whatever of offense there has been to me, I leave here; I carry with me no hostile remembrance. Whatever offense I have given which has not been redressed, or for which satisfaction has not been demanded, I have, Senators, in this hour of our parting, to offer you my apology for any pain which, in heat of discussion, I have inflicted. I go hence unencumbered of the remembrance of any injury received, and having discharged the duty of making the only reparation in my power for any injury offered.

Mr. President and Senators, having made the announcement which the occasion seemed to me to require, it only remains for me to bid you a final adieu. . . .

After this farewell speech Jefferson Davis returned to Mississippi and, soon, at Montgomery, Alabama, was named provisional President of the Confederacy. Following the secession of Virginia, Texas, and other southern states, he was inaugurated President of the Confederate States of America in Richmond, Virginia, in February, 1862.

But was it all worth while? Time has not finalized the States' rights question. The thousands upon thousands who fought and died have not changed man; their blood has not purified him. The War of Secession has not wiped out hatred, or animosity, or bigotry.

All men are born equal? A question unanswered.

FEDERAL POWER V. STATES' RIGHTS— THE DOCTRINE OF INTERPOSITION

THE OLD PRINCIPLE of States' rights is to this day one of the most important and legally disturbing problems of our dual type of government. It is a controversy that is as old as our country and is one that brings hatred, bigotry, and division among our people.

States' rights is uniquely American. The small-state delegates at the Constitutional Convention feared that their identity would be lost in the formation of the Union. The separate states already had long histories as autonomous colonies, with existing traditions of self-government.

James Madison, a Virginian, knew that the large states would grow even more populous as time passed; and if numbers alone dominated the new national government, the smaller states would inevitably be submerged. Hence the elaborate system of checks and balances among the branches of the government. The states, large and small, have an equal legislative voice in the Senate.

The Congress itself, with enumerated powers, lacked authority to enter areas not specifically mentioned in the Constitution. A limited government was created because the states expected to order their own affairs with neither the need nor the desire for outside intervention.

The Tenth Amendment evidences this determination, providing that powers not delegated to the national government are reserved to the states. The amendment clearly leaves a broad residual jurisdiction to state authority.

This is underscored by the historic principle that the states were, and are, sovereign. Sovereignty, admittedly, is one of the more esoteric of legal principles. Yet the states could rightfully claim this status, as the Union was their creation, and no matter what powers they might delegate, their basic constitutional identity remained.

John Marshall dominated the Supreme Court from 1801 to 1835 and, in a series of decisions, enunciated supremacy of congressional law over state legislation. State and nation are not coequal partners, he said, and the states must yield when they come into direct conflict with federal authority.

The Civil War, of course, established that a state, no matter how sovereign, could not secede from the Union.

Since the birth of the republic, the relation between state and federal governments has been characterized by the question of who is boss. The states have found themselves called upon to perform certain services such as education, mental health, professional licensing, banking and insurance regulation, and the maintenance of law and order. None suggest that the national government take over mental hospitals, prisons, or state universities.

Most quarrels over jurisdiction and performance are taken to the courts, where there is occasion for compromise as well as for ultimate adjudication. Federal law is often violated in spirit, but this does not mean that armed troops are sent in at every such juncture. Despite a Supreme Court ruling against the practice, millions of children are continuing to recite prayers in their schools. Call the troops—soldiers are on the way, but the government in a free society cannot invoke the bayonet daily.

States' rights are important to all citizens. They see the federal government as an agency of coercion, while their state government is an instrument of service. State legislators are accessible, often known personally, and generally sympathetic to local needs.

Among the most vocal proponents of States' rights are small businessmen in all sections of the country. In this group there are millions of other Americans, not themselves businessmen, who identify their well-being with that of the business community. They are self-employed professionals, white-collar employees, property owners who constitute a substantial part of the middle class. For them, States' rights are a protecting shield against further federal intrusions in their lives.

To these, the states should have the major jurisdiction over health, housing, education, and all matters of welfare, because the states know the circumstances at the local level and can tailor their laws to suit local problems.

The businessman, in addition, must keep his eye on costs: he realizes that a too generous minimum wage or too powerful unions can easily bankrupt him. As he sees it, the state legislatures have been understanding in these areas. At least a third of them have enacted "right to work" laws and others have refrained from intervening in business affairs.

States' rights, then, give each businessman the freedom to run his shop as he sees fit. To him, this is fundamental. His entire life is identified with the enterprise he owns, has built up, and manages, and he believes if legislation in the economic realm were left to the states, the entire country would prosper.

Thomas Jefferson in 1823 said "we are undone unless we check these unconstitutional invasions of States-Rights by the Federal Government."

Jefferson's words say all there is to say about the doctrine of interposition. It illustrates the deep roots of the clash between state and federal authority.

The use of this doctrine by Governor Ross Barnett in the integration squabble in Mississippi is but one in a long line of dangerous situations in our national history.

Northern as well as southern states have been defiant of federal power from the earliest days of the republic, and this by no means ended with the Civil War. And though federal authority has increased to the point where it may seem certain to prevail, the record shows that Supreme Courts and Presidents haven't always in practice proved victorious.

In 1792, two citizens of South Carolina sued the State of Georgia for seizing the estate of a deceased man; the U.S. Supreme Court ruled in their favor, but Georgia wouldn't respect the ruling. The conflict led not to state capitulation but to the Eleventh Amendment to the Constitution, which declares that federal judicial power doesn't extend to suits by citizens of one state against another state.

Georgia provided the Supreme Court with one of the stiffest early challenges to its authority; the conflict left the federal bench with a paper victory but a practical defeat.

In the early 1800s, the Cherokee Indians established in the western part of the state their own "nation," complete with a government and laws. A crisis arose when a brave named Corn Tassel killed another Indian; he was seized by Georgia authorities, tried in the state court, and sentenced. When the U.S.

Supreme Court in 1831 ordered the Governor to justify this, he ignored the Court and Corn Tassel was hanged. Chief Justice Marshall then skirted a clash by holding that the Supreme Court had no jurisdiction over the case because the Cherokee nation was neither a foreign nor domestic state, but a "domestic dependent."

But this didn't end the matter. Two missionaries, Samuel Worcester and Ilizur Butler, obtained federal licenses to live among the Cherokees. Because they didn't have a Georgia State license, the state sentenced them to four years' hard labor. The missionaries appealed to the Supreme Court; Georgia didn't even bother to appear in defense of its rulings. Instead, the legislature passed a resolution declaring that "any attempt to reverse the decision [of the Georgia court] by the Supreme Court will be held by this state as unconstitutional and arbitrary interference . . . and will be treated as such."

Unable to avoid the issue any longer, Chief Justice Marshall ruled the state action unconstitutional because the federal government had sole jurisdiction over Indian affairs. The furor that followed, with Georgia still refusing to recognize the high court ruling, prompted President Andrew Jackson to remark: "Well, John Marshall has made his decision, now let him enforce it."

Later, however, Georgia officials dropped their defiance; the missionaries, on withdrawal of their Supreme Court suit, were pardoned. And after the Civil War, the Georgia Supreme Court conceded that "after the state has yielded to the Federal Army, it can well afford to yield to the Federal judiciary . . . the doctrine of co-equality and co-ordination, regarded now from a practical stand-point, seems visionary."

Sometimes federal-state struggles have taken decades to decide. One of these was the little-remembered but fascinating "Pennsylvania Rebellion."

What began this conflict was the claim by a Connecticut sea captain named Olmstead against the State of Pennsylvania for the proceeds of the sale of a British ship. He and three other Connecticut seamen had been captured by the British in 1778 and put aboard the sloop *Active*. They overpowered the vessel's command and were heading the ship toward the American coast when it was seized by a warship chartered under Pennsylvania's government. Ashore Mr. Olmstead insisted that he, rather than Pennsylvania, was entitled to the proceeds from the prize, and won a judgment in a federal court. Pennsylvania, however, refused to release the money; it was held by State Treasurer Rittenhouse.

Fifteen years later, in 1803, Mr. Olmstead sued in another federal district court; District Judge Peters told Pennsylvania to pay him. The state legislature belligerently refused the decree. In 1809 Mr. Olmstead, at age eighty-two, won a Supreme Court judgment requiring enforcement. Chief Justice Marshall declared that "if the legislatures of the several states may, at will, annul the judgments of the courts of the United States and destroy the rights acquired . . . the Constitution itself becomes a mockery."

Whereupon, Pennsylvania Governor Thomas McKean declared he would call out the state militia to prevent enforcement of the decree, and won the legislature's approval. When a federal marshal sought to win compliance from executors of then deceased State Treasurer Rittenhouse's estate, he was met with armed resistance from state troops. The marshal summoned a posse of two thousand, and the "Siege of Rittenhouse Castle" ensued.

Governor McKean appealed to President James Madison to uphold Pennsylvania's "rights," but was sternly rebuffed, though Mr. Madison has been considered a co-author of the doctrine that states have an inherent power to "interpose" against a federal order they deem unconstitutional. So state troops were withdrawn, and old Captain Olmstead got his money.

Perhaps the most serious pre-Civil War federal-state crisis came over South Carolina's "Ordinance of Nullification" against the federal tariff laws. The battle was the more dramatic, not only because President Jackson was a native of the state, but because his Vice-President was John C. Calhoun, who espoused the doctrine that it was within the power of the states to declare "null and void" in the state, and warned that if Congress passed any law seeking to force compliance, "the people of this state will thenceforth hold themselves absolved from all further obligation to maintain or preserve their political connection with the people of other states, and will forthwith proceed to organize a separate government." In a word, secession.

With this, the state legislature empowered the Governor to order the entire military force of the state into service and to buy ten thousand rifles.

President Jackson, however, also was moving. He switched troops in Charleston to prevent them from going over to the "Nullies," and sent in armed men to federal forts. His contact with Charleston, Joel Poinsett, the leader of the Union Party, recommended that Mr. Jackson send some three hundred muskets for possible use by his volunteers; President Jackson ordered five thousand to be placed at Mr. Poinsett's disposal. He confided to friends that he could put fifty thousand men in South Carolina in forty days. "I consider the power to annul a law of the U.S. assumed by any one state to be incompatible with the existence of the Union," he declared. "The Union will be preserved."

But while President Jackson was asking Congress for stouter authority to enforce the tariff law, he also requested a downward revision in tariffs. This altered the collision course. On learning that a compromise tariff measure was in the works in Congress, South Carolina suspended nullification. When Mr. Jackson signed both the tariff compromise and the "Force Bill," South Carolina rescinded the nullification; as a face-saver, the "Force Bill" was called null and void. Each side claimed victory.

While southern states' defiance of federal authority was to

rise again, and be smashed in the Civil War, it is easy to forget that Northerners also took a whirl at it—and with considerable success.

Even the Civil War, the greatest of all clashes involving the federal-state struggle for supremacy of powers, didn't prevent continued conflict. A 1932 case involving the Governor of Texas has provided the Kennedy Administration with the precedent that a state governor is subject to the same legal processes as any other citizen when he uses his official position to violate the rights of others.

What prompted the ruling was Governor Ross Sterling's call-up of the state militia to stop oil production in the huge East Texas oil fields.

In August, 1931, the Texas legislature passed a law authorizing the state railroad commission to regulate the flow of oil from Texas wells. Governor Sterling declared operators were violating the commission's orders, wastefully pumping thousands of barrels per day. Public feeling about the overproduction was running so high, he asserted, the citizens might take the law into their own hands. There were threats of dynamiting; "war conditions" were necessary, the Governor insisted. On his proclamation that a state of "insurrection, tumult and a breach of peace" existed, state troops moved in; first closing the wells, then enforcing the railroad commission's production orders, which drastically cut the daily flow per well. A federal district court, in granting the operators an injunction against the commission's orders, held that none of this was true, however.

Though the Supreme Court, under Chief Justice Hughes, ruled that Governor Sterling had used his official position to violate the rights of the complaining oil producers, Texas in the end won what it wanted. In the early New Deal days, the National Recovery Administration permitted state regulatory bodies to set the rate of oil production within their borders. After the NRA was declared unconstitutional, Congress, in 1936, passed the Connally "Hot Oil" Law barring interstate movement of oil in excess of the allowable production set by state regulations.

Northern defiance was displayed shortly before the Civil War. During the 1850s, an escaped slave was discovered by his master in Wisconsin and claimed under the newly passed Fugitive Slave Law. An Abolitionist newspaper editor, Sherman Booth, helped the slave escape from jail, and was brought to court. In 1854, the Wisconsin Supreme Court freed both him and the slave; then the case was taken to the U.S. Supreme Court for review.

When the Court, under Chief Justice Taney, denied the right of the state judiciary to intervene and upheld the federal Fugitive Slave Act, Wisconsin refused to obey; subsequently, some ten other states "interposed" and suspended the slave law within their borders.

Before that again, in 1807, when the British and French were fighting and showing high disregard for the safety of neutral America's ships on the high seas, President Jefferson tried to apply pressure by cutting off U.S. foreign trade via the Embargo Act.

In hard-hit New England, state legislatures declared the act unconstitutional. Connecticut Governor Jonathan Trumbull declared it the duty of state governments to "interpose their protecting shield between the rights and liberties of the people and the assumed power of the Federal Government."

Governors refused to supply militia to enforce the law. After eight months of effort, Mr. Jefferson asserted: "I did not expect a crop of so sudden and rank a growth of fraud and open opposition by force could have grown up in the United States." His attempt to gain stronger authority to enforce the Embargo Act raised such protest that Congress quickly passed, and Mr. Jefferson signed, the Non-Intercourse Law; this repealed the Embargo Act and reopened trade immediately with all countries but France and England.

Recently, of course, the question of federal versus state power has come alive again as a result of the 1954 Supreme Court decision outlawing school desegregation. But even as in the days of President Jackson and John Marshall, judicial decision and practical enforcement aren't always identical.

Seven years ago, when the State of Alabama yielded to court orders to admit Autherine Lucy to the University of Alabama, Miss Lucy was admitted, but ensuing student riots led to her expulsion. While Miss Lucy claimed the expulsion was because of her color, a federal district judge ruled it wasn't. The case wasn't appealed; Alabama still maintains almost complete segregation in all its schools.

Six years ago, Arkansas Governor Orval Faubus precipitated a federal-state crisis when he called out the National Guard to block a court-ordered enrollment of Negro students in Central High School. President Eisenhower federalized the National Guard units and quickly sent in paratroopers to enforce the federal court orders. At this point, Governor Faubus ceased resistance, avoiding the risk of personally defying a federal court order.

Mississippi's Governor Barnett plunged further, into formal contempt of court, and in so fighting admission of a Negro to the state university brought the recurring contest between federal and state authority to its most critical level since the Civil War.

In the area of race relations, the Southerner is not alone in wanting to retain the old system. To put it bluntly, the fear of the Negro is a national fear.

Most states have not legislated on civil rights or, where they have, have not undertaken strict enforcement. Progress must be socially inspired rather than politically motivated. Southerners are franker in stating their anxieties, but their misgivings about racial equality are shared in even the most sophisticated northern suburbs.

The white men constitute the majority in all southern states, but there are the black-belt counties which are predominantly

Negro. In some areas the population is less than 40 per cent white.

It is in places like this that States' rights sentiment is the strongest. For, if the state government is a shield for the minority, the shield flashes in two directions. On one side it protects the black-belt whites from the Negro majority that surrounds them and that could, if given the chance, easily outvote them.

On the other hand, it protects the white South as a whole from the federal government, which many white Southerners see as intent on destroying the entire way of life of a region.

The white Southerners feels beleaguered, even tryrannized, by the fact of national power. The bottles and bricks hurled in Oxford protested an invasion equated by some Mississippians with that of the Soviet tanks stationed in East Berlin.

States' rights, as defined below the Mason-Dixon line, may exist to serve the white man's interests. It is white man's law, enacted by white judges and police.

If Negroes are also citizens of southern states, they neither participate in, nor are benefited by, these laws. Separate facilities, they have discovered, are not and cannot be equal.

This is why James Meredith by-passed Mississippi and sought redress through the federal courts. As Negroes constitute less than a majority in the South today, they can contend that what are States' rights for their white neighbors are a denial of minority rights for them.

Electing a President

WE ELECT A PRESIDENT—
OR DO WE?

WE AMERICANS ELECT a President—or do we? In 1960 the vote was close and might easily have delivered a popular majority for Vice-President Nixon while still delivering the Electoral College to Senator Kennedy. Whenever our nation experiences a close election there is demand that the Electoral College be abolished. This idea always is appealing to the party coming in second in a very close race, but does not do well in the contest for the states.

The writers of the Constitution, by leaving it to the state legislatures to settle how electors should be "appointed," clearly intended to reserve to each state a separate voice in the choosing of a President. This was to be a representative government of sovereign states in a federal system. To wipe out the separate identity of the states in the President-choosing process would weaken their importance in our system.

The Constitution provides for a body of electors whose duty it is to choose a President and Vice-President. Voters in each state vote for electors, who in turn vote for the candidate of the voter's choice. Each state chooses as many electors as it has Senators and Representatives. The total number of electors is now 537. A majority of 269 is required to elect.

At the time of the Constitutional Convention in 1787 there were men who felt that the common people didn't have time or opportunity to get to know their candidates and couldn't, consequently, vote wisely. Another group felt that giving the

265

common people the vote would bring into the government officials who might be unfriendly toward the wealthy. Both of these groups wanted to make sure that the President would be elected by a select group rather than by the common man. The indirect election of the President was set up to accomplish their purpose. Choosing of electors was left up to the states—whose legislatures sometimes made the choice.

In those days the state's electors gathered together, and each named two men on his ballot. A clerk listed all the names with the number of votes for each and forwarded the list to Washington. The person with the most votes became President, if his total vote was the majority of all the electors. The second highest man became Vice-President. If no man received a majority of the electoral votes, the House of Representatives was empowered to choose the President.

But the Electoral College, after the election of Washington, never worked the way it had been intended. People clamored for, and got, the right to vote directly for their electors. Later, when political parties were formed in strength, the election of the President came closer home than ever. Voters then—and since—chose only those electors who promised to support the candidates of the parties. The elector became more and more just a device in the counting of people's votes.

States choose electors by various methods—party primaries, district and state party conventions, executive or central committees—or a combination of them.

Electors cast their votes on the first Monday after the second Wednesday in December, at their state capitals. Legally they may vote for some other man than the party candidate, but generally they do not because of their pledge to party and candidate on the ballot. In 1948 Tennessee's 12 electoral votes were split—11 for Truman, the Democrat; 1 for its States' rights candidate.

The votes of the electors are sent to Congress, where the President of the Senate opens the certificates, and they are counted in the presence of both Houses on January 6. The President is inaugurated on January 20.

Article II, Section I of the United States Constitution provides:

> The Executive Power shall be vested in a President of the United States of America. He shall hold his office during the term of four years, and, together with the Vice President, chosen for the same term, be elected, as follows:
>
> Each State shall appoint, in such manner as the Legislature thereof may direct, a number of Electors, equal to the whole number of Senators and Representatives to which the State may be entitled in the Congress; but no Senator or Representative, or person holding an office of trust or profit under the United States, shall be appointed an Elector.

As has been said hereinabove, originally our Constitution provided that the man who had the most electoral votes would be President and the man with the second highest vote Vice-President. That was changed in 1804, when the Twelfth Amendment to the Constitution was ratified. It provides that separate ballots will be cast for President and Vice-President. It does not require that the two successful men be of the same party. It further provides that presidential electors shall meet in their respective states and vote by ballot separately for President and Vice-President, one of whom at least shall not be an inhabitant of the same state with themselves. A practical effect of the amendment is that the nominees for President and Vice-President are chosen from different states.

A comparative handful of votes often alters the make-up of our government: In 1880, Winfield S. Hancock, Democrat, defeated James A. Garfield, Republican, by 94 votes in California, splitting the state's electoral vote under the then existing law: 1 for Garfield and 5 for Hancock. Garfield won the election.

Theodore Roosevelt, Progressive candidate, in 1912 beat Woodrow Wilson in California by 174 votes. Under the then existing law, the electoral vote was divided, giving Roosevelt 11, Wilson 2. But in 1916 President Wilson received a plurality of 3,773 votes over Republican Charles Evans Hughes and won re-election. Loss of the 13 California electoral votes would have resulted in the election of Hughes.

President Harry S. Truman in 1948 won California over Thomas E. Dewey by 17,865 votes. In 1884 a change of less than 600 popular votes from Grover Cleveland to James G. Blaine would have given Blaine the electoral vote of New York State and the Presidency.

In 1916 a change of 29 votes would have given Hughes, rather than Wilson, the 4 electoral votes of New Hampshire. Democrat William Jennings Bryan would have won Kentucky in 1896 by a change of 141 popular votes. He would have also taken South Dakota by a change of only 92 popular votes.

One election changed the Constitution of our country. Aaron Burr and Thomas Jefferson inadvertently figured in the development of the present system of electing our President and Vice-President. In the election of 1800 Jefferson and Burr received the same number of electoral votes. As a result the House of Representatives had to decide the issue. It soon became clear that the politicians, dominated by angry Federalists who despised Jefferson, would name Burr, despite the fact that it was clearly understood before the election that Burr had been selected as Jefferson's running mate. Burr would have been President save for Alexander Hamilton, who hated Jefferson but believed Burr was not of presidential caliber. He threw his support to Jefferson, who received 10 votes. Burr received 4 and 2 were not cast. Burr became Vice-President. This narrow escape caused enactment of the Twelfth Amendment to the Constitution, and James Madison, in 1808, was the first President elected following its ratification.

In the 1824 election, the voting began October 29 and lasted until November 22. The results gave Andrew Jackson 99 electoral votes; John Quincy Adams, 84; William Crawford, 41; and Henry Clay, 37. Since no one had a majority, the House of Representatives selected the President. Each state had 1 vote, and 13 constituted a majority. Adams received 13 votes, Jackson 7, and Crawford 4.

It was not until 1872 that a President and Vice-President were selected at an election in which every state chose its electors by popular vote. In that year, Ulysses S. Grant, with a popular vote of 3,597,132, won over Horace Greeley, who received 2,834,125 votes. Greeley died November 29, 1872, before his electors had voted, and his electoral votes were then scattered among several of the other candidates.

In 1828, no candidate for Vice-President received a majority of the electoral vote. The Senate, accordingly, elected Richard M. Johnson, who had received 147 electoral votes to Francis Granger's 77.

In the 1876 election, Samuel J. Tilden, Democrat, received 4,285,992, to 4,033,768 for Republican Rutherford B. Hayes, but an election dispute followed. Double sets of returns were received from Oregon, Louisiana, South Carolina, and Florida. An Electoral Commission, composed of five U.S. Supreme Court Justices, five U.S. Senators, and five members of the House of Representatives, decided the Republican electors were the legally chosen ones. The electoral vote therefore resulted in Hayes receiving 185 and Tilden 184.

The closeness of the 1960 election vote (Kennedy won by 112,801 popular votes) resulted in a threat by the Republican Party to withhold electoral votes in some of the contested states. This could not have helped their candidate, Vice-President Nixon. If the Republican Party had succeeded in withholding (for example) the State of Illinois's 27 electoral votes, thus seeking to trim or overturn the electoral vote margin of President-elect John F. Kennedy, it would have only reduced the number Kennedy needed to win.

Kennedy was credited with 303 electoral votes. But if the 27 Illinois votes (for example) had been withdrawn, Kennedy would have had only 276. It has been assumed this would have been 7 more than the 269 needed. But the Republicans were in error. If Illinois had refused to cast its 27 votes, the number of "appointed electors"—the wording in the Constitution—would have dropped from 537 to 510. Kennedy then would have needed only 256—a majority of 510—to win. The same situation applies to other states where the vote outcome might have been contested.

There are many interesting side lights on the office of President.

¶ Only once has there been an effort to remove a President. Andrew Johnson was charged with the corrupt use of the veto power, interference at elections, and breaking the Tenure of Office Law. On the first vote of the major charge the Senate voted 35 to 19 for conviction; one vote short of the necessary two-thirds vote to effect conviction. The two other charges were dropped.

¶ By act of Congress the line of succession to the Presidency is:

The Vice-President	Attorney General
Speaker of the House	Postmaster General
Senate President Pro Tem	Secretary of the Interior
Secretary of State	Secretary of Agriculture
Secretary of the Treasury	Secretary of Commerce
Secretary of Defense	Secretary of Labor

¶ To date only eight Vice-Presidents have been called upon to take over the reins of government. John Tyler (1840) took over after William H. Harrison died, a month after election, and tried to run in 1844 but withdrew. Millard Fillmore took office when Zachary Taylor died July 9, 1850, later was "Know-Nothing" and Whig candidate. Andrew Johnson was the first to take over (April 15, 1865) after an assassination, and the only President who faced impeachment. Chester A. Arthur was sworn in September 20, 1881; James Garfield had been shot on July 2 of that year. Theodore Roosevelt became President September 14, 1904, and was elected, the first of the seven to succeed. Calvin Coolidge took the oath August 3, 1923, after Warren G. Harding's still mysterious death. He ran and was elected in 1924. Harry S. Truman became President April 12, 1945, when

Franklin D. Roosevelt died in his fourth term; and won his election to that office in 1948. Lyndon B. Johnson took the oath of office November 22, 1963, soon after John F. Kennedy was assassinated.

¶ In the 1868 presidential election, 23 electoral votes from the "unreconstructed states" of the South were excluded from balloting in the Electoral College.

¶ The Republican Party first appeared in the 1856 election, with General John C. Fremont as its candidate. He was defeated by the Democrat, James Buchanan. Abraham Lincoln was the second Republican Party candidate and the party's first President.

¶ The Democratic Party was founded by Andrew Jackson supporters before the 1828 election. Jackson was the party's first President.

¶ Nine of the Presidents, including Washington and Lincoln, were not college men.

¶ Six Presidents were born in log cabins. They were Jefferson, Jackson, Fillmore, Lincoln, Buchanan, Garfield, and Arthur.

¶ George Washington was the first President elected under the Constitution, but he was preceded by nine Presidents of the United States in Congress assembled under the Articles of Confederation. They were Thomas McKean, John Hanson, Elias Bordinot, Thomas Mifflin, R. E. Lee, John Hancock, Nathaniel Gorham, Arthur St. Clair, and Cyrus Griffin. They were each elected for one-year terms, and served in the order listed during the period 1781–1789.

¶ The President of the United States cannot be arrested.

¶ Under the presidential succession law of his day, David Rice Atchison, as President Pro Tempore of the Senate, became President of the United States on Sunday, March 4, 1849, and served until Zachary Taylor took the oath of office the next day. President Polk's term expired on Sunday and President-elect Taylor was not inaugurated until Monday.

¶ The largest plurality of electoral votes ever given any President was received by Franklin D. Roosevelt in 1936 at the end of his first term in office. Of the total of 531 votes, he received 523.

¶ Only two men have been elected President while serving in the U.S. Senate: Warren G. Harding in 1920 and John F. Kennedy in 1960.

¶ During the last 124 years no Vice-President has been elected President while serving as Vice-President.

¶ Fourteen candidates received less than 50 per cent of the total popular vote but were successful in becoming President. The percentage of the total votes received by "minority" Presidents are:

YEAR	PRESIDENT	PERCENTAGE OF POPULAR VOTE	PERCENTAGE OF ELECTORAL VOTE
1824	John Q. Adams	29.8	31.8
1844	James K. Polk	49.3	61.8
1848	Zachary Taylor	47.3	56.2
1856	James A. Buchanan	45.3	58.7
1860	Abraham Lincoln	39.9	59.4
1876	Rutherford B. Hayes	47.9	50.1
1880	James A. Garfield	48.3	57.9
1884	Grover Cleveland	48.8	54.6
1888	Benjamin Harrison	47.8	58.1
1892	Grover Cleveland	46.0	62.4
1912	Woodrow Wilson	41.8	81.9
1916	Woodrow Wilson	49.3	52.1
1948	Harry S. Truman	48.5	57.1
1960	John F. Kennedy	49.7	56.5

¶ Kennedy's lead of 84 votes in the Electoral College is not the closest one in history by any means. Hayes in 1876 won by a margin of 1 electoral vote. Cleveland won by 37 electoral votes in 1884 and lost by 65 in 1888. Garfield had a lead of 59 in 1880.

¶ Since 1876 no Republican has been elected without carrying New York State.

¶ Theodore Roosevelt was inaugurated at the age of forty-two. The oldest was William Henry Harrison, who became

President at sixty-eight and served one month before his death. John F. Kennedy was forty-three when inaugurated.

¶ Of all the Presidents, the second, John Adams, attained the greatest age. Ninety years old at death, he had lived to see his own son, John Quincy Adams, inaugurated as the sixth President. Dwight D. Eisenhower, at seventy, was the oldest President to occupy the White House.

¶ In 1789—the first election for President—the New York legislature selected no electors, and therefore the people of New York had no voice in electing our first President.

¶ In the 1888 election Grover Cleveland, Democrat, received 5,540,050; and Benjamin Harrison, Republican, 5,444,337. The electoral vote, however, was Harrison, 233, and Cleveland, 168. Harrison carried the key states of New York and Indiana. The popular vote does not always prevail.

¶ As the Vice-President, Richard M. Nixon was the first man in a hundred years to announce the results of an election in which, as a candidate for President, he was defeated. The last time a defeated presidential candidate officiated at such a ceremony was February 13, 1861, when Vice-President John C. Breckenridge proclaimed Abraham Lincoln the winner in a four-man race. Like Nixon, Breckenridge was a loser, getting 72 of the 303 electoral votes to Lincoln's 180.

We elect a President—or do we?

The Miscellaneous File

A MAN'S HOME IS HIS CASTLE

LAWYERS TOIL DAILY with words and phrases coined over hundreds of years.

It was during the late 1500s that the maxim "a man's home is his castle" came into usage. It is not known exactly when or where the expression originated. We do know why.

England was experiencing a period of turmoil in the sixteenth century. The populace was restless. The Crown was worried. Persons suspected of disloyalty were subject to having their homes entered and searched. To the average Englishman, such acts were unthinkable.

Sir Edward Coke, a great lawyer and an even greater judge, is presumed to be the legal author of the phrase, for in deciding a lawsuit in 1605 he wrote:

> . . . The house of everyone is to him his castle and fortress, as well for his defense against injury and violence as for his repose. . . .

It can be assumed that the phrase had been commonly used before Coke set it down on paper. The Bard of Avon, William Shakespeare, may have alluded to this everyday maxim in *The Merry Wives of Windsor,* when he had the host of the Garter Inn direct Simple to Sir John Falstaff's room:

> . . . There's his chamber, his house, his castle, his standing bed, and his truckle-bed. . . .

The legal principle embodied in the maxim is much more comprehensive than is commonly supposed. It means that a

277

home is inviolable to arbitrary invasion and search. No outward doors of a man's house, wrote William Blackstone in 1765, can in general be broken open to execute any civil process, though in criminal cases the public safety supersedes the private.

In a speech in the House of Commons in 1760, the Elder Pitt graphically illustrated the importance of the maxim when he said:

> . . . The poorest man may in his cottage bid defiance to all the force of the crown. It may be frail, its roof may shake, the wind may blow through it, the storms may enter, but he, King of England, cannot enter, all his forces dare not cross the threshold of the ruined tenement. . . .

Less than two decades later the American Revolution was fought, in order to divorce the people of this nation from certain principles employed by England.

But while we disagreed with England on many points, we took no issue with the fact that a man's home is his castle. The principle was embodied in the Bill of Rights and remains with us today.

TITLE GUARANTEED

GEOGRAPHY PRIMERS teach us that four fifths of the world's surface is water; one fifth is land. This ratio graphically indicates why mankind has established peculiar values regarding ownership of real property.

Gold is precious. But even more precious is the earth in which it is found. Men by the hundreds of thousands have fought and died, singly and in huge numbers, attempting to conquer or defend an area or areas of land.

Perhaps this is why, today, a person buying a piece of property demands a thorough investigation of the title—to insure that he owns what he purchases.

The process known as title search has produced an entertaining, if unbelievable, yarn concerning certain eastern interests considering purchase of some real estate in Louisiana.

An attorney for the eastern syndicate discovered to his horror that the title record ran back only as far as 1803. He wrote the title company and demanded a search of records prior to that date. This was the reply:

> Please be advised the Government of the United States acquired the Territory of Louisiana, including the tract to which your inquiry applies, by purchase, from the Government of France in the year 1803.
>
> The Government of France acquired title by conquest from the Government of Spain.
>
> The Government of Spain acquired title by discovery by one Christopher Columbus, traveler and explorer, a resident of Genoa, Italy, who, by agreement concerning the acquisition of title to any lands discovered, traveled and explored under the sponsorship and patronage of her Majesty, the Queen of Spain.
>
> The Queen of Spain had verified her arrangement and received sanction of her title by consent of the Pope, resident of Rome, Italy, and ex-officio representative and vice-regent on Earth of Jesus Christ.
>
> Jesus Christ was the son and heir-apparent of God.
>
> God made Louisiana.
>
> Trusting that this additional citation complies with your request and assuring you of our willingness to be of service, we are . . .

Who was it who said answers make only as much sense as the question prompting them?

MAN'S BEST FRIEND

GEORGE GRAHAM VEST (1830–1904) was a Missouri lawyer. His practice was limited to civil cases of little significance. Stacked up against the legal giants of the last century, George Graham Vest was a nobody.

A nobody until one day he walked into a Missouri courtroom and delivered an unusual argument in an unusual case. Vest represented a client suing a man who had wantonly shot and killed his dog. The facts of the case were presented in routine manner. They merit no attention. It was the summation that lifted Vest from obscurity to immortality.

He stood before the jury box and made the usual opening remarks. Then he paused. When he began again, his voice took a richness never heard before and never heard after. These were his words:

> . . . The best friend a man has in the world may turn against him and become his enemy. His son or daughter that he has reared with loving care may prove ungrateful. Those who are nearest and dearest to us, those whom we trust with our happiness and our good name may become traitors to their faith.
>
> The money that a man has he may lose. It flies away from him, perhaps when he needs it most. A man's reputation may be sacrificed in a moment of ill-considered action. The people who are prone to fall on their knees when success is with us, may be the first to throw the stone of malice when failure settles its cloud upon our head.
>
> The one absolutely unselfish friend that man can have in this selfish world, the one that never deserts him, the one that never proves ungrateful or treacherous, is his dog. A man's dog stands by him in prosperity and in poverty, in health and in

sickness. He will sleep on the cold ground, where the wintry winds blow and the snow drives fiercely, if only he may be near his master's side. He will kiss the hand that has no food to offer; he will lick the wounds and sores that come in encounters with the roughness of the world. He guards the sleep of his pauper master as if he were a prince.

When all other friends desert, he remains. When riches take wing, and reputation falls to pieces, he is as constant in his love as the sun in its journey through the heavens.

If fortune drive his master forth an outcast in the world, friendless and homeless, the faithful dog asks no higher privilege than that of accompanying him, to guard him against danger, to fight his enemies. And when the last scene of all comes, and death takes his master in its embrace and his body is laid away in the cold ground, no matter if all other friends pursue their way, there by the graveside will the noble dog be found, his head between his paws, his eyes sad but open in alert watchfulness, faithful and true even in death. . . .

George Graham Vest's words won him the admiration of the world as well as the case. They may have played a part in his becoming a United States Senator, a position of respect he held for twenty-four years.

But his service in the Senate proved to be as obscure as his career as a lawyer. He is remembered only for his tribute to a dog. No greater monument to his memory can be built; nor need it be.

THE VICTIM OF MURDER

THE FOLLOWING is a true story. Only the names of the persons involved and the actual locations have been changed.

This was not a greatly publicized case; it was a murder, so said the People of California, and both the victim and the suspect were persons of little importance. The newspapers devoted a scant few inches of space to the entire affair. As murder cases go, it was a run-of-the-mill affair. At first glance only two ingredients were missing to make it airtight: The accused never confessed the crime to the police and there were no eyewitnesses.

On a late December evening, a little over thirteen years ago, an obscure, two-time loser named Willis Jewel, a Negro, went driving about Oakland, California, with an acquaintance, one Jesse Ransom. Jewel had not been long out of prison; at thirty-three he had two prior felony convictions, one in New Orleans for larceny and another in Los Angeles for robbery.

As the police later pieced the story together, Jewel wanted sex and he had told Ransom that he expected to meet a certain Anne Fort, whom he had known only a short time, for this purpose. About midnight of the same day Jewel met Anne at a café and Ransom then drove them to the apartment of a Sarah Lee. The Fort woman got out of the car at the Lee apartment and Ransom and Jewel remained inside the automobile for a while. After some time had passed, Jewel got out of the car and went into the Lee apartment, where he joined Anne. After a brief conversation about Anne's aching feet had taken place, the two rejoined Ransom.

Ransom then drove Jewel and Anne to the home of a Mark Hatfield. After staying a short time, Anne and Willis Jewel left, getting back into Ransom's car. According to the police, Jewel and the Fort woman had some kind of a verbal altercation at this point, though Ransom and Hatfield both later admitted they were drunk and befuddled at the time this alleged incident took place.

What then followed is hazy and obscure. The police contended that Anne got out of the car and went back into the Hatfield place, with Willis Jewel following her shortly thereafter. Ransom, now rather drunk, made a statement some time later that a car had driven up behind his automobile, that a man looked at Anne and that Willis then left, walking down the street *away* from the Hatfield house.

Between 2:30 and 3:00 A.M. on the following morning, a Mrs. Ruth Hodges, who lived on Mills Street facing the Baker School, in Oakland, testified she heard some screams coming from the direction of the school. She later admitted she could not identify the person who was allegedly screaming.

At about 3:00 A.M. on the same morning, the defendant's mother later testified she saw her son, Willis Jewel, in their home, located a number of blocks away from the Baker School.

At 4:00 P.M. on the afternoon of this same day, the body of Anne Fort was found lying in the yard of the Baker School. According to the police reports, she had died of a subarachnoid hemorrhage with accompanying brain injury. It was the opinion of the medical examiner that her injuries had been caused by a "blunt instrument." Her undergarments had been removed and part of one stocking was wrapped around her neck. When the body of this twenty-one-year-old girl was subsequently autopsied it was discovered that human spermatozoa were present in her vaginal tract.

Willis Jewel was arrested by the police on December 27. He admitted he had been with Anne and Ransom on the evening in question, but claimed he had left Anne at an intersection some distance from the Hatfield home at about 3:30 in the morning. He also testified that he had "wandered around" after that, arriving home between 4:00 and 5:00 A.M. In another statement made to the police he testified he had been with a prostitute earlier in the evening.

The police divested Willis Jewel of his clothing and, after an examination of his shoes, located blood on the forward portion of each shoe. A mineralogist testified that soil found on Jewel's shoe matched soil in the yard of the Baker School.

Shortly after his arrest, Jewel was placed in a cell with one Arthur Raymond, who was released by the police shortly thereafter—*after* making a statement to the police to the effect that Jewel had told him to go to his, Jewel's, home and dispose of some bloody clothing. Later, at the time Jewel was tried, Raymond did not appear as a People's witness, the People stipulating that "this witness could not be found within the State after due and diligent search." Raymond's statement to the police, however, *was* read into the official court record.

Jewel was tried by a jury of his peers in accordance with the laws of the State of California. After he was found guilty of the crime of murder in the first degree, the sentence of death was passed upon him. An automatic appeal taken before the Supreme Court of the State of California later held that Willis Jewel had received a fair trial, that the sentence of death must be upheld.

Let us backtrack for a moment before we follow Willis Jewel—now #A-4400-A—to his final place of confinement, Death Row, San Quentin State Prison, San Quentin, California.

We know that the defendant could and did offer an alibi as to his presence at home, through the testimony of his mother. We also know that both Hatfield and Ransom were, on the night of the death of Anne Fort, under the influence of alcohol, through statements they later made to the police. It was the holiday season in the city's Negro ghetto and all of the principals in this case had been celebrating for the better part of the day. Indeed, Ransom later claimed he had dozed in his car, from time to time, after Anne and Jewel went into Hatfield's place of residence.

As to the soil found on Willis Jewel's shoes, it was established during the trial that Jewel had worked as a janitor at the Baker School about a week before the murder. His route to and from the school took him over the same path, daily, where the suspect sample of soil had been found, thus seemingly negating the People's evidence on this account.

As to the blood found on Willis Jewel's shoes, it is possible to classify such blood with respect to the type. If the blood was

Anne's, why didn't the People enter this into the evidence against Jewel? Could it have been that the blood found on Willis Jewel's shoes came from another person? We know Willis Jewel had a previous criminal record and no apology is made for it, but is the existence of a criminal record, a tainted past, enough to cause the State to assume, automatically, that this blood was Anne's? Why didn't the State follow through on these blood samples? Could the bare mention of this evidence, worthless without further analysis, have been a "red herring"?

Another piece of evidence the People did not feel disposed to comment upon was the seminal fluid found in Anne's vaginal tract. This substance, like blood, may be classified as to type and origin. While such a forensic investigation is fairly complex, the People had both the time and the resources to follow through on it. This was a murder case and it would be expected that the People would do everything in their power to insure that the case against Willis Jewel was airtight. Why, then, was this important evidence excluded at the trial?

And now for Raymond's testimony. The most important piece of evidence against Jewel was unquestionably Raymond's deposition, the statement that Willis Jewel had verbally admitted his guilt in the slaying of Anne Fort, while the two men were confined together in the city jail. As you know, the credibility of a witness in court—especially in a murder case—is of the utmost importance. And in the Willis Jewel case, you will remember, we are dealing with a most peculiar set of circumstances; aside from Raymond's statement to the police, all of the People's evidence against Willis Jewel is meaningless! At the very best, without Raymond's statement, the People had the flimsiest kind of case, a case that would seem to demand an acquittal.

And what kind of man was this Arthur Raymond? Well, in order to establish his truthfulness as a witness in a capital case, one would assume that his past surely must be as pure as driven snow! To believe a man whose testimony, by itself, is enough to send another to the gas chamber, we should have to suppose that this Arthur Raymond was a paragon of honesty and virtue. Therefore, let us take a close look at the dossier of the informant, Raymond.

Police records show him as RAYMOND, Arthur. His FBI identification number, fingerprint number, and California Bureau of Identification number are also given. I know this, for I have his complete police record in my office.

The first entry against Arthur Raymond goes back to September 16, 1936. He was arrested in El Centro, California, and turned over to the sheriff's office for investigation.

On September 15, 1938, Mr. Raymond was arrested in Los Angeles, California. The charge against him was burglary. He was convicted and sent to the Ione Reformatory. His length of sentence is not shown.

In May, 1942, Raymond was arrested by the Tucumcari, New Mexico, Police Department. The charge: Trespassing on railroad property. He received fifteen days in the county jail for this offense.

The El Centro Police Department picked Raymond up on May 3, 1946. At this time he was fingerprinted and subsequently released.

In February, 1947, the Oakland Police Department made Mr. Raymond's acquaintance for the first time. He was held for "investigation" and released on February 5, 1947.

On February 20, 1947, Arthur Raymond was again arrested by the Oakland police. This time the charges against him were grand theft and auto theft. The charge of grand theft was dismissed; he was found guilty of auto theft, however. He was sentenced to San Quentin State Prison on April 11, 1947, his term of sentence fixed at between one and five years. On August 16, 1948, he was paroled.

The Los Angeles County Sheriff's Office arrested Raymond on March 17, 1949; the charge was listed as violation of parole. He was returned to prison—this time Folsom State Penitentiary

—and was discharged, his full term completed, on November 23, 1950.

And now comes the fateful moment when Raymond met Willis Jewel for the first time. The Oakland Police Department arrested Raymond on December 30, 1950. The charge against Raymond was "Investigation of Burglary." Raymond and Jewel were placed together in the same cell; we know the rest of the sordid story.

. . . and what we also know is that on January 3, 1951, Mr. Arthur Raymond was released from custody. Why was he released? Was the evidence against him insufficient? And are we entirely sure he wasn't on parole at this time? Finally, is it possible that the charges against Raymond were quite valid and that he was simply released because of "certain services rendered"?

Arthur Raymond's exploits continued after he left Willis Jewel alone in his cell in the Oakland city jail. The record shows a vagrancy charge against him in Sacramento in June, 1951. A drunk charge in Oakland, the same year, is also shown. Another drunk charge on January 12, 1952, in Oakland, follows. Another charge of drunkenness on February 18, 1952. A charge of theft on March 31, 1952.

Two felony convictions follow on counts of robbery and grand theft. After being in and out of the penitentiary, Raymond was finally returned to Folsom State Prison on April 21, 1961, where he is presently confined. During the brief periods of time he was at liberty his record is dotted with many arrests for drunkenness. I wonder: Why was Raymond drinking so much? Was it because of something that was eating at his vitals? Was it because he knew he had been instrumental in sending a man to the gas chamber? I cannot speak for what went on, for what is going on, in the mind of Arthur Raymond. Like all of us, someday he will have to make peace with himself.

While Willis Jewel was confined in San Quentin, the State took the time and the trouble to make some lengthy and detailed studies of his general mental and physical state of health. You see, while little or no attention is usually paid to those serving sentence, the People become exceedingly concerned with the welfare and general etiology of those about to die. Perhaps this is a morbid curiosity, somewhat akin to that of a small boy torturing a beetle with a lit match. I do not know what motivates the State to spend large sums of money in these studies, using the material gleaned only to stuff their files in Sacramento, rather than to make some constructive benefit of it, but I do know that the authorities in San Quentin State Prison had the following to say about Willis Jewel:

. . . here is an adolescent with a dull intelligence and a superior physique who comes from an unsatisfactory background . . . he appears to be an inadequate and poorly integrated individual who failed to achieve any sustained semblance of social adjustment and probably could never achieve this to any satisfactory degree . . .

. . . subject is estimated to have a dull normal intelligence with a Beta I.Q. of approximately 80 . . . The CSI indicated 28 aberrant answers, this number quite high and suggesting marked emotional maladjustment. Subject indicates that he has been under observation as a mental patient, and a doctor has told him he has stomach ulcers . . .

In the interview he was friendly and co-operative. He revealed no remorse for the victim and seemed considerably frightened by the prospect of his sentence . . .

. . . subject has a history of syphilis. He is now negative but should have periodic checkups . . .

He is friendly and co-operative, but his stream of mental activity and speech is slow and laboring and sad and depressed. He states his mother doesn't have money for an appeal and he has written to the NAACP to get him a lawyer. He claims he is not guilty and the witnesses contradicted themselves and denies that he struck or killed the victim.

We are agreed that he has some handicap in intelligence, that he is overly concerned about his physical condition and has some somatization reactions but he is not insane.

He is quiet—never demanding and has adjusted fairly well to his situation on Condemned Row.

He has expressed no bitterness nor has he shown any special religious inclination. He has impressed this writer as being quiet, soft spoken, and well mannered.

If the National Association for the Advancement of Colored People answered Willis Jewel's plea for help, it is not shown within the mass of documentation the State amassed prior to his execution. Perhaps this group did not consider Jewel sufficiently "advanced" to warrant any consideration.

There were no special, last-minute writs filed as Willis Jewel waited for the executioner to kill him. There was no national campaign, no high-priced speaker, no well-known movie star to plead his cause, to fill page after page of petitions demanding his release. There were no pickets to keep the lonely death watch in front of the prison's main gate on the morning Willis Jewel was led to the gas chamber. The newspapers offered the public no photographs, no special pen-and-ink drawings of the accused or the apparatus that was to take his life. No one was on hand from any of the syndicated wire services to report what Jewel ate or drank as he waited to die. No one alive, today, remembers his last words as he was led from the holding cell and thence into the gas chamber.

Willis Jewel was a poor, simple-minded Negro who never had a chance. A man of limited intelligence and no financial means, he was a loser from birth. During his life he made no great contribution to society; indeed, he was never called upon for such. He spent much of his life as a ward of the State and from the State he deserved far better than he received. While he received a "fair trial" in the strictest sense of that cold legalism, it is obvious that much could have—and should have—been done to destroy the informer Raymond's credibility; to attack what flimsy evidence the People offered against him.

The Reverend Byron Eshelman, Chaplain of San Quentin State Prison, has expressed doubt that Jewel was guilty. While having no concrete proof that Jewel was innocent, Reverend Eshelman came to know him well before the State took his life. Reverend Eshelman has indicated, in public and in private, that it could be that the State took the life of the wrong man.

Willis Jewel has been dead, now, for over ten years. He was killed in accordance with the laws of the State of California. His last words were not recorded; we know of him only from the yellowed records that the State, out of a curiosity hard to fathom, bothered to keep as a kind of chronicle of his life. Had there been no such records, we would not know of Willis Jewel, for he died, as he had lived, in a mute and terrified kind of silence.

This is a murder story. I leave it to you to decide who was truly the victim.

THURSDAY'S CHILD

I WISH TO TALK about a subject that has long been troubling my mind; a problem that transcends race, creed, color, and all the other barriers that often separate one man from the other. I speak about a tragedy that is not an American tragedy, but a universal tragedy—the tragedy of unwanted human life.

When a child is old enough to begin questioning its own existence it will ask its parents: "How did I get here?" Depending upon their own notions of child-rearing, the parents may reply that the child was found on a lily pad, that it was a star before it was born, or if the parent is wise and remembers his own childhood, he will tell the child something that is approximately the truth: that its mother carried it beneath her heart for long months, that both the mother and the father wanted that child more than anyone in the whole world.

Now, a child who is wanted and who has been told, to the best of its ability to comprehend, how its existence came about will be a happy child. A child does not think like an adult, true, but a child is a powerful lie detector; like all of us, a child knows when it is loved, when it is wanted. It also knows when it is unwanted. And it suffers perhaps more terribly than we do when it knows it is alone and alien, in a place where it was never wanted and never will be wanted.

What a happy world this would be if all of us were able to control the size of our family, the degree of our income, the facilities with which we could raise our children. But we cannot control these things any more than we can control our temper, our taxes, our faltering heart that will someday cease to beat; for we are human, and to be human is to make mistakes, to err, to act more often upon the advice of the heart than the mind. The mistakes we make, daily, are legion; fortunately, most of these mistakes are of little consequence and the damage resulting from them is easily corrected. For the greater mistakes —the taking of a life, the stealing of property—we are punished. This time it is Society, not we, who does the correcting.

It has always been my belief that one of the most sacred responsibilities any human being can ever be charged with is that of being the creator, and later the guardian, of a human being. I know of no single thing that is more precious, more irreplaceable than a single human being. From the moment a child is born its fate is, largely, in the hands of its parents. True, many things can happen from the time the child is born until the child becomes a man, and over many of these things a parent has little control. In such instances the parent becomes somewhat like the attorney in the play *A View from the Bridge,* who says: "There are times when you want to cry out in alarm, but there is nothing you can say. . . ."

The actual act of creation—the act of love—is a beautiful thing that I make no attempt to describe or to explain. It is there and it has been done since man and woman first existed. Each religion has its own beliefs on the significance of this act, and that is as it should be. We know, for example, that one holds that the act is made beautiful only so that man and woman will couple and, in so doing, produce a child. Certainly that is part of it, and perhaps if there were no beauty in it we should all be dwelling in the ocean, still. I don't really know.

I *do* know that the result of this act is a child, in many cases, and in too many cases it is an unwanted child. In many instances the child is as much a product of ignorance or religious proscription as it is anything else. Or the child may be the product of violence, where there was no love, only a brutal act of rape that culminated in the implanting of an alien seed in the belly of a broken, bleeding woman. But the seed is there, for whatever the reason, and if it finds nourishment it grows and grows, and the thing within the womb that in the first month resembles a kind of invertebrate animal later becomes a human being that will be forcibly ejected from the womb to begin life in our society.

Hopefully, most of us were wanted. Our parents made some sort of plan for our existence. In some cases our parents did without so that we would have enough to eat, shoes to wear to school, a warm bed, and sympathy and understanding for our heartache, our tears. We have all been knocked about in this world in the years that followed our birth but there are few of us who did not know that the old folks at home loved us, would send us a few dollars when we needed them and, when they were alive, would always have a place for us at home if we failed in the big city. We accept the love our parents had for us and perhaps this is what blinds us, to such a great degree, to the plight of our less fortunate brethren: the unwanted child. Thursday's child.

At common law and by statute in most, if not all, of the states, the word "abortion" describes an offense. It is not the mere expulsion of the fetus. The gist of it is the artificial means employed to procure expulsion. Under the varying statutory provisions, the accomplishment of the desired result, the quickening of the child, or the death of the woman may or may not be elements of the crime. In brief, it means that the life of the fetus or embryo shall be destroyed in the woman's womb, or that a premature birth thereof be caused before it is capable of sustaining life.

Although we have no reliable statistics on the matter, we know that literally hundreds of thousands of abortions are performed yearly in the United States. The manner in which these operations are carried out ranges from the single woman attempting to curette herself with a knitting needle to the wealthy married matron going to an expensive private clinic and having the operation performed by a highly skilled physician, under the most sterile and modern conditions. In the two cases I have just mentioned, the Colonel's lady and Judy O'Grady are sisters under the skin; they have participated in a criminal act, a felony, and they could be sent to the penitentiary.

There are few states in our land that actually sanction the so-called criminal surgery, or abortion. In many instances such acts have the left-handed approval of legislators and medical people, but sanctions vary. For example, in California, in the recent Sherry Finkbine matter, the State Medical Association held that to abort Mrs. Finkbine, who was at the time carrying a child disfigured in utero by the drug thalidomide, would be a criminal act. Mrs. Finkbine did no better in finding help elsewhere in America. Finally she was obliged to go to Europe, where the unborn fetus was medically aborted and was discovered to be disfigured in a terrible and tragic manner.

The practice of abortion is, if anything, increasing in this country. It is increasing for many reasons, I suspect, but it can be said that, ultimately, there are hundreds of thousands of women in this country who do not, on the face of it, want a child. Their reasons vary, naturally. Many of these women are unmarried and the responsible male has either left town or otherwise refused to accept liability for his part in the pregnancy. In many other cases the parents may have some hereditary defect such as diabetes, epilepsy, or incompatible blood types that will result in a defective child. A few states allow what is called therapeutic abortion for such unfortunate people as these, but in the main the average physician is deathly afraid to abort a woman, sometimes even if her life is in danger, so great are the penalties that may be levied against him.

In my life as a trial lawyer I have talked to thousands of physicians and I can recall few, if any, of these gentlemen, who took a positive stand against abortion. These men, learned in medicine and the ways of human beings, are sympathetic but powerless when a woman comes to them, asking for help, asking that a two-month-old unwanted lump of life be expelled from her body. The physician knows that if he helps this woman, performs a curettage of her uterus, he risks losing his practice, disgracing himself, and probably going to prison. The physician also knows that by being unable to do anything for this woman she will, no doubt, go to a quack who will, in the most crude and distasteful manner imaginable, scrape out her uterus, pack her vagina with caustic and dangerous chemicals, and very likely cost her her life. There are hundreds of cases each year all over the nation where lives are lost due to the bungling of a quack— usually a lay person with no formal training in medicine—performing an abortion. At best, if the woman is not killed she will probably require medical attention sometime after such an operation. In many cases the ultimate result will be an infection that will lead to female castration and all of the problems and complications that are attendant on this form of surgery.

A small minority of women in this country are able to board a boat or an airplane and fly to Mexico or some other foreign land where abortion is sanctioned by law. Here, such an operation is performed in a modern hospital and there is little danger involved. But such women are in the minority. Indeed, the majority of women in this country who are unable to afford a trip abroad are equally unable to afford a child, purely on the basis of economics. In most cases there would be no father to care for the child and, if a father is present, he is for one reason or the other unable to provide decently for the care of a child.

The point that everyone seems to miss when the controversial subject of abortions is raised is that, by the very act of seeking an abortion, the woman is saying: "I do not want this child." The woman's attitude is negative, for whatever reason, and it is unlikely that anyone is going to change her mind. And, as I said earlier, the reasons for her attitude are most frequently dictated by porkchop economics; she cannot *afford* the child. In any case, she *does not* want the child and that is the crux of the issue: Are we going to bring unwanted children into this unhappy world of ours?

What are the results of the prohibitions against abortion? Look at the relief rolls. Over half of the families on relief have unwanted and illegitimate children. What is the future of these children. Walk into any jailhouse, any penitentiary, and Condemned Row, and you shall see their future. Walk into any court of law, look at the defendant, and most often you will see what the end of the line is for this never-wanted child.

There was a time, centuries ago, when man was dying at about the same rate he was being born. And because wars were still being fought by masses of men in the field—and because human labor had not yet been replaced by machines—both the Church and the State decreed that he who had the most children was the best citizen. That was all a long time ago. Today, man has become, tragically enough, a kind of superfluous commodity. There is not enough work for him. There is not enough good housing for him. There is not enough land left for him to till and there are few who care for him. And, in the case of Thursday's Child, there are none who love him. And to my way of thinking, this is the highest form of tragedy. He who enters the world without love is he who would have been better off if he had not been born.

The law says that the still-unformed thing in a woman's womb is not a human being. In our own hearts we, too, know this. We also know that to punish a person for a mistake that can be corrected, that has yet done no one any harm, is wicked and useless. And yet we punish not only the woman but the child, for we allow this tiny, unwanted lump of living plasma to become a child. An unwanted child. But if we do anything to this woman in her second or third month of pregnancy we have become criminals. We are not punished for murder—the thing is not yet human, so there can be no murder—but merely for the *act of expelling it!*

I wonder: which is the greatest crime? Expelling a still-unformed, still-unthinking, and still-nonbreathing piece of unwanted matter—or allowing it to form into a formed, thinking, breathing, and unwanted human being?

I BELIEVE

¶ It is not so important to know which question to ask the witness as it is to know which question not to ask.

¶ When a man says he is innocent, he does so with reference to a witness, and not to his conscience.

¶ The history of persecution shows the human race in all the pomp of its misery, and in all the splendor of its colossal pettiness.

¶ Let us abolish the death penalty until the infallibility of human judgment is established beyond a reasonable doubt.

¶ To some, every pleasure in life is vulgar, obscene, corrupt, and appealing only to man's prurient interest.

¶ Today there is a wave of prosecution and persecution never before known in our history as a nation. I wonder if any of our holier-than-thou's remember the words of Justice Oliver Wendell Holmes, who said: "About 75 years ago, I learned that I was not God. And so when the people want to do something I can't find anything in the Constitution expressly forbidding them to do, I say, whether I like it or not, Goddamit, let 'em do it."

¶ In a courtroom, it takes twelve men to find out if a woman is innocent. On a country lane in the moonlight, it takes one.

¶ Acquisitiveness may make a man either a bank robber or a bank president.

¶ We impute evil to those against whom we hold prejudices.

¶ Mercy is seasonable in the time of affliction, as clouds of rain in the time of drought.

¶ The smallest bit of trust represents some man's bitter toil.

¶ In court, the officers, the jury, the judge are akin to the gods of mythology, manipulating the vast mysterious force that is the Law, looming suddenly and inexorably against the gaiety of life, to smash families—even to mark for death.

¶ The greatest dangers to liberty lurk in insidious encroachment by men of zeal, well-meaning but without understanding.

¶ It is a violation of the law to walk against a red light at a street crossing. It is not against the law for one to allow his benefactor to die in the poorhouse.

¶ Don't be fooled by somebody always looking you straight in the eye. Looking you straight in the eye is the first lesson learned by the successful swindler.

¶ Some men, after causing an injury, soon reach the point of forgiving you for what they did.

¶ Don't lose faith because a few laws are being broken—look at the Ten Commandments.

ABOUT THE AUTHOR

J. W. Ehrlich is best known to millions of Americans as one of the country's most celebrated trial lawyers. Only recently the National Broadcasting Company's television series *Sam Benedict* depicted some of his life's experiences over the many years he has spent in civil and criminal litigation.

A man of many facets and a multitude of interests, the public is probably less aware of another of Mr. Ehrlich's accomplishments: legal writing and a series of works devoted to the religious as well as the historical analysis of the law.

Since admittance to the Bar in San Francisco in 1922, Mr. Ehrlich has written *Ehrlich's Blackstone, Ehrlich's Criminal Law,* and *Ehrlich's Criminal Evidence,* scholarly legal works that are frequently used by judges and lawyers as courtroom guides. Mr. Ehrlich is also the author of *What Is Wrong with the Jury System, The Lost Art of Cross-Examination, The Educated Lawyer,* and *The Contested Divorce Case.*

Between his busy court schedule and his many other activities, he finds time to write for the University of California's Continuing Education of the Bar series. One of his most recent and celebrated San Francisco cases—one involving censorship—has been published under the title of *Howl of the Censor.* Finally, Mr. Ehrlich's competence as a biblical scholar may be seen in his *The Holy Bible and the Law.*

Mr. Ehrlich's active professional life includes membership in the Scribes, The National Law Writers Association, The Board of Editorial Advisors of the Lawyers Literary Club, The Authors League of America, the Dramatists Guild, and The American

Society for Legal History. When time permits, Mr. Ehrlich is a much-sought-after speaker before bar associations all over America.

Athough his reputation as a criminal lawyer is widely known, Mr. Ehrlich's practice in the field of civil litigation is varied and wide. He is a director and general counsel of the San Francisco National Bank and president of the Hobart Estate Company.

An informal and entertaining account of his life, as well as many of his more celebrated criminal cases, may be found in his biography, *Never Plead Guilty.*

LOUIS R. LURIE

San Francisco, California

THIS BOOK WAS SET IN

CALEDONIA AND GARAMOND TYPES BY

HARRY SWEETMAN TYPESETTING CORPORATION.

IT WAS PRINTED AND BOUND AT THE PRESS OF

THE WORLD PUBLISHING COMPANY.

DESIGN IS BY LARRY KAMP.